To my mother, Patricia, who is always in my thoughts.

—Stephen McGregor

Contents

Acknowledgments

We would like to express our heartfelt gratitude to the following people for their various contributions to this project: Hunter Allen, Kevin Beck, Gale Bernhardt, Mike Busa, Andrew Coggan, Jeremy Duerksen, John Duke, Gear Fisher, Nataki Fitzgerald, Joe Friel, Donavon Guyot, Corey Hart, Hal Higdon, Brad Hudson, Asker Jeukendrup, Dean Karnazes, Linda Konner, Steven Lawrence, Cynthia McEntire, Bobby McGee, Greg McMillan, Hannu Kinnunen, Laurel Plotzke, Ian Ratz, Kevin Sullivan, Rachael Weese, and Roberto Veneziani.

Introduction

One of the virtues of the sport of running is how little equipment it requires. Shoes, socks, shorts, and a top are the essentials. Among competitive runners, a stopwatch has also been considered essential, because it allows runners to quantitatively monitor and control their training in ways that ultimately enable them to train more effectively and race faster.

The days of the stopwatch may be numbered, however. That's because a new type of device, commonly known as a speed and distance device, is now able to do what a stopwatch does and much more. A speed and distance device such as the Timex Ironman Triathlon Bodylink is able to measure not just elapsed time but also distance covered, speed (or pace), and elevation change. Many devices also have the capability of estimating calories burned and monitoring heart rate. Other special features vary by brand. For example, Polar speed and distance devices can be used to estimate and track changes in $\dot{V}O_2$max, or the maximum rate at which the body consumes oxygen during running—an important indicator of running fitness. What's more, the software applications that come bundled with speed and distance devices, as well as those that are purchased separately, allow runners to compile and analyze workout and race data in all kinds of helpful ways.

You don't have to be a supercompetitive runner or a gadget whiz to benefit from these technologies. They have something to offer every runner who wants to improve. In fact, thousands of runners of all abilities and levels of experience have already used the tools described in these pages to build greater speed and endurance. Few of these runners can be described as computer geeks. If you can work a stopwatch, you can learn how to manage your performance with a speed and distance device. And don't worry: This process will not strip running of its charming simplicity. In fact, it will allow you to run with an even greater sense of freedom that comes from acquiring the knowledge to truly coach yourself—with a little help from technology.

When the first modern speed and distance devices hit the market in 2002, some running coaches and exercise scientists, including us, quickly realized that they could be much more than just a better stopwatch. We saw that these devices had the potential to revolutionize how runners manage their performance. Essentially, the devices created the possibility for runners of all abilities to digitally coach themselves and to do so as effectively as the top professional coaches train their athletes.

Over the past several years we have worked independently and collaboratively to unleash the full potential of speed and distance devices. Stephen McGregor has done so by developing new training concepts and software tools that runners can use with a speed and distance device to monitor, analyze, and plan their training in ways that are impossible with a mere stopwatch. For example, a feature called normalized graded pace (NGP) or flat pace converts the actual pace on a running route with elevation change to an equivalent pace for level terrain so that runners can compare the challenge level of (and their performance in) workouts performed in different environments. Matt Fitzgerald created a tool called the pace zone index (PZI) that allows runners to easily score their current fitness level and choose the appropriate pace at which to perform each type of workout. Matt also created the first generation of training plains that are downloadable onto a speed and distance device.

Most runners are still unaware that such tools exist; even fewer know how to use them effectively. That's why we wrote this book. The typical runner uses a speed and distance device in more or less the same way drivers use the speedometer and odometer: as a source of basic information that is used in real time to stay within certain vaguely defined parameters. Only a fraction of runners even bother to download workout and race data from the speed and distance device to the computer. That's unfortunate, because the real power of the technology really begins with this action. The performance management software (as we call it) that works with a speed and distance device enables runners to analyze their runs more accurately and far more in depthly than ever before. As a runner, you can use this type of analysis to determine appropriate pace targets for all of your workouts and refine these targets as your fitness changes. You can also program workouts and even complete training plans based on your personal target pace zones and upload them to your speed and distance device.

And this is only the beginning. As you collect run data over time, you can use your software to determine your optimal long-term training load, identify and address strengths and weaknesses in your running fitness, identify periods of overreaching resulting in illness or overtraining, determine your optimal balance of training intensities, identify periods of stagnation in your training, ensure that your training is truly progressive, plan a taper, and define an optimal weekly training regimen. In other words, by learning how to fully exploit the power of your running technology you can achieve total digital performance management of your running. Your confidence and skill as a self-coached runner will reach a whole new level.

This book takes you through the whole process, from choosing a speed and distance device to using it in races. We begin in chapter 1 by describing the uses of speed and distance devices and heart-rate monitors (which may be purchased separately but are integrated within many speed and distance units) and the benefits of using them to their potential. In chapter 2 we present a comprehensive buyer's guide for speed and distance devices and performance management software programs that help runners get more out of their technologies. Chapters 3 through 6 describe the performance management system that we created to help you get the most out of your speed and distance device and the three steps of this system: monitor, analyze, and plan (or MAP). Chapters 7 to 9 will show you how to race with your speed and distance device and create pace-based training plans. We also provide a selection of ready-made plans for various types of runners. Chapter 10 presents specific advice for triathletes. You'll find guidelines on integrating swim, bike, and run training within a unified performance management system.

The workouts, examples, and scenarios presented in this text use a combination of metric and English measurements, such as meters, miles, 5K, 10K, half marathon, and marathon. If you use metric as the standard unit of measurement in all your training, know that all speed and distance devices feature metric options. You can easily convert the English measurements in the text to metric. A few metric conversions are included after imperial measurements in the text.

Acronyms and Abbreviations

ATL: acute training load

bpm: beats per minute

CTL: chronic training load

CV: critical velocity

DEXA: dual-energy X-ray absorptiometry

EPOC: excess postexercise oxygen consumption

FTP: functional threshold pace

GPS: global positioning system

GTC: Garmin Training Center

HRmax: maximum heart rate

IF: intensity factor

kpm: kilometers per hour

LT: lactate threshold

MAP: monitor, analyze, and plan

MLSSv: maximal lactate steady state velocity

mph: miles per hour

NGP: normalized graded pace

PZI: pace zone index

spm: strides per minute

TSB: training stress balance

TSS: training stress score

1

Gaining the Technological Advantage

A run can be measured, or quantified, using two basic types of measurement. *Performance measurements*—which we might also call *external measurements*—put into numbers the work accomplished in a run. The two most familiar performance measurements are distance and pace. When you say something like "I ran 6 miles" or "I averaged 7 minutes per mile," you are speaking in terms of performance measurements. The other type of measurement is physiological, or internal. *Physiological measurements* may be used to quantify the effects of a run on the body—that is, how hard the body's various systems are working or how much stress they are being exposed to. Common physiological measurements in running include blood lactate levels, rate of oxygen consumption, and heart rate.

Both external and internal measurements are useful in planning and executing training. For example, by tracking your split times for intervals performed in a certain type of track workout, you can quantify improvements in performance as you periodically repeat the workout. Or by working with a coach who provides lactate testing, which involves giving tiny blood samples during a treadmill workout of increasing intensity, you can quantify improvements in your body's ability to handle the stress of running at any given pace.

Recent technologies have given runners the ability to use performance and physiological measurements more easily and effectively than in the past. Specifically, heart-rate monitors allow runners to monitor the contraction rate of the

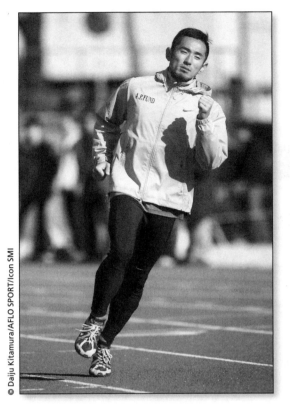

© Daiju Kitamura/AFLO SPORT/Icon SMI

Dai Tamesue trains at Hosei University in Tokyo. Training devices can be used to quantify the work performed during training.

heart—a commonly used indicator of the overall physiological stress of a run—in real time throughout each run as well as during recovery periods in runs and at rest. Before the advent of modern heart-rate monitor technologies, there were no tools for physiological measurements that runners could use on their own. They had to go to university laboratories for $\dot{V}O_2$max tests and other tests.

More recently, a new generation of speed and distance devices based on global positioning system (GPS) and accelerometer technologies has given runners the ability to make accurate and continuous performance measurements in every run. Previously, the best we could do was go to the local track and get split times at the end of every lap or measure road routes with a car odometer and make paint marks at every mile or kilometer.

Heart-rate monitors and speed and distance devices each have several specific uses that help runners train more effectively. But the greatest benefits accrue when runners integrate all of these individual uses within a cohesive system that we call performance management. Chapter 3 presents an overview of the three-step performance management system. Chapters 4, 5, and 6 provide concrete guidelines for executing each of these three steps: monitoring, analyzing, and planning. In this chapter, we focus on the specific uses of heart-rate monitors and speed and distance devices. This is a general overview of the benefits of running and racing with technology. The specific guidelines you will need in order to realize these benefits are detailed in subsequent chapters.

HEART RATE 101

A Finnish company, Polar Electro, developed the first wireless heart-rate monitor in 1977. This device used electrodes contained in a strap worn around the chest to capture the spikes in electrical activity that occur each time the heart muscle contracts. This captured information was then transmitted to a display watch worn on the wrist, which provided a real-time readout of heart rate. Today's heart-rate monitors offer many more bells and whistles, but they still perform their basic function of monitoring heart rate in the same way.

Heart-rate monitors became very popular among runners, cyclists, triathletes, other endurance athletes, and even general exercisers after the late 1970s. The rationale for their use was readily understood, especially by endurance athletes. Runners, for example, are accustomed to targeting one or more specific running intensities in workouts to stimulate a desired training effect—as each running intensity triggers slightly different physiological adaptations. Heart rate has a well-known positive correlation with exercise intensity. The more rapidly and forcefully the working muscles contract during exercise, the more rapidly the heart muscle must contract to provide enough oxygen to enable the working muscles to continue working as hard as they are trying to work. When consumer heart-rate monitors hit the market, runners immediately recognized these devices as tools enabling them to aim at fairly precise numerical targets in their efforts to perform each run at the correct physiological intensity for the workout's purpose, instead of just going by feel. For example, research has shown that the working muscles metabolize fat as fuel at the highest rate at an intensity that corresponds with 75 to 80 percent of maximum heart rate in the average trained endurance athlete. A runner with a heart-rate monitor can use this knowledge to control his or her pace to stay within this heart-rate zone when performing long runs designed to increase fat-burning ability. This physiological approach enhances endurance because fat is a far more abundant muscle fuel source than the other major muscle fuel, carbohydrate. Fatigue in prolonged efforts often occurs when the carbohydrate stores of the working muscles are depleted. When fat-burning capacity is increased, the runner is able to rely more on fat to fuel running and thereby spare carbohydrate and delay the point of fatigue.

The runners who chose to use heart-rate monitors, their coaches, and exercise scientists who conducted research with heart-rate monitors quickly developed a set of standard uses for the devices. Over the past 20 years or so, these standard uses have evolved slightly to account for certain limitations of heart-rate monitoring as a tool for physiological measurement. And most recently, the advent of speed and distance devices has provided runners with new uses for heart-rate monitoring in its rightful role as an adjunct to pace monitoring.

FOUR USES OF A HEART-RATE MONITOR

Heart-rate monitors have four main uses. Use the device to maintain target heart rates in workouts, track changes in fitness, monitor your recovery status, and quantify the stress of individual workouts.

Maintain Target Heart Rates in Workouts

By far the most common use for heart-rate monitors is to facilitate training at the appropriate intensity in workouts. If you know the heart-rate range that is associated with the specific training stimulus you seek in a given run, or segment of a run, then you can check your display watch periodically throughout the workout and adjust your pace as necessary without having to worry about your pace or having to rely entirely on perceived exertion to control your effort. Table 1.1 presents a summary of the primary physiological training effects associated with training at various heart rates.

Table 1.1 Physiological Adaptations Associated With Training at Various Heart Rates

Percentage of maximum heart rate	Physiological adaptation	Fitness benefit
60–70	Increased muscle mitochondria density Increased capillary density Increased aerobic enzyme activity Increased fat oxidation capacity	Increased aerobic capacity (minimal) Increased endurance (moderate)
71–75	Increased muscle mitochondria density Increased capillary density Increased aerobic enzyme activity Increase carbohydrate oxidation capacity Increased muscle glycogen storage	Increased aerobic capacity (minimal) Increased fatigue resistance at moderate paces (moderate)
76–80	Increased heart stroke volume Increased muscle mitochondria density Increased capillary density Increased aerobic enzyme activity Increase carbohydrate oxidation capacity Increased muscle glycogen storage Increased oxygen transport capacity	Increased aerobic capacity (moderate) Increased resistance to fatigue at marathon pace (strong)
81–90	Increased heart stroke volume Increased oxygen transport capacity Increased carbohydrate oxidation capacity Increased neuromuscular coordination Increased lactate shuttling and metabolism	Increased aerobic capacity (moderate) Increased running economy Increased fatigue resistance at half-marathon to 10K pace (strong)
91–100	Increased heart stroke volume Increased fast-twitch muscle fiber recruitment Increased resistance to muscle cell depolarization Increased stride power Increased neuromuscular coordination	Increased aerobic capacity (strong) Increased anaerobic capacity (moderate) Increased speed Increased running economy Increased fatigue resistance at 5K to 1,500 m pace (strong)

The earliest attempts to develop target heart-rate training methodologies were aimed at producing one-size-fits-all protocols that worked for people at all fitness levels in every sport. Simple formulas were used to establish heart-rate zones that divided the heart-rate continuum into levels between recovery intensity and maximum intensity. The simplest and most primitive methodology used the formula of 220 beats per minute (bpm) minus age in years to determine an individual maximum heart rate and a table such as table 1.1 to establish individual target heart-rate zones based on the maximum heart-rate value.

It didn't take very long for athletes, coaches, and exercise scientists to discover major flaws in such one-size-fits-all protocols. First of all, it was observed that maximum heart-rate values, as well as the percentage of maximum heart rate (HRmax) that could be sustained for any given time, varied considerably from activity to activity. For example, runners can generally achieve higher heart rates than cyclists, who in turn can achieve higher heart rates than swimmers.

Further complicating matters, testing showed that the formula of 220 minus age was inaccurate for most athletes. What's more, it was discovered that uniform target heart-rate zones based on percentages of maximum heart rate often were not appropriate for individual athletes, and typically became more or less appropriate for individual athletes as their fitness levels changed. For example, some target heart-rate zone tables established lactate threshold heart rate as 81 to 90 percent of HRmax. (Lactate threshold is the exercise intensity level above which lactate begins to accumulate rapidly in the blood, and it usually corresponds to roughly one hour of maximum effort in trained athletes.) There are three major problems with these zones:

1. The actual lactate threshold heart rate for any individual athlete is much more specific than a full 10 percentage point range.

2. As a percentage of maximum heart rate, lactate threshold values vary considerably among athletes, from as low as 70 percent of HRmax to more than 90 percent.

3. The lactate threshold heart rate of each athlete changes with his or her fitness level.

Fortunately, a few noteworthy experts have since developed better methodologies for establishing target heart-rate zones that overcome these flaws. One of the best was developed by our colleague Joe Friel. It ignores HRmax completely and instead bases target heart-rate zones on lactate threshold heart rate, which is determined through field testing. The simplest field test for lactate threshold heart rate is to run a 30-minute time trial (after a thorough warm-up) at a steady pace. Your average heart rate for the final 10 minutes is considered your lactate threshold heart rate, although it's actually somewhat higher than the value that would be arrived at through laboratory testing. You then look up this value on a table for your specific sport—in this case running—which gives you target heart-rate zones for all of the training zones in Friel's system. Following is a listing of the approximate heart-rate range associated with each zone for running. To establish your zones, you would multiply your lactate threshold heart rate (LT HR) by the percentage associated with the bottom and top of each zone.

Zone 1: Active recovery (>80% of LT HR)

Zone 2: Aerobic threshold (81 to 89% of LT HR)

Zone 3: Tempo (90 to 95% LT HR)

Zone 4: Sublactate threshold (96 to 99% LT HR)

Zone 5a: Lactate threshold (100 to 101% LT HR)

Zone 5b: Aerobic capacity (102 to 105% LT HR)

Zone 5c: Anaerobic capacity (>106% LT HR)

The final step in the process is to repeat your lactate threshold field test every few weeks and adjust your target heart-rate zones to match changes in your fitness level.

The advent of speed and distance technology has made possible an even simpler and more accurate way to establish target heart-rate zones. All you have to do is wear your heart-rate monitor while performing pace-based workouts such as those using the pace zone index (PZI) system presented in chapter 4. Press the Lap button on the display watch at the beginning and end of a segment of the run that is performed at a given target pace. After completing the workout, download the data and inspect the graph of each workout to determine the heart rate that is associated with each target pace. Since no single workout ever encompasses every target pace (there are six separate target pace zones in the PZI system), repeat this process in different workouts until you have covered all of the target pace zones and found the heart rate associated with each.

While we recommend that you rely mainly on pace to monitor and control the intensity of your runs, heart-rate zones established through pace-based training can be a good substitute whenever you are unable to train with your speed and distance device.

Track Changes in Fitness

You can use heart-rate monitors in a few different ways to track changes in fitness level. One way is called *orthostatic testing*. Put on your heart-rate monitor, lie down for a few minutes, and note your heart rate. Now stand up, wait 15 seconds, and note your heart rate again. Your second heart-rate measurement most likely will be 15 to 30 bpm higher than the first. If you perform orthostatic testing regularly while training toward peak fitness, the difference between the two measurements likely will decrease as your heart becomes more powerful and efficient.

An alternative to orthostatic testing that you can use in the context of workouts is heart-rate recovery testing. At the end of a run, cool down with easy jogging until your heart rate levels off at a round number, say 120 bpm, and then stop. After stopping, note how long it takes for your heart rate to drop to 100 bpm. As you gain fitness, your heart rate will drop faster. Be sure to use the same starting heart rate each time you repeat the test. The precise heart rate you choose as a starting number is unimportant. It should just be a heart rate within the range associated with your recovery jogging pace. Choosing a round number within this range might make it easier to remember.

There are other ways of using a heart-rate monitor to track changes in your fitness level that require simultaneous performance measurement. One of the more sophisticated ways of combining these two types of measurement involves tracking the alignment of your goal race pace for a particular event and your heart rate at race pace. If you are training to achieve a certain time goal in an upcoming race, a specific pace per mile associated with that time represents your goal race pace. For example, if your goal is to run a 3:10:00 marathon, your goal race pace is 7:15 per mile.

When you run the race, your performance also will be associated with a certain average heart rate. At the beginning of the process of training for this race, when performing race-pace workouts, your average heart rate will be higher, indicating that you are not yet efficient enough at your goal pace to sustain it for the full race distance. As the training process unfolds, you should observe a lowering trend in your average heart rate at this pace. You also can flip it around and perform workouts at your race-pace heart rate (this requires that you have heart-rate data from previous races at the same distance that were run at peak fitness) and look for a trend toward increasing average speed at this heart rate. There is some debate about whether the information derived from this sort of analysis is worth the bother, and in fact we do not use it in our own coaching, but there are some very successful coaches, including Bobby McGee, who do. (Read about Bobby McGee's approach to balancing pace and heart rate in the sidebar.)

Using the software that comes with your device, or an aftermarket product such as Training Peaks WKO+, you can perform this type of analysis with every run. Just download your workout, look at the graph, and note the average heart rate associated with your average pace for a segment of the workout in which you ran at a steady pace. Then go back to a similar workout performed a few weeks earlier and note the pace associated with the same heart rate or the heart rate associated with the same pace. If you're getting fitter, you will find that in your recent workout, you either ran at a faster pace at the same heart rate or had

Bobby McGee on Balancing Pace and Heart Rate

Originally from South Africa and now based in Boulder, Colorado, Bobby McGee has coached runners at all levels since the late 1970s, and he has coached with speed and distance devices since the Timex Speed and Distance first hit the market in 2002. Before that time, McGee had used heart-rate monitors with his athletes. When the new generation of speed and distance devices came along, he put a lot of thought into how best to balance and integrate the two types of measurement, which can be taken with a single hybrid device such as the Polar RS800. The results of this process are very interesting.

McGee now relies heavily on heart rate–pace relationships to monitor, analyze, and plan the training of his athletes. "With the combination of heart rate and pace, you can triangulate a single workout that allows you to say, 'If I hit these numbers, I know I can accomplish my race goal.'" McGee's training plans culminate in highly race-specific workouts in which runners monitor both pace and heart rate and try to sustain the goal race pace and hope to not exceed their race heart rates. (An example of such a workout for a 10K runner is 5 × 2K with 3-minute walking recoveries.)

Velocity and heart rate are seldom given equal weight in this process, however. "I do heart-rate workouts in the early part of the season," he explains. "At that time, we're training the central physiology—the heart and lungs—and we don't really care about leg speed. But when we get closer to racing, I have them focus on velocity, and heart rate moves into the background. Then I'll say, 'Run at your goal pace and ignore your heart rate. But keep your heart-rate monitor going, and afterward we can see if you had the heart rate we need.'"

For example, McGee's marathon runners often begin their focused race preparation by running 3 or 4 kilometers at precisely their goal marathon pace and note the heart rate associated with that pace. For the next several weeks, they will do workouts that target that heart rate. Speed is not used to control the workout intensity, but it is monitored, and McGee looks to see the runner moving faster and faster at the same heart rate.

In the latter part of the training process, this pattern is inverted. The runner performs increasingly challenging workouts at his or her goal race pace. Heart rate is ignored during the workout, but not afterward. McGee looks to see the heart rate coming down as the pace remains the same over longer distances.

"Heart-rate numbers by themselves never meant much to me," McGee says. "Comparing heart rate and velocity numbers is very instructive, however. And speed and distance devices are quite useful for that purpose."

a lower heart rate at the same pace. It should be noted, though, that heart rate can be affected by various factors, such as temperature, sleep, and emotional arousal, so there will be some variability in this response.

Monitor Recovery Status

Adequate physiological recovery between workouts is critical to the process of fitness development. The central nervous system plays an important role in various recovery processes. The nervous system has two components. The sympathetic nervous system specializes in handling stress and is therefore highly active during exercise. It raises the heart rate, among other things. The parasympathetic nervous system specializes in recovering from stress and becomes most active after exercise. It lowers the heart rate, among other things. When an athlete trains too hard or gets too little recovery between workouts, the sympathetic nervous system becomes chronically overexcited, one consequence of which is an elevated heart rate between workouts.

Based on this fact, you can use the orthostatic testing method described previously to monitor your recovery status. If the difference between your lying and standing heart rates fails to decrease over time despite increasing training, you have reason to suspect that you are not getting enough recovery and should scale back your training.

Quantify the Stress of Workouts

In the 1970s, an exercise scientist named Eric Banister created a heart rate-based system of quantifying the stress of workouts. In this system, the duration and average heart rate of a workout are plugged into a complex formula that yields a training impulse score. What's cool about the training impulse model is that it enables athletes to make "apples to apples" comparisons of all types of workouts. For example, you can figure out just how far you have to run at a low heart rate to achieve a training impulse that is equal to a short, high-intensity interval workout. Banister and other scientists who built on his work used the training impulse model primarily to establish precise quantitative relationships between training stress and performance. This work yielded valuable insights into the most effective rate of training stress increase, the time course of recovery from training stress, and other such matters that can help athletes shape their future training in a manner that maximizes the likelihood of peak performance at the right times.

As powerful as it is, the training impulse model has several drawbacks, including the fact that it is incredibly complex and impractical for everyone except a few experts on the model. A few years ago, in an effort to salvage the strengths of the training impulse model and discard its weaknesses, Andrew Coggan created a new way of quantifying the training stress of workouts that is specific to cyclists and uses power data instead of heart rate. In this model, each workout is assigned a training stress score (TSS). Impressed by the simplicity and power of TSS, Stephen McGregor subsequently created a formula to determine TSS in running based on pace data from a speed and distance device. Most recently, Stephen's colleagues at Training Peaks found an accurate way to translate power-based and pace-derived TSS scores into heart rate-based TSS scores, which allow cyclists and runners to quantify the stress of workouts when they don't have pace or power data.

Training stress score is one of the most important performance management concepts. You can use it to gather all kinds of information and insights that will help you train more effectively. In coming chapters you will learn how to use TSS and other related concepts to achieve performance management objectives such as determining how long you should train for a marathon and how often you should schedule recovery weeks.

LIMITATIONS OF HEART-RATE MONITORS

As useful as they are, heart-rate monitors have significant limitations for runners. Even in the most sophisticated heart rate-based training systems, the prescribed target heart-rate zones do not always fit the individual runner. In addition, heart-rate monitoring is not useful in short intervals and very high-intensity efforts, and as previously stated, heart rate is affected by factors such as temperature and emotional status. And most important, heart-rate data are not performance-relevant for runners. Let's take a closer look at each of these limitations.

Zones Don't Always Fit

The relationship between heart rate and exercise intensity varies considerably among individual runners. Even runners who have the same lactate threshold heart rate as determined through testing might find that their heart rates behave very differently at exercise intensities above and below the lactate threshold. For this reason, the heart-rate zones that any given heart rate-based training system prescribes for runners who share a certain lactate threshold heart rate might fit one runner better than another.

For example, a relatively unfit runner and a very fit runner might both have a lactate threshold heart rate of 170 bpm. However, this number might represent only 75 percent of the unfit runner's maximum heart rate, whereas it might be 85 percent of the very fit runner's maximum heart rate. Yet while the unfit runner would struggle to sustain efforts at a slightly higher heart rate—say, 177 bpm—the fitter runner might be able to sustain such efforts much more easily. In some heart rate-based training systems, a heart rate of 177 bpm falls within the aerobic capacity or $\dot{V}O_2$max training zone for all runners sharing a lactate threshold heart rate. But in this example, a heart rate of 177 bpm is probably not an appropriate target heart rate in $\dot{V}O_2$max intervals for both the unfit and the very fit runner. The unfit runner should aim a few beats lower and the very fit runner a few beats higher.

Based on the uniqueness of each runner's heart-rate profile, we believe it's best to skip the heart-rate zone formulas and do pace-based workouts using the pace zone index. As suggested previously, if you wear a heart-rate monitor during your workouts, you can hit the Lap button at the beginning and end of segments at various target paces and then review your workout data after completing your runs to determine the heart rate associated with each target pace. With this information, you can use heart rate as a secondary means of gauging the intensity of your workouts.

Not Useful in Short Intervals and Very High-Intensity Efforts

In running, the maximum heart rate is reached at submaximal paces—usually 3,000-meter to 800-meter race pace, depending on the runner. When running speed is increased further, the heart rate does not increase because it has already hit a ceiling. Further, the heart rate response is quite slow compared to changes in pace. Thus, at the end of a 200-meter sprint, your heart rate likely will be no higher, and may actually be lower, than it is at the end of a 3,000-meter race, despite the fact that you run 20 to 25 percent faster in the sprint.

Because heart rate plateaus at submaximal running paces, heart-rate monitoring cannot be used to quantify and control exercise intensity during very high-intensity training intervals or shorter races. What's more, heart rate does not rise instantaneously to match sudden increases in pace. For this reason, when you run shorter intervals—which, of course, tend to be very fast intervals—your heart rate will not reach a level that is truly indicative of your exercise intensity until you're 30 or more seconds into it. Due to this phenomenon of cardiac lag, as well as that of the heart-rate plateau, heart-rate monitoring is not useful in your fastest and shortest training efforts.

Not Relevant to Performance

The greatest limitation of heart-rate monitoring is that it's not relevant to a runner's performance. Heart rate alone tells you nothing about your capacity to perform as a runner. Races are run by time. The only performance-relevant variables are time over distance and pace. You can't set heart-rate goals. Well, you could, but such goals wouldn't make much sense! As Joe Friel says, "They don't give out medals for the highest heart rate. They give out medals for crossing the finish line first." For this reason, heart rate can't motivate you to train harder or push yourself more in races.

Perhaps the most significant advantage of training by pace over training by heart rate is simply that training by pace—if done properly—pushes you to run harder in your key workouts and thus get more benefit from those workouts. Pace and time over distance are meaningful to runners. For this reason, you almost always will perform better in your harder workouts if, instead of just running hard by feel, you run in pursuit of a goal time or pace that forces you to run a

© Nick Laham/Getty Images Sport

Shannon Rowbury wins the women's 1500m at the Adidas Track Classic. Races are won based on time over distance and pace, not heart rate.

bit faster than you would run by feel—just as you will almost always run the homestretch of a race faster if you're battling another runner for position than if you're all alone.

Naturally, you're not supposed to push your limits in every workout. Heart rate and pace monitoring alike actually should be used to moderate your effort in many workouts. But your fitness gets the greatest boost from those key workouts in which you do push your limits; pace monitoring will help you push your limits and get more out of these workouts, whereas heart-rate monitoring will not.

SPEED AND DISTANCE 101

Two types of speed and distance devices provide real-time measurements of running distance, time, and pace. Devices such as the Timex Bodylink use GPS technology. Signals are sent between the device and satellites in outer space to triangulate your precise position to within a foot, and changes in your position are used to calculate the information you're interested in tracking. Devices such as the Nike Triax use accelerometer technology. An accelerometer is a device that measures changes in the rate of forward movement. Unlike pedometers—more primitive devices that merely count steps and can't account for variability in stride length— accelerometer-based devices contain sensors that you attach to the laces of your shoe and make several hundred measurements per second for more accurate data.

SEVEN USES OF A SPEED AND DISTANCE DEVICE

Speed and distance devices of both types—GPS based and accelerometer based—can benefit your training in more ways than you probably ever imagined. We briefly discuss seven uses for speed and distance devices here. You will learn how to execute these uses in later chapters.

Maintain Target Pace in Workouts and Races

The most basic use of a speed and distance device is for monitoring your pace during runs. While it is interesting to know how fast you are running at any given time, this information is not intrinsically helpful. To make pace monitoring beneficial to your training, you need to start each run with one or more specific target pace levels in mind and use your speed and distance device to ensure that you hit these targets. If you perform appropriately structured workouts and select pace targets that are appropriate for your current fitness level, you will get exactly the fitness benefit you seek from each run.

Controlling workout intensity by pace is more effective than controlling it by heart rate because pace is directly relevant to performance. While it's enlightening to know your heart rate, oxygen consumption rate, blood lactate level, and other physiological parameters when running, the relationship between each of these physiological parameters and performance is complex. And in the end, performance is what really matters. Consider two runners who are both capable of running a 20:00 5K. When running side by side during a 5K race, these runners would likely have different heart rates, oxygen consumption rates, blood lactates, and so forth. It is the sum of these disparate physiological variables in each runner that makes both capable of running a 20:00 5K. Therefore it would not be appropriate for either of them to do workouts based entirely on just one of these variables. Only performance accounts for all of them.

These two runners will get the best results from their training if they do pace-based workouts scaled to their performance level. Since they race at the same pace, they should perform every type of workout at more or less the same pace, regardless of how each of them achieves these pace levels physiologically.

The pace zone index is a simple tool that was developed by Matt Fitzgerald with Training Peaks to enable runners with speed and distance devices to select appropriate target pace levels for each workout and execute their pace-based runs correctly. This tool is based on the VDOT pace-based training system developed by Jack Daniels and described in his 2005 book *Daniels' Running Formula*. There are other pace-based training systems, but we recommend that you use the pace zone index because of its compatibility with speed and distance devices. To get started on this system, our hypothetical 20:00 5K runners would simply look up their 5K time in table 4.1 (see page 63), find the PZI level associated with it, and then move to table 4.2 on page 68 to locate the target pace zones for various workout intensities.

Develop a Sense of Pace

Pacing is a critical and underappreciated factor in running performance. Achieving maximum performance in races requires that you have a good feel for exactly how much to restrain your pace in the early part of a race so that you reach the finish line just before fatigue forces you to slow down. No runner has a perfect sense of his or her performance limits, but some have a better sense than others, and every runner becomes a better self-pacer with experience. Workouts and races calibrate your sense of pace by enabling the largely subconscious parts of your brain that regulate pace to create associations between the feeling of running at different paces and the amount of time it takes for fatigue to develop at each of these paces.

Training by pace facilitates this important process by feeding your brain with additional objective information that it can use to calibrate its pacing mechanism. For example, if you are training to break 3:10:00 in a marathon, a finishing time that's associated with a pace of 7:15 per mile, you will develop a much better feel for this pace if you wear a speed and distance device during marathon-pace workouts and see uninterrupted visual confirmation of the fact that you are running at 7:15 pace while simultaneously experiencing the feeling of running at this pace. A stopwatch is not as useful for this purpose because it allows you to check your pace only when you reach distance markers (usually once every mile or km), whereas a speed and distance device allows you to monitor your pace continuously.

Design and Execute Pace-Based Training Plans

The pace zone index features six target training pace zones. There are 10 total pace zones, but four of them are gray zones that are not targeted in workouts. The appropriate distribution of your weekly training among the six target pace zones depends on your goal race distance and how far along you are in the training process. Using the pace zone index and the proven principles and methods of training for races of various distances, you can design training regimens in which your pace zone distribution is planned and varied optimally from the very first week of training to the very last.

Among the cool features of some of the performance management software programs for runners is one that shows you how much time you have spent running in each pace zone over the last week, or four weeks, or other time period. This feature enables you to determine whether your actual training pace distribution matches what you had planned. Any discrepancy might explain a weakness in your running fitness. Then you can make adjustments to correct it. Figure 1.1 shows a sample 28-day pace zone distribution graph.

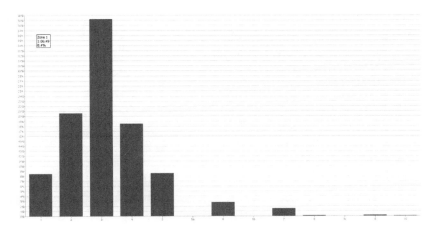

Figure 1.1 Sample pace zone distribution graph.

Courtesy of TrainingPeaks (www.trainingpeaks.com).

Get Encouragement to Train Harder

As suggested previously, one advantage of pace monitoring over heart-rate monitoring is that pace monitoring tends to encourage you to run harder in those
key workouts in which it is appropriate to test your limits. The performance-
enhancing effect of feedback has been demonstrated scientifically. In a British
study, 40 healthy male subjects performed a challenging shuttle run test both
with and without performance feedback—specifically, pace and time information—provided by observers. The researchers found that the subjects performed
significantly better in the test with performance feedback. Clearly, they were
motivated by the numbers.

Seldom should you push yourself truly as hard as you can in workouts. Such
efforts would be counterproductive; they would take a long time to recover from
and would therefore sabotage your performance in your next few runs. A much
more productive way to use the performance data from a speed and distance
device in key workouts is to aim toward slightly exceeding your performance in
the last key workout of the same type. For example, if you ran a 10K tempo run
in 43:12 two weeks ago and today you do another 10K tempo run, you should
aim to complete it in slightly under 43:12. A tempo run is not a time trial. The
goal is never to run as fast as you can. But by running the first key workout of
each type at the appropriate pace for your PZI level and then pushing to raise
the bar a bit in each subsequent workout of that type, you generally will train
a little harder and gain fitness slightly faster without overtaxing yourself and
failing to get the desired training effect from these workouts.

Track Training Workload

Although technically pace is an external measurement, it can serve as a useful
proxy of internal measurement. Earlier we explained that no single physiological

variable (heart rate, rate of oxygen consumption, blood lactate level, and so on) presents a complete picture of how much stress the body as a whole experiences during a run. However, pace, when considered in relation to the individual runner's performance level, does provide a complete picture of workout stress because running pace and the duration spent running at that pace are the only inputs that determine the totality of workout stress on the whole body.

Most runners keep track of their total running distance (also referred to as mileage and expressed either in miles or kilometers) and use their mileage numbers to quantify how hard they are training. But total distance does not account for the intensity of running, which also has a significant impact on total training stress. Thirty miles of fast running per week would likely be more stressful than 50 slow miles. It's really the combination of running mileage and running intensity, or pace relative to performance level, that determines your training load, or total training stress. Speed and distance devices and their associated software make it possible to track your training workload, thus defined. The most sophisticated example is the training stress score system mentioned previously, which is explained fully in chapter 5.

Tracking your training workload enables you to analyze the effect of training on your fitness and performance in all kinds of ways. For example, Training Peaks allows you to plot your best workout performances on a graph that shows fluctuations in your training stress balance, which is essentially your fitness level minus your fatigue level, over time. By looking at this simple picture, you can readily determine the training stress balance that is optimal for your performance.

Track Changes in Performance

Every runner with a stopwatch, access to a track or other measured running courses, and a decent memory is able to track changes in his or her running performance in a rudimentary way. For example, perhaps you ran 400-meter intervals at the track three weeks ago and completed each lap in 86 to 89 seconds. Yesterday you ran 400-meter intervals again and completed each lap in 84 to 87 seconds. The difference between your split times in these two workouts provides a solid indication that at least one aspect of your running fitness is improving.

A speed and distance device, in combination with performance management software, enables you to track changes in performance in more varied and sophisticated ways. For example, if you use a speed and distance device with heart-rate monitoring capability, every stride of every run you do can be used to measure changes in performance. Simply choose a segment of a very recent run in which you maintained a fairly steady pace and note the corresponding average heart rate. Now go back a few weeks and find a segment of a run in which you averaged the same pace over the same distance. If the corresponding average heart rate is higher in this earlier workout, you have pretty good evidence that you've gained efficiency at that particular pace. You can make this type of comparison for any pace: a very fast-pace run in short intervals, your goal pace for an upcoming marathon, your standard aerobic pace, or any other pace you run with regularity.

Analyze and Assess Workout and Race Performances

With a speed and distance device, you can analyze your workout and race performances in more sophisticated ways than you could without one. You can use the information and insights drawn from such analyses to shore up weaknesses and avoid repeating mistakes. For example, in interval workouts performed without a speed and distance device, you cannot analyze your pacing very deeply. If you run intervals on a track, you can look at each 400-meter split time for intervals that are 400 meters in length or longer. But with a speed and distance device and the accompanying software, you can look at your pace in segments of any length within each interval. Suppose you run 1-kilometer (2.5-lap) intervals at the track. You could look at your pace for each 100-meter segment of each interval to see how well you paced yourself.

A common tendency in such workouts is to run the first 200 to 300 meters very fast, then slow considerably, and finally rebound a bit in the final 200 to 300 meters. This uneven pacing pattern may indicate poor fatigue resistance and pain tolerance at the pace level that usually is targeted in intervals of this length: pace zone 8 in the PZI system, or roughly 5K race pace. Making a conscious effort to run slightly slower at the start of these intervals and to prevent a sagging of pace in the middle segment may help to address these weaknesses. Alternatively, it may simply be that the sagging of pace in the middle of these intervals is indicative that the first part is too fast. Regardless, by slowing the first portion, a more appropriate pace for the interval can be achieved.

Another way to identify weaknesses is to compare your performance in different types of workouts. For example, when you train using the PZI, most of your key workouts are performed in pace zones 4, 6, 8, and 10. It can be instructive to look at your average pace in workouts targeting each of these four pace zones. If you tend to run toward the top end (that is, the slow end) of one of these four target zones while running toward the low end (that is, the fast end) of the others, then you are probably weak at that one particular intensity level and should consider increasing your training at that intensity level to address the problem.

LIMITATIONS OF SPEED AND DISTANCE DEVICES

The usefulness of speed and distance devices in run training is limited in two ways. First, pace is affected by hills; therefore the relationship between pace and physiological intensity changes with the gradient of your running surface. The variable of normalized graded pace (NGP), or flat pace, corrects for this effect, but only after the fact (when you analyze the workout in your performance management software), so you can't use it to adjust your pace appropriately while you run. In the future, flat pace may be integrated into one or more brands of speed and distance devices. In the meantime, it is best to use heart rate to control pace on hill climbs and descents. For example, as you approach a hill running at a target pace, note your heart rate. As you begin climbing the hill, you can reduce your pace as necessary to keep your heart rate fairly constant to maintain approximately the same physiological effort, as opposed to overdoing it by trying to run the hill at the same pace as on the flats, causing you to fatigue prematurely.

A second limitation of speed and distance devices is their accuracy. Most are only 97 to 99 percent accurate. This level of accuracy is adequate for most circumstances, but there are times when perfect accuracy would make a difference. For example, suppose you perform an interval workout on a road route, having performed the same workout on a different road two weeks earlier. A 1 percent improvement in your interval pace between the first workout and the second would be a good sign, but since your device's margin of error is probably greater than 1 percent, you can't know with certainty whether this improvement was real.

Different types of speed and distance devices, and different ways of using them, are more or less accurate than others in various running environments. For the casual runner, these differences, while they do have a measurable effect on accuracy, are not worth worrying about. However, for a serious competitive runner who trains with precise target paces for various workout types and wants the greatest possible degree of accuracy in recorded workout data, these differences need to be accounted for and addressed as much as possible.

Roads

In normal training on the roads, all of the speed and distance devices from major brands have an acceptable level of accuracy. For example, Matt Fitzgerald's Garmin 405 is consistently 99 percent accurate on the roads, which translates to being roughly 4 seconds per mile off his actual pace.

That said, it's useful to know *exactly* how accurate your device is. You can determine your unit's level of accuracy by using a bike computer to measure off a mile on a stretch of road you frequently run, and then run it to see how your speed and distance device's measurement compares. Using this method and other similar comparison methods, Matt has found that his Garmin is not really accurate to within ±1 percent, as you might expect. Rather, it *consistently overestimates* distance by roughly 1 percent. This knowledge allows him to make a mental correction of the data his device gives him in every road run. For example, if it tells him he ran 18 miles at 6:56 per mile, he knows he really ran something closer to 17.82 miles at 7:00 per mile.

Tracks

Most GPS-based speed and distance devices grossly overestimate distance on standard 400-meter running tracks. The GPS tracking resolution just isn't adequate for reading those tight counterclockwise turns precisely. Since perfect accuracy is paramount in track workouts, these devices are essentially useless in that environment. However, some GPS-based speed and distance devices can be converted to accelerometer-based devices with the purchase of a foot pod. The foot pod can be calibrated on the track itself, providing better accuracy there in some circumstances. Because this depends on the consistency of the individual's cadence and stride length, there are limitations to foot pod accuracy as well. If you make a habit of running on tracks, you should either purchase an accelerometer-based device such as the Suunto t6 or convert your device with a foot pod.

We have been assured that the performance of GPS-based speed and distance devices on the track will improve in the future. It's a matter of waiting for a full switchover to a dual-frequency GPS platform.

Treadmills

Naturally, you can't use a GPS-based speed and distance device indoors on a treadmill. Since a properly calibrated treadmill provides accurate information on speed and distance, you might wonder why you would even need to use a speed and distance device on a treadmill. The reason is data capture. Monitoring and controlling speed and distance are only half the purpose of using a speed and distance device. Capturing data to download onto your training log is the other purpose, and for that you need a speed and distance device.

If you run regularly on a treadmill, purchase either an accelerometer-based speed and distance device or a foot pod that converts your GPS-based device for use indoors. This will allow you to capture pace, distance, and possibly also heart rate data throughout your treadmill workouts, just as you do on the track and on the road.

Hilly Routes

Some speed and distance devices record changes in elevation more accurately than others. This is something you'll want to consider if you make a habit of running on hilly routes. Accelerometers actually can't measure elevation changes at all. Accelerometer-based speed and distance devices rely on built-in barometric pressure sensors to measure changes in elevation. Not all accelerometer-based speed and distance devices have built-in barometric pressure sensors, however, and among those that do, some are better than others. The best ones are in high-end units such as the Polar RS800CX.

A good barometric pressure sensor generally measures elevation changes more accurately than GPS, which does a poor job of it. Fortunately, mapping technologies available in some performance management software applications can largely correct for the inaccuracy of elevation-change data collected on a run with a GPS-based speed and distance device. These elevation-correction tools match the coordinates of your route (as mapped by your device) against precise topographical maps of those coordinates to determine the actual elevation changes you experienced during the run. So if you use a GPS-based speed and distance device, be sure to use a performance management software application with elevation-correction capability.

YOUR DIGITAL COACH

Speed and distance devices and heart-rate monitors allow you to do for yourself many of the things that a good running coach does for his or her athletes, but in somewhat different and often more powerful ways. The main job of a running coach is to manage the athlete's performance. The latest running technologies make effective performance management easy to do without a coach. Indeed, using these technologies is like having your own digital coach that you can stuff in a drawer between workouts and analysis sessions.

Heart-rate monitoring alone is not adequate for effective performance management. Pace monitoring provides enough information for a self-coached runner to plan and execute training for optimal results, but combined pace and heart-rate monitoring will allow a runner to do even more. If you can afford the $150 to $250 price tag of a device that combines speed and distance monitoring and heart-rate monitoring capabilities, we suggest you get one. It's still a lot cheaper than hiring a coach!

Choosing the Right Technology

Before you can train with a speed and distance device, you have to own one. The purchase of such a device is one you'll want to make carefully. These tools are not cheap, so it's important that you know as much as possible about the model you favor before you take it home, lest you suffer from $150 or more worth of buyer's remorse. There are significant differences between models, and none of them is every runner's favorite. You will greatly increase the odds of purchasing a device you're happy with if you first educate yourself about all of the major brands. This chapter gives you that education.

The six major players in the market for speed and distance devices for runners are Garmin, Nike, Polar, Silva, Suunto, and Timex. Except for Polar, all of these companies make both stand-alone speed and distance devices and speed and distance devices with integrated heart-rate monitors. Polar includes a heart-rate monitor with all of its speed and distance devices and also sells heart-rate monitors separately. New models are being introduced and existing models modified and phased out rapidly, so we avoid mentioning specific models in the following pages and instead focus our discussion on the key characteristics of each brand, which are manifest in most if not all of the brand's individual models and are less likely to change in the future.

GARMIN

Founded in 1989, Garmin is a Kansas-based company that specializes in developing and selling GPS devices. It won't surprise you, then, to learn that most of Garmin's run speed and distance devices use GPS technology. In our experience, Garmin makes the most reliable GPS devices. They are quite accurate and are the least likely to have their signals interrupted midrun by clouds, trees, and other obstructions. Garmin was also the first manufacturer of speed and distance devices to install the GPS inside the wrist display unit, so there is only one piece of hardware to worry about (besides the heart-rate monitor strap). Many runners prefer this design to that of the Timex Bodylink, which has a separate wristwatch and GPS unit worn strapped around the upper arm.

In our testing, the Garmin Forerunner's distance readings were consistently 98 to 99 percent accurate on roads. They were considerably less accurate on running tracks, however. If you purchase a Forerunner with plans to use it regularly on running tracks, we strongly recommend that you also buy the foot pod accessory that allows you to instantly convert the Forerunner into an accelerometer-based speed and distance device. The foot pod looks like a miniature computer mouse and is attached to the top of either shoe through the laces. It also can be placed in the accelerometer pockets of those running shoes that have them, such as certain Adidas models. When the foot pod and the Garmin speed and distance device are both switched on, the device detects the foot pod and prompts the user to link to it so that it receives speed and distance data from the foot pod instead of its built-in GPS. You can calibrate the accelerometer right on the track for better accuracy. The foot pod enables you to use the unit indoors on a treadmill, as well. There is also a Garmin speed and distance device that contains no GPS and is strictly accelerometer based.

Garmin's Forerunner line deserves high marks for accuracy, reliability, and ease of use. What it lacks is any cool proprietary features to compete with Polar's Running Index and Suunto's Training Effect, which more fully realize the potential power of this type of technology.

With the purchase of MotionBased, now called Garmin Connect, a Web application that imports GPS data into functional analysis and online mapping tools, Garmin offers the most sophisticated mapping features of any company in the business. It allows you to do all kinds of cool things, such as wirelessly share workout information with other Garmin users and replay past workouts on a map, with a moving dot representing your progress along the route, to compare your pacing in different workouts on the same course at various points in the training process.

Some of the most useful tools on the device are more basic. A Virtual Partner helps you maintain a predetermined target pace in workouts and races by showing you exactly where you are in relation to a little stick figure who maintains that pace perfectly (for example, "You are ahead by 0:15"). An autolap feature can be used to collect split times at any distance automatically as you run. You also can store a large number of preprogrammed workouts on the device, which guides you through the specific workout you've selected as you execute it. You can even download entire training plans onto the device, which then coaches you through each workout day by day. Finally, Garmins are the only speed and distance devices that allow the user to program 10 pace zones—for example, all 10 zones of the Pace Zone Index.

Garmin speed and distance devices come with a performance management software application called Garmin Training Center (GTC). With GTC you can view detailed graphs of your workout data plotted over time or distance and create customized workouts with specific goals and rest intervals.

Some Garmin speed and distance devices can be mounted on a bike handlebar and used as a cycling computer. All models are sold either as stand-alone speed and distance devices or with an integrated heart-rate monitor.

NIKE

The world's largest sporting goods brand entered the speed and distance device market with the Triax Elite, which, like competing devices made by other brands, consists of an accelerometer foot pod, a wristwatch, and a heart-rate monitor strap. The Triax Elite is still on the market, but it has been hugely overshadowed by Nike+, which has radically changed the face of the speed and distance device market. Nike+ has taken this technology to the masses. Companies such as Timex and Polar number their annual sales of speed and distance devices in the tens of thousands of units. Codeveloped by the Apple computer company, the Nike+ was purchased by nearly half a million runners in its first three months on the market in 2006.

Nike has taken the bold step of making nearly all of its running shoes Nike+ compatible, which means they are designed with a recess underneath the insole where a small Nike+ accelerometer, sold separately, can be placed. It sends information on speed and distance either to an Apple iPod, which transmits the data audibly to the runner through headphones, or to a wristband for visual display. Workout data can then be uploaded onto a Mac or PC and, from there, uploaded onto a personal online training log. Nike has created a lot of excitement around the Nike+ with a brilliant marketing campaign that includes online team challenges, in which groups of runners vie to log the highest cumulative Nike+ distance over a designated time period.

The Nike+ is not suitable for serious performance management, however. In general it is less accurate than most other speed and distance devices and becomes increasingly inaccurate as the runner's speed increases above or decreases below the pace that was run during the device's initial calibration. Thus the data collected in variable-pace workouts such as the typical interval session are worthless. In addition, the Nike+ Web site's data analysis tools lack sophistication.

For all of these reasons, we recommend that Nike fans wanting to commit to digital performance management purchase the Triax Elite. It is significantly more accurate than the Nike+ system and it comes with full-featured performance management software. The foot pod, which must be attached to the laces of a shoe, is rather bulky compared to the Nike+ accelerometer unit, however.

POLAR

Polar made athlete heart-rate monitors for many years before the company produced its first running speed and distance device. Given Polar's technological heritage, it was only to be expected that the company would decide to include an integrated heart-rate monitor with each of its speed and distance devices. And they are the best heart-rate monitors on the market, featuring comfortable, durable chest straps, smooth heart-rate readings, and cool proprietary features. Among these features (not all of which are available on every model) are recovery measurement time, which measures how quickly your heart rate drops at the end of a workout; OwnOptimizer, which is a built-in modified version of orthostatic testing; and the Running Index, which rates each run through a complex analysis of the relationship between your pace and heart rate in a given run.

Most of Polar's speed and distance devices use accelerometer technology. As with other brands, the accelerometer is contained in a foot pod that is attached to the shoe, but it's smaller and easier to attach and remove than most. One downside of this convenience, however, is that even a slight shift in the positioning of the foot pod from one installation to the next may result in the need for recalibration.

Runners who wear Adidas running shoes and apparel have another option. Adidas and Polar have teamed up to provide an integrated system, called WearLink, in which the heart-rate monitor is affixed to the running top and the accelerometer is placed inside the shoe, as in the Nike+ system.

Just as some of Garmin's GPS-based speed and distance devices can be converted into accelerometers with the purchase of an optional foot pod, some of Polar's accelerometer-based models can be converted into GPS devices with the purchase of an optional GPS unit that is worn strapped to the upper arm. There's no significant difference in accuracy between the two options, and Polar's GPS unit lacks the sophisticated mapping support that Garmin's has. What's more, only the accelerometer option allows the user to monitor stride cadence and length, which can be useful. Throw in the greater versatility of the accelerometer (more accurate on running tracks, usable indoors), and we think that with Polar's speed and distance devices, the foot pod is the way to go.

Polar's performance management application, Polar Personal Trainer, is among the best. It is hosted online at www.polarpersonaltrainer.com. When you connect the device to your computer and download a workout, it is logged into your online training calendar. Use the application to track your training by the day, week, or month through any variable from mileage to Running Index score. You also can use it to create complete training plans and then download them onto your device to follow day by day.

John Stanton on the Intimidation Factor

John Stanton has known about and advocated run speed and distance devices longer than almost anyone else. Stanton is the founder of Canada's largest chain of running specialty stores, The Running Room, which is headquartered in Calgary, Alberta, Canada, just down the road from the University of Alberta, where the accelerometer technology that is used in many devices was developed. Thanks to his connections there, Stanton enjoyed the opportunity to be among the first runners and coaches to test the technology.

To say that Stanton is a fan of the technology is to be guilty of a gross understatement. "I think it's the best thing to come along since the stopwatch," he says.

The Running Room sells more speed and distance devices than any other Canadian retailer. Besides its strong advocacy of the technology, the key to The Running Room's success in selling speed and distance devices is its efforts to help customers overcome feelings of intimidation about the newness of the technology, its proper use, and even the price of some products.

The primary means by which Stanton and his staff help their customers overcome their worries about the difficulty of using a speed and distance device is by taking the time to show them how to operate the device. "Nobody gets much out of user's manuals," he says. "It always seems so much easier when someone who understands how to operate the product guides you through the process in person." Stanton recommends that all runners in the market for their first speed and distance device do their shopping at stores that provide the same level of service or learn to use a product from a fellow runner who already owns it, preferably before buying it.

Stanton believes that some brands of speed and distance devices are easier to use than others, and considers Garmin the most user-friendly brand. Manufacturers have an obligation to create products that are not intimidating, he says, and he in turn feels an obligation to steer customers toward the most user-friendly products, unless they are more concerned about having specific features than about ease of use. Virtually all manufacturers are making increasingly easy-to-use devices, notes Stanton, and he urges runners who were turned off by the difficulty of earlier devices to give them a second chance.

In Stanton's experience, younger runners and beginning runners are the most receptive to the new technology. "Today's young people have grown up with so much technology that they are very comfortable using it in every part of their lives, running included," he says. Novice runners like speed and distance devices for a different reason. "I believe the number-one factor that prevents people from exercising is fear of embarrassment," says Stanton. "Speed and distance devices help new runners overcome that by giving them the ability to easily guide their own training."

Stanton foresees a day, not too far in the future, when every sports watch is also a speed and distance device. The technology will continue to become cheaper and easier to use until speed and distance monitors are simply standard features of better running watches, and the only runners who are intimidated by these devices are the few who are intimidated by regular sports watches today. In the meantime, Stanton is doing his part to make runners comfortable with the products that currently exist. Indeed, the future is now at The Running Room store in Alberta. "We have a group that meets regularly for workouts, and about 80 percent of them use speed and distance devices," he says.

Triathletes will be happy to know that Polar makes one speed and distance device that can be purchased with options that allow it to function as a bike computer and power meter. For more information about this model, see page 185, under the heading Polar, in chapter 10.

SUUNTO

Suunto is the "other" Finnish company that manufactures speed and distance devices for running. It was founded in 1936 as a compass maker. Suunto later began to supply divers with watches specially designed for their needs. Only within the past few years did the brand enter the endurance sport market. But while Suunto is a latecomer to the speed and distance device market, and their share of that market is but a sliver, it is widely agreed that their running products are as high quality as any.

© Walt Middleton/Icon SMI

Galen Rupp sprints to the finish line at the NCAA Cross-Country Championship in Terra Haute, Indiana. Speed and distance devices are useful in monitoring all types of running.

Suunto offers both accelerometer-based and GPS-based devices. However, only the accelerometer-based devices, which use a foot pod that is clipped to the laces of a shoe, is marketed specifically to runners. The GPS-based device is sold as a general outdoor sport unit. The easy attachment and removal of the foot pod make it convenient for runners who use more than one pair of shoes, but even slight discrepancies in placement create the need for recalibration, which requires a trip to the local running track.

All models have the features runners want, including programmable pace and heart-rate zones and an auto-split feature. But some unique advanced features make Suunto's offerings special. Most notably, these devices estimate excess postexercise oxygen consumption (EPOC) and use these data to calculate the training effect of each workout (that is, how stressful it was). The devices also estimate respiration rate and oxygen consumption during workouts.

The performance management software that is bundled with Suunto's speed and distance devices is called Suunto Training Manager. It allows you to graph EPOC, training effect, oxygen consumption, pace, and other variables from a specific workout or across any chosen period.

Suunto also sells packages for triathletes. Along with a heart-rate monitor strap and foot pod, they include a pedaling cadence sensor and a spoke-mounted sensor that delivers bike speed and distance data to the display watch, which is worn during both cycling and running. This setup allows you to easily capture data for a complete brick workout or triathlon event.

TIMEX

Timex introduced the first GPS-based speed and distance device for runners in 2002, but they got an assist from Garmin, who supplied the actual GPS unit. Timex contributed the wristwatch and the software. Runners and triathletes, many of whom had wished for such a technology for years, were enthralled by the Timex Ironman Speed + Distance, but it wasn't perfect. The flow of data from communication between the GPS and satellites was easily interrupted by trees and cloud cover, and the GPS unit was cumbersome and bulky.

The latest generation of Timex speed and distance devices exists in two lines: Timex Speed + Distance (no heart-rate monitor) and Timex Ironman Triathlon Bodylink (with integrated heart-rate monitor). These devices are significantly more refined than the first generation of Timex devices. The GPS unit is about half the size of the original, and the satellite connections are more reliable. In our experience, Garmin's own branded speed and distance devices have fewer signal interruptions.

Timex's specialty is watches, and their speed and distance display watches are probably the best. They are light and stylish enough to be worn all day, they have the "takes a lickin' and keeps on tickin'" factor, and they have a better variety of information display options than other devices. You can even configure your own custom display so that the watch shows the information you want to see where you want to see it.

If you want to use your Timex speed and distance device for complete performance management, you will need to purchase an optional data recorder, a very small unit that you can clip to the waistband of your shorts, to collect all of the navigation and heart-rate data from each run. It is from this unit that you will download data onto your computer for use with Timex Trainer software, which is compatible with PCs and Macs. This software has all of the basic summary and graphing features plus a few unusual features, including a Course Statistics page that allows you to inspect the gradient of hill climbs. Triathletes may purchase a bike mount that allows them to use a single device for all of their workouts.

BRAND-AGNOSTIC PERFORMANCE MANAGEMENT PROGRAMS

The performance management computer programs that come with speed and distance devices work only with devices of the same brand. But there are a few brand-agnostic programs that can be purchased separately. Some, such as PC Coach, are software applications that you load onto your computer. Others, such as Phys Farm, are Internet-based services. One performance management program, Training Peaks WKO+ at www.trainingpeaks.com, works with all speed and distance devices.

Training Peaks has cooperative relationships with most of the device manufacturers, who readily admit that WKO+ is far more powerful and sophisticated than their own performance management offerings. Because of this fact, and because you can create a basic Training Peaks account for free, we encourage every runner who uses a speed and distance device to also use Training Peaks WKO+, whether or not they use their device-specific performance management application as well.

Training Peaks is an online platform of tools for endurance sport coaches and athletes. The business began as an enhanced online training log that allowed coaches and athletes to plan future training and record completed training. The calendar (figure 2.1) remains the core of the platform, but it is quite a bit more sophisticated today than it was when it first went live in 1999.

WKO+ is a software application that you can download onto your computer from the Web site. It is compatible with both PCs and Macs. WKO+ mostly duplicates the features that are available on the Web site, but the Web site has valuable extras. Since Training Peaks WKO+ is brand agnostic, you can download data from any speed and distance device to the program, and from there upload it to your Training Peaks account. Training Peaks WKO+ also offers a more sophisticated set of training data analysis features than the performance management software applications that come with the devices.

The tables and graphs that can be generated with the application enable runners to monitor and control their training workload. Training Peaks WKO+ automatically assigns a training stress score (TSS) to every run that is downloaded from a device. Then TSS from multiple runs are used to calculate your chronic training load (CTL), or how hard you've been training over the past several weeks, which quantifies your fitness level, and your acute training load (ATL), or how hard you've been training over the past week, which quantifies your fatigue level. The difference between your CTL and ATL is your training stress balance (TSB), which quantifies your form, or how well you can expect to be able to perform in your next run (fitness minus fatigue equals form). The tables and charts produced through these calculations make it fairly easy to assess how close you are to peak fitness, how quickly your workload is increasing, whether you need more rest, and so forth.

Additional features allow you to analyze your training in other ways. For example, a pace zone distribution chart provides insight into how balanced your training is in the dimension of intensity, and a mean minimal pace graph plots performance benchmarks, such as your 10 fastest 5-minute blocks of running over the past 28 days, providing at-a-glance evidence of fitness improvements. You also can create an infinite variety of customized charts and graphs to suit your particular needs.

The planning tools are equally sophisticated. You may purchase complete training plans from well-known coaches, which are loaded straight onto your calendar, to create your own plan using a vast library of ready-made workouts and even to design your own workouts from scratch. You also can trade workouts with other Training Peaks members. Your planned training is replaced with actual training data as you download workout files from your device each day.

Training Peaks also offers highly advanced mapping features. You can export route data from GPS-based devices to Google Earth, so you can see your entire run from a bird's-eye view. A feature called Ground Control provides instantaneous correction of the elevation information from your GPS-based device. This enables Training Peaks to calculate a more accurate normalized graded pace, which converts your actual pace on hill climbs and descents into an equivalent pace for level ground. This, in turn, allows Training Peaks to generate a more accurate training stress score for each run. Another handy feature is an elevation override, which allows you to manually cancel out elevation information that you know to be inaccurate. To remove false elevation changes from your workout file, use this feature whenever you run on a track.

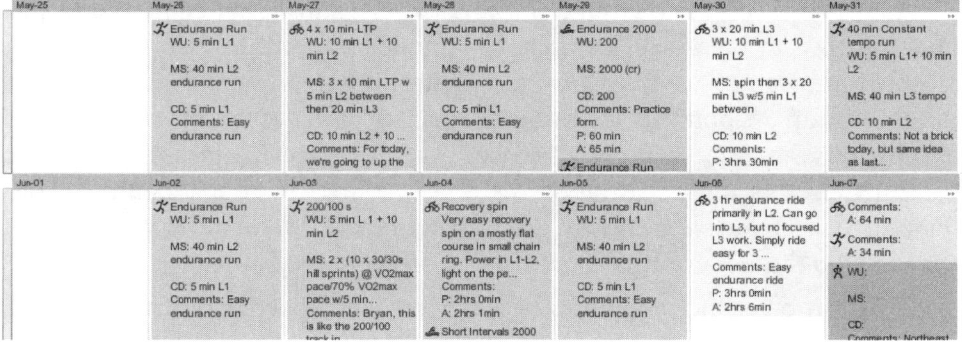

Figure 2.1   Training Peaks personal account summary page.
Courtesy of TrainingPeaks (www.trainingpeaks.com).

The nutrition features of Training Peaks quickly add up the carbohydrate, fat, protein, and calories in each meal and snack consumed, as well as daily totals. There are also nutritionist-designed meal plans that you can purchase and load onto your calendar to follow just as you do with training plans. These features make it possible to monitor, analyze, and plan your nutrition as carefully as you do your training. Meals and workouts sit side by side on your calendar, and you can even view charts that compare the calories you take in through food against those you burn at rest and in training to help you achieve and maintain your optimal race weight (figure 2.1).

GETTING STARTED

All too often, those who buy a suitable speed and distance device never tap into its full potential or they get frustrated with simple problems like not being able to get the darn thing started and end up tossing it into a drawer. To get the most out of your speed and distance device, you need to learn how to properly use it. Don't worry—it's not difficult to do. Here are the first five steps:

1. **Read the user's manual.** The first step toward getting the most from your speed and distance device is to read the directions. Perhaps this point sounds too obvious to bear mentioning, but you'd be surprised at how many people purchase a speed and distance device and then ignore the manual. Spend an hour reading the manual. It's worth every minute. With the manual in front of you, move on to the following steps that will ensure your speed and distance device doesn't end up as another forgotten piece of workout gear at the back of a closet.

2. **Try it on and turn it on.** Follow the instructions to put on the components of your device (strap the display watch onto your wrist, strap the GPS to your upper arm, attach the foot pod to your shoes, and so on). Now turn on the device and get your first pace reading. If your device is GPS based, you'll have to go outdoors to take this step.

If your device has an integrated heart-rate monitor, put that on too. To ensure an accurate reading, wet the sensor pads on the chest strap before you put them on. Adjust the chest strap around the ribs so it fits snugly, yet comfortably, just underneath your breasts (or for men, right underneath the bulges of your chest muscles) and center the sensor over your sternum. Many first-time users find the chest strap uncomfortable. This is normal and will not last beyond the third or fourth use. It's not unlike getting accustomed to wearing glasses, braces, or anything else not quite natural on the body. At first you're maddeningly conscious of its feel, but soon enough you forget it's there. We've never worked with anyone who did not eventually get used to wearing the strap.

3. **Try it out.** Once you know how to wear your speed and distance device and get pace and heart-rate readings, and you have a feel for the buttons, you're

ready to begin working out with it. In your first workout with your speed and distance device, we suggest you just put it on, do your normal workout, and look at the display every few minutes without yet worrying about your target pace or any other function. Simply get used to running with it.

4. **Download your run data onto your computer.** To do this, of course, you will have to have first installed the performance management software that came with your device. Don't wait to accumulate a bunch of workouts on your device before your first download. Analyzing your pace and heart-rate data is just as important as using the device to monitor your pace and heart rate. You don't want to delay the process of getting comfortable with your software.

5. **Explore your performance management software.** After you've downloaded your first workout, start fiddling around with the various features of the application to get a basic feel for how it works. Use any instructions included with the software to facilitate this process. Don't expect to absorb every feature in your first sitting. Pace yourself and try to learn another analysis, mapping, or planning feature each time you download another workout until you've mastered your performance management software.

We recommend that you use not only the software that comes with your device but Training Peaks WKO+ as well. This will allow you to take advantage of the unique performance management tools in each. For example, if you use a Suunto speed and distance device, you can use Suunto's performance management software to follow graphs of the training effect of your workouts and Training Peaks WKO+ to study your acute and chronic training loads and training stress balance. Once your manufacturer's performance management software is installed, you can easily download workout files from your device to this software and Training Peaks WKO+ simultaneously. From there only one more step is required to upload your workout file to your online training log.

Having a speed and distance device is better than not having one. Actually using your device is better than not using it. And using it to actively manage your running performance is better than using it merely to observe your runs. Very few runners who do own speed and distance devices reach the level of active performance management. That's because digital performance management is a skill that must be learned, just like effective training. But since the technology is new, not many folks are qualified to teach computer-assisted running performance management. We are! Are you ready to learn?

Managing Performance for Optimal Results

Performance management is a systematic approach to making the pursuit of improved running performance more controllable and predictable. Speed and distance devices and performance management software enable runners to practice performance management more easily and more effectively.

The performance management process is divided into three steps. Step 1 is monitoring, step 2 is analysis, and step 3 is planning. Planning leads to additional monitoring, and this additional monitoring leads to fresh analysis, so performance management becomes a never-ending cycle. In chapters 4 through 6, we address these three steps of the performance management process individually. This chapter provides an overview of performance management and where technology fits into it.

PERFORMANCE MANAGEMENT EDGE

Improvement comes easily for beginning runners and for more experienced runners who are out of shape as the result of a long layoff. When you first take up regular training, almost anything you do will enhance your running performance. As long as you avoid injury, you can train in any number of ways, even somewhat chaotic and backward ways, and still gain speed and endurance, because when your body is at its starting point on the path toward peak running fitness, anything is better than nothing.

But these days don't last long. Every step you take in your development as a runner shortens the list of training options that will cause you to improve further. In the beginning, you could improve for some time simply by gradually increasing the volume of running you do at a moderate pace. Eventually, though, you will reach a limit (only a temporary limit, if you play your cards right) in the amount of moderate-paced running you can do each week without becoming overtrained (that is, chronically fatigued) or injured. At that point you could continue to improve by staying within your volume limit and introducing a little high-intensity running into your weekly schedule and then gradually increasing the amount of high-intensity running you do.

Before long, however, you will reach another limit. Further improvement may then require that you begin doing different types of high-intensity training—such as short, very fast intervals or longer, moderately fast intervals. When you hit your next plateau, your only remaining option for improvement might be finding effective ways to periodize your training—that is, to modulate your training workload and change your main training emphasis over time. This last-ditch strategy to enhance your development is a lot trickier than the preceding strategies in the sense that you can't always be sure that your body will respond positively to any given periodization pattern that you try. In other words, at this advanced stage of your development as a runner, the training process becomes somewhat experimental.

SCIENTIFIC METHOD

If the process of developing as a runner is an ongoing experiment, then maximizing your progress in this process requires that you become a sort of scientist. In scientific disciplines such as physics and medicine, researchers discover truth by creating hypotheses and then testing those hypotheses in carefully designed experiments. As a runner, the truth you seek is knowledge about which specific training practices make you faster and which ones stand in the way of making you faster. The most effective way to gain such knowledge is to continuously gather quantitative data about the amount and types of training you're doing and about how your fitness is changing in response to these variables. As you gather such data, you can begin to observe apparent cause–effect relationships between specific training practices and your fitness development. You can discard ineffective practices and retain or emphasize effective ones on the basis of these observations.

It's actually very difficult to conduct truly valid scientific studies on the general effectiveness of specific training practices because it's hard to adequately control the training of large groups of runners over extended periods. Some of the best studies on the effects of specific training practices in runners have been conducted by Esteve-Lanao, Foster, Sieler and Lucia (2007) at the University of Madrid, Spain. A summary of one of these studies will give you a good sense of how the application of a scientific approach to training can yield knowledge that has great practical value.

In a 2007 study published in the *Journal of Strength and Conditioning Research,* these researchers divided 10 high-level male runners into two groups. At the beginning of the study period, all 10 runners completed a 10.4-kilometer time trial and their times were recorded. Over the next five months, the runners in the two groups trained identically except for one key difference. The members of one group did two threshold runs (or runs at approximately their one-hour race pace) per week, while the members of the other group did just one. Their total training mileage, speed training schedules, and strength training regimens were the same. The only difference was that the members of one group did more threshold running and less easy running than the members of the second group. At the end of the study period, all 10 runners repeated the 10.4-kilometer time trial. The members of the threshold group improved their time by 2:01, on average, while those in the easy group improved by 2:37. Statistical analyses revealed that such a large discrepancy was extremely unlikely to occur by chance. Therefore the researchers concluded that a training program in which 81 percent of running is easy, 10.5 percent is done at threshold pace, and 8.5 percent is done at speeds exceeding race pace is more effective than an equal-distance program in which only 67 percent of running is easy, 24.5 percent is at threshold pace, and 8.5 percent is fast.

On the other hand, in a 2004 study by French exercise physiologist Veronique Billat and colleagues, 11 experienced runners who had performed only slow, long-distance runs and who had not experienced any recent training improvements incorporated higher-intensity training at their maximal lactate steady state velocity (MLSSv), which is slightly higher than lactate threshold speed, two times weekly for six weeks. After the conclusion of the six weeks, the runners' $\dot{V}O_2$max, speed at $\dot{V}O_2$max, lactate threshold speed, and MLSSv had improved significantly. Further, the time to exhaustion at MLSSv increased 50 percent after the training period. These results clearly indicate that training at or above the LT two times per week is better than strictly training by long, easy runs alone.

Although there was some degree of individual variation in the extent to which runners in the 2007 Spanish study improved over five months, no runner in the threshold group improved as much as any runner in the easy group. On the other hand, in the 2004 French study, as a group, the runners improved a number of parameters in only six weeks, when no improvements had recently been observed using only slow training. Therefore, it appears that some training at or around the LT is of benefit, but the question is how much. Further, there is a lot of variability in how individual runners respond to the same training. For this reason, each runner must perform his or her own experiments to figure out what works, what doesn't, and how to improve.

The more controllable and predictable you can make the experiment of training, the more you will improve. To master the experiment, you must know what you've done and how it has affected you so that you can connect cause and effect. That's where technology can make a big difference. With a speed and distance device that includes heart-rate monitoring capability and performance management software, you can quantify your training and fitness in more diverse and useful ways than you can by merely tracking your running mileage and workout split times.

NUMBERS THAT MATTER

Previously we noted that the training process is like a science experiment. It's also like a math equation, with input and output. The input is the work you do, which can be viewed in objective terms (distance and time) or physiological terms (such as training stress score). The output is the results of the work you do. Technology is useful in relation to both sides of the training equation. Let's start with a look at the input side. Here are several of the more useful metrics you can use to quantify your training. Others are discussed in later chapters.

Miles, or Kilometers, per Week

Miles per week (or kilometers per week, for those on the metric system) is the most commonly used metric for training load. It is a perfectly legitimate measurement of absolute work performed and has a variety of practical uses. For example, collective evidence suggests that first-time marathon runners should aim for a peak weekly training distance of at least 40 miles (64 km) to ensure a successful marathon experience, while those reaching for the elite level must exceed 100 miles per week in their heaviest training period.

Running mileage doesn't tell the whole story, however. A mile can be run at a variety of speeds. The faster it is run, of course, the more stressful it is on the body. Thus, a 40-mile week of exclusively easy running is less stressful than a 40-mile week in which 15 miles are run at threshold pace and faster. Similarly, an uphill mile run in 8 minutes is more stressful than a flat mile run in the same time. So the most revealing possible metric for training workload would be one that incorporated mileage, pace, and elevation gain and loss. Training stress score (described a little later in this chapter) is one such metric.

A speed and distance device makes it easy to track training mileage. While these devices are not 100 percent accurate, they are far more accurate than the ballpark estimates we used to make when running on nonmeasured routes before such devices existed. And since speed and distance devices also record pace and—in many units—elevation change, they can also be used to produce a training stress score for each run.

It's also worthwhile to track your increase in rate of weekly running mileage during periods when your running mileage is increasing. Injuries and overtraining symptoms are most likely to occur during periods when you aggressively increase your running mileage. Some runners are able to increase their mileage faster than others without consequences, but all runners have their limits. The maximum safe rate of increase in total running distance tends to stay relatively consistent for each runner. By tracking your weekly distance consistently, you can identify your own maximum safe rate of weekly increase in mileage. Unfortunately, the only way to identify your true limit is by exceeding it and getting injured or sick, but this is something that's bound to happen to every competitive runner sooner or later. Once you know your limit, you can use this knowledge to ensure that you don't exceed it again.

A speed and distance device supports this type of monitoring by enabling you to accurately and consistently track your running mileage and record mileage data in your performance management software for later reference. For most runners the maximum safe rate of increase in total distance is roughly 10 percent per week (for example, 20 miles this week, 22 miles next week, 24.2 miles the week after that).

Hours per Week

The amount of time you spend running in a week is another volume metric that is closely related to total weekly running distance. Changes in the number of hours and minutes you run each week will tend to follow changes in the number of miles or kilometers you run each week in linear fashion, whether upward or downward. Because there is a large degree of individual variation in the average pace that runners maintain in training, however, there is an equally large degree of variation in the relationship between total distance per week and hours per week. For example, if José and Jane both ran 50 miles last week, but José's average pace is 7:00 per mile and Jane's is 9:00 per mile, then there's a 1-hour 40-minute difference in the amount of time José and Jane spent running in that week (5 hours 50 minutes for José versus 7 hours 30 minutes for Jane).

Miles, or kilometers, per week is a truer measure of the absolute work performed in a week of training, because it takes the same amount of work to run a mile regardless of your pace. But hours per week may be a truer measure of the relative stress that a given volume of running imposes on your body. And since weekly running time is not an exact substitute for weekly running distance, it's not a bad idea to monitor both. If you do, it's not unlikely that you will notice time-based patterns in addition to mileage-based patterns. For example, you might notice that you tend to show signs of overtraining when your running time exceeds eight hours per week.

Time in Heart-Rate Zones

If your speed and distance device has heart-rate monitoring capability, the software that comes with it may allow you to view a graph that shows the distribution of time you've spent running in different heart-rate training zones within a given run or over the past week or four weeks. This graph—especially the longer, 28-day version—provides information about the intensity of your training. In a well-designed and well-executed training program, this graph will show a balance that is appropriate to your race distance and training phase. The precise look of the graph will depend on how your heart-rate training zones are defined, but in any case the graph should show that you do most of your running at an easy pace, a moderate amount in your threshold range, and a small but not insignificant amount at faster paces. Common errors that are identifiable in graphs of time distribution in heart-rate zones include spending too much time running in the high aerobic heart-rate range (between your moderate aerobic and threshold heart-rate zones) and spending too little time running above your threshold heart-rate range.

As you know already, we do not recommend that you train primarily by heart rate. Your heart-rate training zones should merely reflect your heart rate within your training pace zones, which serve as your primary means of monitoring and controlling your running intensity.

Time in Pace Zones

A graph of your running time distribution in the various pace zones does the same thing that a time in heart-rate zones graph does, only better. It gives you a clear picture of how balanced your training is in terms of intensity. Lack of adequate balance is one of the most common training errors among runners. Once you understand how your time in pace zones graph should look given your race focus and phase of training, you can look at this graph often to ensure that your training maintains the right balance. To ensure the greatest accuracy in this graph, be sure to adjust your pace zones as your fitness increases or decreases. This is very easy to do with the pace zone index system described fully in chapter 4.

Training Stress Score

The best tools to quantify how hard you're training are those metrics that account for both the volume and the intensity of your running. A new and powerful tool of this sort is training stress score (TSS). As mentioned in chapter 1, this new metric generates a score that quantifies the overall stressfulness of a run by considering how much time you spend running at every pace level touched during the run. The stressfulness of any given pace is determined in relation

Brad Hudson on Race-Pace Training

Brad Hudson is a former world-class runner who now coaches a new generation of world-class runners, including multiple national champion James Carney in Boulder, Colorado. He is also the author of the 2008 book *Run Faster From the 5K to the Marathon: How to Be Your Own Best Coach,* which shares the secrets of his training philosophy, called *adaptive running.*

One of the tenets of this philosophy is that runners should train from generality toward specificity. "At the beginning of the training process, you need to focus on building a foundation," says Hudson. That foundation has two components: aerobic fitness, which is developed through a high volume of moderate-intensity running, and neuromuscular fitness (speed, strength, and power), which is developed through a small volume of very high-intensity running. "As you get closer to racing, you shift from building a foundation to maintaining it while adding a layer of specific endurance on top of it," Hudson says.

Specific endurance is Hudson's term for the capacity to resist fatigue at race pace. As such, it incorporates both the aerobic and neuromuscular components of the fitness foundation. To develop specific endurance, you go faster and faster in some of your aerobic workouts and go longer and longer in some of your neuromuscular workouts while also doing more and more training within the race-pace range itself. You can think of the whole process as one of zeroing in on race pace from opposite sides. In the beginning you do some very fast running and a lot of very slow running and not much in between. Then your slow running gets faster and faster and your fast running gets slower and slower until there is no distinction between your fast and your slow running. That's an oversimplification, of course, but it conveys the general idea.

Hudson's approach to marathon-specific long runs provides a concrete example of this process. Try using the following workout progression in training for your next marathon: Warm up by running 2 miles (3.2 km) at an easy pace. Then run a mile (1.6 km) at your marathon pace minus 10 seconds followed by a mile at your marathon pace plus 45 seconds. (For example, if your goal marathon pace is 8:00 per mile, run a mile in 7:50 followed by a mile in 8:45.) Repeat this pattern six times for 14 total miles (22.5 km), including the warm-up. The next time you do the workout, warm up with 2 easy miles and then run 1.5 miles (2.4 km) at your marathon pace minus 5 seconds per mile followed by a mile at your marathon pace plus 30 seconds. Repeat this pattern six times for 17 total miles (27.4 km). Do the workout one last time two to three weeks before your marathon. Warm up with 2 easy miles and then run 2 miles at your marathon pace followed by 1 mile at your marathon pace plus 15 seconds. Again, repeat the pattern six times for 20 total miles (32.2 km).

Such workouts are much easier to do with a speed and distance device such as a Garmin Forerunner 405 than without, because you can run on roads that simulate the course of your upcoming marathon without sacrificing accurate pace measurements. A growing number of Hudson's athletes, including 2008 U.S. half-marathon champion James Carney, use these devices. "They're not quite as accurate as a track," says Hudson, "but they're pretty close, and the ability they give runners to do race-specific training on courses that simulate the courses they race on more than makes up for their small degree of inaccuracy."

Dathan Ritzenhein (left) at the USA Track and Field cross-country championships.

to your current functional threshold pace (that is, the fastest running pace you could sustain for one hour), thus ensuring that each TSS is accurate with respect to your current fitness level. The calculation makes adjustments for hills (for example, a hilly 40-minute run at a steady pace of 8:00 per mile, or 5:00 per km, would generate a higher TSS than a flat version of the same run) and even for the fact that running at any given pace becomes more physiologically stressful the longer that pace is sustained.

Aside from the stand-alone quantitative value that can be assigned to a given workout to represent the stress that the workout produces, TSS also can be used for calculating other parameters that are used for more complex performance planning and analysis, which are discussed in chapters 4 through 6.

Chronic training load (CTL) is calculated as an exponentially weighted moving average of your run-by-run training stress score over time (typically the past 42 days) with a decay constant that gives your most recent training greater weight than less recent training. In colloquial terms, CTL represents fitness. The acute training load (ATL) is calculated as an exponentially weighted moving average of your TSS over the past 7 days with a much steeper decay constant, the result of which is that your ATL tends to increase and decrease much faster than your

CTL with fluctuations in your training. In colloquial terms, ATL represents fatigue. Finally, training stress balance (TSB) is simply the difference between your chronic training load (how hard you've been training over the past several weeks) and your acute training load (how hard you've been training within the past week). In colloquial terms, TSB represents form, or how well you can expect to perform at any given point in the training process based on your current levels of fitness and fatigue.

Training Peaks WKO+ software calculates all of these variables automatically. When you download a workout file from your speed and distance device into the application, it looks at your pace and at changes in elevation throughout the run and converts your real pace into flat pace, which is the level-ground equivalent in terms of physiological stressfulness of running uphill or downhill at a particular pace. This process is known as *normalization*. For example, if during a recent run you ran up a hill with a 5 percent grade at a real pace of 9:14 per mile, WKO+ might convert this stretch of running into a flat pace of 8:20 per mile, signifying that running uphill at 9:14 per mile was equivalent in terms of physiological stress to running 8:20 per mile on level ground.

The program then breaks your run into 30-second segments, looks at the normalized or flat pace for each segment, and then raises that pace (actually speed in meters per second) to the fourth power. This exponential weighting of the pace for each 30-second segment is a way to account for the fact that the stressfulness of running increases exponentially as running speed increases. The program then averages the exponentially weighted pace for all of the 30-second segments and takes the fourth root to yield a fully normalized and graded average pace for the workout that indicates its true physiological stressfulness. Next, the software divides this corrected average pace by your functional threshold pace (FTP), which is the fastest pace you can sustain for 60 minutes at your current fitness level. The result of this division is a variable known as the intensity factor (IF), which represents the overall intensity of a run relative to your current fitness level. Now the software multiplies the average (uncorrected) flat pace of the workout by its duration to calculate the absolute total amount of work performed in the run and then multiplies that number by the IF to convert it into a more relative measure of the work performed. Finally, this number is divided by the total amount of work you are capable of performing in 60 minutes of running at your current FTP and the product is multiplied by 100 to yield a measure of the total relative stressfulness of the workout, or training stress score. WKO+ then uses accumulated TSS to calculate your acute training load, chronic training load, and training stress balance day by day.

As you see, the TSS calculations are rather complex, so it's nice to have a software program to do all of them for you. If you do not use WKO+, you can still generate rough TSS, ATL, CTL, and TSB scores on your own. The first step is to determine or estimate your current functional threshold pace. The hard way to do this is to run a 60-minute time trial. An easier way is to estimate it based on recent race performances. For example, suppose that you recently ran a 10K race in 42:40. This time converts to a pace of 6:51 per mile. According to one popular race time conversion calculator, a 42:40 10K is equivalent to a half-marathon time of 1:34:56, which is 7:15 per mile. So your fastest pace for one hour is likely to be somewhere between 6:51 and 7:15 per mile—probably closer to 6:51 because your 10K time is less than 18 minutes shorter than 60 minutes and your half-marathon time is almost 35 minutes longer. So 7:00 per mile would be a good estimate of your current FTP in this example.

Once you know your FTP, you can calculate the TSS for any run using the following equation:

$$\text{TSS} = \text{duration (in hours)} \times \text{IF}^2 \times 100$$

The trickiest part of this calculation is determining the run's intensity factor, which is your normalized graded pace for the workout divided by your functional threshold pace. As described previously, WKO+ normalizes pace by converting real pace into flat pace and then grades the normalized average by dividing the run into 30-second segments and weighting the pace of each segment to account for the fact that the physiological stress of running increases exponentially as speed increases. Without WKO+, there is no easy way to normalize pace—that is, to convert real pace into flat pace. This is not a problem in runs performed on relatively flat terrain, but in hilly runs it will result in inaccuracy.

In runs that are performed at a relatively steady pace, you can skip the step of dividing the run into 30-second segments and simply use the average pace for the entire run in the IF calculation. But in interval workouts and other variable-pace workouts, dividing it up, although tedious, will yield far more accurate results.

Find the average pace for each 30-second segment in meters per minute, raise this number to the fourth power, and then divide it by 0.5 (representing that segment's half-minute duration). Add together the weighted pace for all of the 30-second segments, divide the sum by the total number of segments, and then take the fourth root of the result. This is your graded pace for the entire workout. Divide this number (expressed in meters per minute) by your functional threshold pace (also expressed in meters per minute) to determine the run's intensity factor. Now plug this number into the TSS equation.

All of this can be done with a calculator, but if you're handy with spreadsheets, that is the way to go. The setup takes some time but once you have the spreadsheet structured, calculating the TSS of individual runs is relatively painless.

Here are the formulas you need in order to calculate your CTL, ATL, and TSB on the basis of TSS scores from day to day:

$$\text{CTL}_{\text{today}} = \text{CTL}_{\text{yesterday}} + (\text{TSS} - \text{CTL}_{\text{yesterday}}) \times [1/\text{time constant (42 days)}]$$

$$\text{ATL}_{\text{today}} = \text{ATL}_{\text{yesterday}} + (\text{TSS} - \text{ATL}_{\text{yesterday}}) \times [1/\text{time constant (7 days)}]$$

Because generally it takes more time to gain or lose fitness than to accumulate or overcome fatigue, the time constants for the parameters that represent these two constructs (CTL and ATL, respectively) are proportionally different. The significance of this will become clear in later presentation, but taking these different time responses into effect, we can derive the relationship for the TSB as such:

$$TSB = CTL - ATL$$

Therefore, on a given day, the training stress balance depends on the fitness accumulated over time minus the fatigue incurred through recent training, and this should be indicative of relative performance on the given day. In other words, a slightly positive TSB should correspond to a better performance on a given day compared to a performance on a day when the TSB is negative.

Calories

Some speed and distance devices enable you to track how many calories of energy your body uses during each run. This feature is clearly useful for those who are trying to lose weight or maintain a certain weight, but it's a good metric for your overall training workload, or the combined volume and intensity of your training. The number of calories your body uses in a run is, of course, a function of both how far you run and how fast you run. Thus, if you run 50 easy miles this week and 50 miles again next week, but include 10 miles of running at threshold pace and above, you will record a greater total number of calories burned in the second week, indicating a greater metabolic stress level thanks to those fast miles.

Tracking the number of calories you burn in each run also allows you to compare the stress level of workouts of different types. For example, you might find that you burn an equal number of calories in a 90-minute long run at an easy pace and in a one-hour speed workout including 800-meter intervals run at 5K race pace. From this comparison, you may infer that each of these workouts will produce similar recovery requirements.

Training Effect

Training effect is a variable that is calculated exclusively by Suunto speed and distance devices. Training effect is an estimate of excess postexercise oxygen consumption (EPOC), which is akin to the more familiar term *oxygen debt*. This is defined as the difference between the amount of oxygen that is consumed after a workout is completed and your normal rate of oxygen consumption at rest. A high level of EPOC indicates that the workout just completed applied significant stress to your body and thus can be expected to stimulate a cardiorespiratory training effect. EPOC depends on the duration of exercise (the longer the workout, the greater EPOC will be), the intensity of exercise (the higher the intensity, the greater the EPOC), and your fitness level (the higher the fitness level, the longer or more intense a workout has to be to generate significant EPOC). Thus, if your fitness level is known, EPOC can be used to estimate the strength of the cardiorespiratory training effect of a completed workout.

Heart rate and rate of oxygen consumption are closely related. The exercise scientists who developed training effect on behalf of Suunto took advantage of the well known correlation between heart rate and rate of oxygen consumption to derive a formula that allows a heart-rate monitor to generate an estimate of EPOC. You might think that it does so by counting excess heartbeats above your normal resting heart rate after completion of a workout. But instead, it does so by continuously measuring changes in heart rate throughout exercise. Suunto argues that in this way, its speed and distance devices are able to monitor the approximate cardiorespiratory training effect of a workout in real time, allowing you to do things such as stop a given workout when a certain desired training effect has been achieved. Training effect is measured on a scale of 0 to 5, where 5 represents the maximal possible cardiorespiratory training effect of a workout.

The training software that comes with Suunto speed and distance devices allows you to manipulate training effect data in sophisticated ways. For example, it will help you plan your future training to increase your cardiorespiratory fitness based on the accumulated training effect of completed training. This variable has a few limitations, however. First, because EPOC is influenced by fitness level, Suunto devices require users to classify their fitness on a seven-level scale to produce more accurate training effect scores, but in reality fitness does not fall into a few discrete levels, but lies on a continuum that seven levels may not sufficiently represent.

Therefore, training effect scores are likely to be a little too high or a little too low for most athletes. And because the fitness level of any single athlete changes over time, it can be difficult to determine the degree to which changes in EPOC in a single athlete over time represent true differences in the stressfulness of workouts or changes in the athlete's fitness level. Monitoring pace along with training effect can help you draw this distinction more clearly. For example, if a 10-mile run at 9:00 per mile produces a lower EPOC today than the same run did a month ago, you can have more confidence that the lower EPOC score reflects improved fitness.

EFFECTS OF TRAINING

Quantifying the training you've done is only one half of the process of training scientifically. The other half is quantifying how this training has affected your body, your fitness level, and your running performance. By practicing both halves of the process consistently, you can connect cause and effect in your training and make better decisions about your future training. Following are seven ways to measure how your training has affected you. Six of them—pace zone index, performance in similar workouts, race and time trial performance, heart rate and pace relationships, running index, and body weight—are quantitative. The seventh—injuries—is qualitative.

Pace Zone Index Score

The pace zone index (PZI) is a generalized rating of your current fitness level based on a recent performance in a standard race distance. At any given time, you can associate a PZI score with your present fitness level by running a race, doing a time trial, or making an experience-based estimate of the finish time you would achieve in a race of a given distance today. Your PZI score will change as your fitness level does. Because your PZI score is used to set pace targets for various types of workouts, it is important that you formally adjust your PZI score periodically as the training process unfolds to ensure that your pace targets remain appropriate throughout the process.

The most natural time to tweak your PZI score is when you run a race, but you don't have to—and in many cases shouldn't—wait until you race to do so. In the normal course of performing your planned workouts, you will find yourself consistently beating your PZI-based pace targets at the same level of perceived effort as your fitness improves. When this pattern stretches beyond a couple of weeks, go ahead and lower your PZI score one level and begin using the pace targets associated with this lower score.

Running fitness seldom improves at a consistent rate. Even in well-designed and properly executed training programs, there are periods of relatively rapid improvement and other periods of relatively slow improvement. Nevertheless, your fitness level should improve uninterrupted, if not always at the same rate, as you train toward a peak race. Tracking changes in your PZI score is a way to monitor the effectiveness of your training. If your PZI score fails to improve for a long period, you have cause to believe that your training is not as effective as it should be and must be sensibly modified. Periods of rapid improvement in your PZI score also provide valuable information about your training. The key characteristics of your training approach in such periods clearly work well for you and should be retained in your future training.

For example, in analyzing the data in your performance management software, you might determine that an increase in the amount of easy running in your weekly schedule appears to be responsible for the breakthrough represented in the rapid lowering of your PZI score. Based on this information, you'll want to ensure that your future training continues to include plenty of easy running.

Performance in Similar Workouts

Run training features a fair amount of redundancy. As you work on developing specific aspects of your fitness, you tend to repeat the particular key workout formats that drive this development on a weekly basis, increasing the challenge level or pushing for better performance each time. Comparing similar workouts in your performance management software enables you to observe and quantify progress.

Suppose one week you perform a workout consisting of 6 × 1-mile intervals at 10K race pace with 400-meter jogging recoveries and then the next week do a slightly more challenging version of the workout, consisting of 5 × 2-kilometer intervals at 10K pace with 400-meter jogging recoveries. (The second workout is slightly harder primarily because the intervals are longer—2K equals 1.2 miles—and secondarily because the total amount of interval running is slightly greater—10K, or 6.2 miles, versus 6 miles.) Naturally, in this workout you will use the split function on your speed and distance device display watch to capture distance, time, and pace information for each interval. Suppose your average mile interval time is 6:24 in the first workout, and you average a 6:22 pace in the longer intervals the next week. The latter performance is slightly but definitely better than the former, indicating improved fitness.

In the past it was impossible to accurately compare performances in workouts on routes with different topography, but at least one performance management software application available now converts actual pace on routes with elevation changes to an equivalent flat pace. In other words, the application calculates what a certain pace on a particular uphill or downhill gradient would have been without the hill. Suppose you do the first of the two workouts described previously on a track and the second on an ascending hill. Perhaps your average pace for the 2-kilometer intervals in the second workout is 6:56—much slower than the 6:24 average in the first workout's 1-mile intervals. But when you download the workout data into your performance management software, you might find that the flat pace for the uphill intervals is 6:22, again indicating slight improvement from the previous week.

Time Trial and Race Performance

At the end of the day, the only effect of your training that really matters is your performance in races. The whole reason you train is to race to the best of your ability. When you achieve your race goals, you know that the training you did in preparation for the race was effective. When you fail to achieve your race goals, you know that something was wrong with your training and needs to be changed, unless the cause of your disappointment was hot weather, a wrong turn, or some other non-training-related factor.

For example, you might look back at your training after a disappointing race and notice that your training stress balance (TSB) was just barely positive with a reading of +1. Training stress balance is the difference between the workload of your last several weeks of training (chronic training load) and that of your recent training (acute training load). Thus, a positive TSB indicates that you are relatively rested, because you have not trained as hard within the past week or two as you have over the past month or so. Most runners race best when their TSB is moderately positive, in the range of 5 to 15. (When your TSB becomes too positive, you've begun to lose fitness, which obviously negates the benefits of being rested.) Based on your observation that your TSB was on the low side, you might conclude that you did not taper adequately for your race and should rest up more before the next one.

Races are also the best source of data about your true fitness level, because the stimulation of racing (not to mention the relative rest that usually precedes a race) enables a higher level of performance than is achievable in any workout. Running a race at a standard distance is certainly the best way to determine your current PZI level. When you do not race for an extended time, you might want to do the occasional time trial (for example, 10K at maximum intensity on the track) to get a better reading on your current fitness level (and a better training stimulus) than your everyday workouts provide.

Heart Rate and Pace Relationships

Often the relationship between your pace and your heart rate changes as you gain or lose fitness. Tracking these changes through your performance management software is a reasonable way to assess the effectiveness of your training. As you train toward peak race fitness, you may find that your heart rate decreases at any given pace and that, at any given heart rate, your running pace gets faster. You also should find that you can sustain any given heart rate for a longer period before fatiguing. Finally, you should find that you are able to sustain a higher heart rate over a given distance or time. Note that all of these changes are relatively small and gradual, so don't look for improvement between Tuesday and Wednesday.

The most precise way to identify changes in your heart rate and pace relationship is to compare equal-duration segments of running at a given pace or heart rate in two runs undertaken a few weeks apart. A somewhat less rigorous but still informative alternative possible with Training Peaks is to divide the average heart rate of a run by the intensity factor (IF) of the run. Intensity factor is the average intensity of a run relative to functional threshold pace. If your average pace during a given run is exactly equal to your threshold pace, then that run's IF is 1.0. Dividing your average heart rate in a run by its intensity factor yields a rough measurement of your cardiorespiratory fitness at different intensity levels. Performing this calculation periodically will help you track changes in your efficiency at different intensity levels. As always, the same caveats presented earlier regarding heart rate and performance apply.

You may also use heart rate and pace relationships to track changes in your endurance. During prolonged running at any steady pace, your heart rate will hold steady for a while and then begin to increase slowly because of dehydration or because of decreasing mechanical efficiency or cardiovascular effectiveness. Joe Friel has termed this phenomenon *decoupling*. He proposes that as your endurance increases, you will be able to go longer at a given pace before the heart rate and pace lines on a workout graph in your performance management software become decoupled.

Running Index

Running index is a feature that is exclusive to Polar speed and distance devices. It is essentially an estimate of a runner's current $\dot{V}O_2max$, which is determined largely by genetics but also is affected by training. Therefore, tracking running index is a way for Polar users to monitor the effects of their training on their fitness levels.

Polar speed and distance devices calculate running index by comparing heart rate and speed. The device notes your heart rate and speed when you reach the 12-minute mark of a run. It converts your heart rate into a percentage of heart-rate reserve. Your heart-rate reserve is the difference between your maximum and resting heart rates. This requires that you enter your maximum heart rate into the device before using it. The more accurate this number is, the more accurate your running index scores will be. The following formula is used to calculate your current running heart rate as a percentage of reserve:

$$\text{(current HR} - \text{resting HR)} \div \text{heart-rate reserve}$$

The device then divides your speed by your percentage of heart-rate reserve to yield an estimate of the maximum running speed you could sustain for 12 minutes, which will be close to your $\dot{V}O_2max$ running speed. Finally, the device converts this value into an estimate of your current $\dot{V}O_2max$; scores typically range from 40 to 80 (the higher, the better). After 12 minutes, the device continuously recalculates your running index as a rolling average up to the present moment, so your final running index score at the end of the run may be slightly different from your initial score at 12 minutes.

For example, suppose that, 12 minutes into a run, your heart rate is 130 and your speed is 7 mph (or 11.3 kph). The device knows that your maximum heart rate is 186 bpm and your resting heart rate is 55 bpm; hence it also knows your heart-rate reserve (186 − 55 = 131 bpm). At 130 bpm, your heart rate is at 57 percent of reserve ([130 − 55] ÷ 131 = 0.57). Your estimated speed at $\dot{V}O_2max$ is your running speed divided by your percentage of heart-rate reserve at that speed (7 ÷ 0.57), or 12.28 mph (19.76 kph) in this case.

Heart rate normally drifts slowly upward as any given pace is sustained, and the faster you run, the faster the drift. Polar speed and distance devices filter out this drift as best they can in calculating running index scores. They also try to filter out the effects of hills on pace. However, they are not able to filter out the effects of environmental conditions such as heat and terrain on heart rate, and this limitation affects the comparability of running index scores from different runs.

Nevertheless, Polar claims testing has shown that running index scores are reasonably accurate predictors of actual $\dot{V}O_2$max. Further, they claim they are even better predictors of maximum running speed at $\dot{V}O_2$max, which is an even more important variable because it factors together both aerobic capacity and running economy and is therefore a better predictor of actual running performance than $\dot{V}O_2$max. High running index scores result from having a relatively low heart rate at relatively high running speeds, and running economy makes a significant contribution to this capacity. Again, Polar claims tests have shown that running index scores predict running economy separately almost as well as they predict $\dot{V}O_2$max.

If you don't use a Polar speed and distance device, you cannot get running index scores but you can still calculate estimated $\dot{V}O_2$max speeds from training data in individual runs. Just note your speed and heart rate at an appropriate point in a run and perform the calculations exactly as illustrated in the example given. For the best results, note your speed and HR on level, smooth terrain at a relatively early point when running at a given speed. During sustained, moderate-intensity runs, the 12-minute point is ideal. When doing short, high-speed intervals, it's actually better to note your heart rate at the end of a given interval, because heart rate tends to lag behind speed in such circumstances.

Body Weight and Composition

Many people jog for weight loss. As a competitive runner, your main motivation for running is probably not weight loss but the thrill of pushing your personal limits in a primal sport. However, your body weight is relevant to that goal. The more you weigh, the more weight you have to carry when you run. That's why elite runners are always very light. As you increase your training workload in pursuit of peak race fitness, your body will automatically shed the dead weight of excess body fat. In most cases you don't (and shouldn't) make any special effort to lose weight. By simply training right and eating right, you will enable your body to find its optimal race weight in time for your next peak race.

Because changes in your body weight are an effect of training, and because body weight is relevant to performance, it's worth monitoring. Step on a bathroom scale once a week or so and record this information in your training log. This will enable you to establish cause–effect relationships between training patterns and changes in your body weight whenever necessary. For example, if you always found it easy to drop weight in the past, but you're finding it difficult during your present training cycle, you might want to compare your current training patterns against past ones in search of some discrepancy that might explain your present difficulties. If you track your weekly calories burned and training stress score, this process will be somewhat easier than it would be otherwise. Of course, it's entirely possible that the cause of your current weight frustrations is dietary and has nothing to do with training. In this case, you'll be better off analyzing your diet and looking for problems there that you can fix with specific changes.

An alternative or supplement to monitoring your body weight is monitoring your body fat percentage. When it comes to optimizing your body for running performance, leanness (defined as a low percentage of body fat) is more beneficial than lightness. The problem with relying too much on the bathroom scale is that it doesn't distinguish muscle mass, which enhances performance, from fat mass, which hinders performance. Research has shown that in endurance athletes, leanness is a better predictor of performance than lightness.

There is no single ideal body fat percentage for everyone. Nor is there any way to predict the body fat percentage that is best for you. Optimal body fat levels depend on individual factors including sex, age, genetic makeup, and your starting point. The only way to find your optimal level is to eat well and train smart and see where you end up. One thing is certain, though: As you train toward peak fitness, your body fat percentage should always decrease, or at least hold steady, because your fitness will almost always increase as your body becomes leaner.

Until recently, there was no affordable and convenient way for the average person to monitor body composition. Nowadays, body fat scales are available at pharmacies, department stores, and sporting goods stores. They cost about the same as a regular bathroom scale (U.S. $40 to $100), and they're just as easy to use. All you have to do is step on the scale and read the numbers.

A body fat scale uses a technology called bioelectrical impedance to estimate body fat percentage. The device sends a weak electrical current into your body and measures the degree to which your body tissues resist it. Muscle impedes the current more than fat does. Bioelectrical impedance is not quite as accurate as some other methods of estimating body fat percentage, such as dual-energy X-ray absorptiometry (DEXA) scans. But what body fat scales lack in precision, they make up for with consistency, so they're very useful for tracking changes in your body composition.

If you're already fairly lean, be sure to purchase a body fat scale with an athlete mode. This feature uses a slightly different formula to calculate a body fat percentage from raw data. Units without this feature tend to be less accurate for athletes, because they use a formula that is most appropriate for people with higher body fat levels. Also, read the instructions that come with your body fat scale. Your results may be way off the mark if you fail to follow basic guidelines such as emptying your bladder and moistening the soles of your feet before using the device.

Injuries

Injuries are the most undesirable outcome, or effect, of training. Common overuse injuries such as runner's knee and iliotibial band syndrome are seldom strictly effects of training errors such as training too much or resting too little. In almost every case, an underlying weakness—most commonly a stride abnormality, a muscle strength imbalance, or a poor choice of footwear—makes you susceptible to injury. In other words, any underlying weakness reduces the amount of training you can do without developing an injury. When you exceed this threshold, you get injured and may reflexively put the blame on the training itself, but the true cause is rarely singular.

Nevertheless, even the most biomechanically and structurally sound runners get injured sometimes, and training does contribute to every injury, so it's a good idea to note injuries, aches, and pains in your performance management software so that you can identify the training patterns that contributed to the injury. The most common training pattern leading to injury is rapidly increasing running volume. The second most common cause of injury is introducing high-intensity running too abruptly, or increasing the volume of high-intensity running too quickly.

CAUSE AND EFFECT

As you can see, theoretically there are many ways to connect cause and effect. But how do you make the connections in practice? Some of them are made very easily with performance management software. Unfortunately, however, with the notable exception of Training Peaks WKO+, most applications offer limited functionality of this kind. This means that if you want to make meaningful graphic connections between most training inputs and outputs, you will have to show off or cultivate some spreadsheet skills and create your own graphs. It's worth the effort, and once you get in the habit it takes little effort to create graphics that provide very useful information.

Consider the case of Roberto Veneziani, a talented Italian age-group runner living in Hong Kong whom we encountered through his blog. Roberto trains with a Polar speed and distance device that is capable of measuring stride cadence. Over the course of a full racing season, Roberto tracked his average running cadence against his IAAF points in races. (IAAF points are a handy way to compare race performances within and across race distances.) Figure 3.1 is the very graph that he came up with. As you can see, it demonstrates a clear correlation between his average cadence in training and his race performances. (The fastest runners tend to have the fastest stride rate at any speed). Roberto's efforts to increase his running cadence were thus validated.

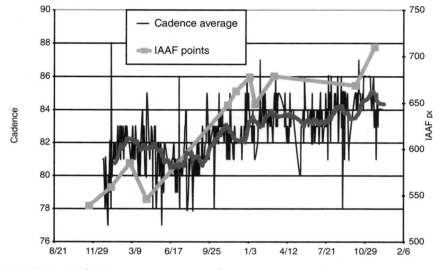

Figure 3.1 Cadence versus race performance over a two-year span.
Courtesy of Roberto Veneziani.

Roberto is a self-described data-obsessed runner. Not all of us are. But we encourage you to draw inspiration from Roberto and play around with making your own graphical cause–effect connections. If you'd rather not, though, never fear. As you will see in the coming chapters, you can manage your running performance perfectly well using the available hardware and software.

MONITOR, ANALYZE, AND PLAN (MAP)

This chapter provides a broad overview of the various ways you can link cause and effect in your training, which is the essence of performance management, or the systematic process of making the pursuit of improved running performance more predictable and controllable. This process has three steps: monitoring, analyzing, and planning. Now we will take a detailed look at how to do each of these things, starting with monitoring in chapter 4.

CHAPTER

Monitoring Training for Pace-Perfect Workouts

An effective training program must incorporate a variety of workout types, including recovery runs, long runs, threshold runs, and interval runs. The various workout types are distinguished by their duration, structure, and pace levels that are targeted. Running at each pace level contributes to the objective of building fitness in its own way. For example, running intervals at approximately 5K race pace increases the body's capacity to use oxygen to release muscle energy (or $\dot{V}O_2max$) more effectively than running at significantly faster or slower pace levels.

Naturally, the absolute pace that is most appropriate for any single type of workout depends on your natural ability and current fitness level. Consider the example of two runners, one of whom runs a 15:30 5K (5:00 per mile) and the other of whom runs a 21:45 5K (7:00 per mile). In workouts where 5K race pace is targeted, the first runner will run 2 minutes per mile faster than the second runner, yet they will both do the workout at a similar *relative* intensity and they will both derive similar benefits from the workout.

(This is a slight oversimplification, because technically these two runners would have to run at either the fastest pace each could sustain for approximately 15:30 or the fastest pace each could sustain for 21:45 to truly train at the same relative intensity in this type of workout. Further, since $\dot{V}O_2max$ pace generally corresponds to a pace that can be maintained for 5 to 8 min, both runners are under their true $\dot{V}O_2$max pace, and the 21:45 runner is substantially below. Still, for workouts of such high aerobic intensity, it is typically better to undershoot the pace rather than overshoot. So, for the purposes of convention and simplicity, we generally use 5K pace as the benchmark for $\dot{V}O_2$max work.)

To train effectively, you need to know how fast to run—given your natural ability and your current fitness level—in each type of workout, and you also need to have some way of monitoring your pace to ensure you're running neither too fast nor too slow when performing each workout. The monitoring part is very easy if you own a speed and distance device. You can simply glance at the display unit every once in a while to check your pace or you can even program your target pace zones into the device so that the device can guide you through structured workouts.

Determining the various pace levels that are most appropriate for you is a matter of somewhat greater complexity, but it's not rocket science. A number of running coaches and experts have devised systems that runners can use to determine appropriate pace targets for various types of workouts given their current fitness levels. Most of these systems use a recent or projected race time as the basis for individual recommendations. For example Arizona-based running coach Greg McMillan created an online tool called the McMillan Running Calculator that employs a special formula to produce recommended pace targets for long runs, tempo runs, intervals of various lengths, and other workouts when a finish time for any standard race distance from 1 mile to the marathon is entered. The McMillan Running Calculator is one of the best tools of its kind, but we favor our own pace zone index (PZI) not because we created it, but because it is especially designed for use with speed and distance devices.

MOVING FROM VDOT TO PZI

More than 30 years ago, legendary coach and exercise physiologist Jack Daniels developed the first system that runners can use to determine the appropriate pace target for each type of workout based on performance level. A score known as VDOT is associated with each performance level. Runners use recent race performances, time trials, or experience-based estimates to determine their VDOT scores and then look up the target pace levels on a table for each workout type associated with this score.

In 2004, Matt Fitzgerald teamed up with Training Peaks to create a modified version of the VDOT system—the pace zone index—that makes this approach to setting workout pace targets more compatible with the use of a speed and distance device. Specifically, whereas the VDOT system coaches runners to target very specific pace levels (for example, threshold pace for a runner capable of 37:00 10K performance is exactly 6:15 per mile), the PZI system invites runners to target pace ranges at each level (for example, the threshold pace zone for the same runner is 6:15 to 6:04). This modification mitigates the annoyance of having your speed and distance device beep at you to tell you that you are running outside your target zone when you're performing PZI-based workouts that have been programmed into the device. Obviously, it's much easier to stay within a zone of 6:15 to 6:04 per mile, assuming that's an appropriate target pace range for you to begin with, than it is to maintain a pace of exactly 6:15 per mile.

Another difference between the VDOT and PZI systems is that the former includes five target pace levels, whereas the latter includes six pace zones. The slowest of Daniels' five levels, easy pace, is essentially divided into two zones—low aerobic pace and moderate aerobic pace—in the PZI system. A third difference is that the fastest VDOT pace level—repetition pace—corresponds rather narrowly to 1,500-meter race pace, but in the PZI system it ranges from 1,500-meter pace all the way to a full sprint, for the simple reason that there is a small place for sprinting in the training of a long-distance runner.

In the pace zone index system, each pace zone corresponds to a physiological intensity level that stimulates fitness adaptations that are at least slightly different from the adaptations associated with any other intensity. While the actual numbers that make up each pace zone are unique for each runner (there are 50 levels, ranging from back of the pack to world class), what's going on inside any given runner's body while running in the various pace zones is basically the same. The pace zone index gives runners of every ability a simple tool they can use to get the most out of their training time by allowing them to zero in on the right running intensities.

There are 10 pace zones. Six of them are target zones used in various types of workouts. There are also four pace zones, called gray zones, that competitive runners should generally avoid in training. The first of these gray zones, gray zone 1, is the pace zone that is simply too slow to qualify as exercise—from standing still to a slow jog. It is never targeted in any workout, but it does exist. The other three gray zones are plenty intense, but they do not conform well to the workout formats that have been proven most effective through many decades of collective trial and error undertaken by runners worldwide. Why bother to create these gray zones if they are not targeted in any workouts? Because these gray zones are useful for the purpose of analysis. No matter how scrupulously the gray zones are avoided, every runner is bound to do some training at pace levels associated with the gray zones. When you upload your training data into the PZI-based performance management software, it automatically determines how much of your running was done in each zone and creates a pace zone distribution chart. This information shows you how much running you did in each of the six targeted zones, allowing you to determine whether your actual training matched your planned training. It also shows you how much training you accidentally did in the four gray zones that are never targeted.

Here are descriptions of the 10 pace zones, including the six target intensities and four gray zones. Corresponding $\dot{V}O_2$ and heart-rate values are given for each as points of reference, in case you are familiar with $\dot{V}O_2$- and heart rate-based intensities, but these metrics were not actually used to determine the PZI pace zones, nor were they used by Jack Daniels to create the VDOT zones on which the PZI zones are based. Both are entirely pace-based systems. Daniels created the VDOT zones using a mathematical formula that predicts the pace that runners of any ability level will run in any type of workout or race given how fast they run in any single type of workout or race.

■ **Pace zone 1: gray zone 1.** This pace zone is too slow to qualify as exercise and too slow to stimulate fitness benefits except in totally untrained people. In most trained runners it corresponds to walking or jogging paces below 55 percent $\dot{V}O_2$max and below 60 percent of maximum heart rate (HRmax).

■ **Pace zone 2: low aerobic.** Low aerobic pace is used almost exclusively in recovery runs, warm-ups, cool-downs, and active recoveries between high-intensity intervals. In trained runners, low aerobic pace corresponds to roughly 55 to 65 percent $\dot{V}O_2$max and 60 to 70 percent of HRmax.

In the low aerobic pace zone (pace zone 2), energy is supplied equally by fat and carbohydrate, whereas carbohydrate is the primary muscle fuel in each of the higher pace zones.

Whenever runners use fat as a fuel source, they spare carbohydrate, a precious energy resource for exercise, in the form of muscle glycogen. Muscle glycogen stores are the primary criteria for the sustainability of submaximal efforts, and restoration of those stores is the primary criterion for the ability to perform subsequent training and racing sessions. Therefore, running at low aerobic pace stimulates systems and components of the muscles necessary to burn fat and also spares glycogen, so runners can train longer or more frequently. As a result, the primary benefit of low aerobic-pace running is that it enables you to run more distance without greatly increasing stress on your body. Doing low aerobic-pace recovery runs between faster, harder runs gives you the aerobic and neuromuscular benefits of additional running without compromising your recovery from the preceding hard run or sabotaging your performance in the next one. If you ran faster on your easy days, you would feel and perform worse on your harder days. On the other hand, if you simply rested between harder runs, you would miss out on the fitness-boosting benefits resulting from the higher mileage that recovery runs provide.

■ **Pace zone 3: moderate aerobic.** Moderate aerobic running is slightly faster than low aerobic running. When you walk out your front door and just start running at the pace that feels most natural, you're running in the moderate aerobic pace zone (pace zone 3). It corresponds to about 65 to 75 percent $\dot{V}O_2$max and HRmax in trained runners.

At this intensity level, energy comes predominantly from carbohydrate, but the body is still metabolizing a fair amount of fat. Moderate aerobic-pace running is appropriate for aerobic base-building runs (base runs) and endurance-building long runs. You have to run frequently or far at this pace to derive significant fitness benefits, but when you do, the benefits are indeed significant: greater injury resistance, improved running economy, increased aerobic capacity, and better endurance.

■ **Pace zone 4: high aerobic.** In trained runners, high aerobic pace ranges between roughly 10 percent slower than marathon race pace on the high (slow) end and marathon race pace on the low end. For the typical fit runner, this range corresponds to 75 to 85 percent $\dot{V}O_2$max and HRmax. In this pace zone, carbohydrate provides virtually all of the energy for muscle contractions in a majority of runners.

High aerobic-pace training provides essentially the same benefits as moderate aerobic running but in greater measure. It is most appropriate for base runs and long runs performed in the later phases of training, after a foundation of aerobic fitness and stamina has been established primarily with moderate aerobic-pace running. High aerobic pace is also useful in progression runs, which begin with steady, moderate aerobic-pace running and finish with a relatively short segment (usually 1 to 3 miles, or 1.6 to 4.8 km) at high aerobic, or threshold, pace. Progression runs are a great way to add a little extra intensity to your training without overtaxing yourself.

■ **Pace zone 5: gray zone 2.** This pace zone falls between marathon race pace on the high end and, on the low end, the pace associated with the lactate threshold. It's a little too fast for sustained workouts such as foundation runs and long runs and a little too slow for workouts such as tempo runs that are intended to target the lactate threshold.

■ **Pace zone 6: threshold.** Threshold pace is traditionally defined as the running pace at which the blood lactate level begins to spike—that is, the lactate threshold. This spiking of the blood lactate level was previously considered important because lactate accumulation in the muscles was believed to cause muscle fatigue. It is now argued by some that lactate may actually delay muscle fatigue by providing an extra energy source to the muscles and also by combating a phenomenon known as muscle depolarization, which is similar to the way a battery runs out of energy. Further, it's clear that the metabolic adaptations that result in decreased lactate accumulation, and hence an increased lactate threshold, contribute to increased fat oxidation and reduced glycogen utilization. As previously discussed, this enhances performance by sparing glycogen for longer or harder efforts. What hasn't changed is the fact that running at lactate-threshold pace is an effective way to boost running fitness.

There are several competing and conflicting definitions of the lactate threshold. A commonly used reference standard is an arbitrary blood lactate level of 4 mmol. Although it is true that using certain criteria this definition will hold on average for many runners, this definition is problematic as there is great variability among individual runners. For those using blood lactate measures to determine the lactate threshold for themselves or athletes they coach, this definition could mislead them into using inappropriate training paces for some individuals. In trained runners, though, the lactate threshold corresponds, and will track, to roughly the fastest pace that can be sustained for one hour. Therefore we simply define threshold pace functionally as the fastest pace that fit runners can sustain for one hour. Less fit runners who may struggle to run an hour at any pace may run their threshold workouts initially at the fastest pace they believe they could sustain for 30 minutes.

Training at your current threshold pace is an effective way to increase your threshold pace, which happens to be one of the strongest predictors of race performance, and also to increase the duration or distance you can sustain your current threshold pace, known as time limit at threshold pace. Threshold pace falls between 85 percent and 90 percent of $\dot{V}O_2$max and HRmax in a typical trained runner. The threshold pace zone (pace zone 6) is the appropriate target pace for threshold runs, also known as tempo runs, which most runners should do regularly throughout the training cycle, except in the early weeks of formal training for an event, when short, threshold-pace progressions at the end of easy runs serve to prepare the body for threshold runs later.

■ **Pace zone 7: gray zone 3.** Gray zone 3 (pace zone 7) corresponds to roughly 10K to 5K race pace for most runners. It's a little too fast for tempo runs and other workouts designed to elevate the threshold pace and threshold pace time limit, and a little too slow for interval workouts designed to boost $\dot{V}O_2$max. You won't spontaneously combust if you run within the gray zone 3 pace range, but your time will be best spent running a bit slower and slightly faster.

■ **Pace zone 8: $\dot{V}O_2$max.** $\dot{V}O_2$max is the maximum rate of oxygen consumption a runner can achieve while running. In most trained runners, this rate of oxygen consumption is reached after a few minutes of running at the fastest pace that can be sustained for 5 to 8 minutes. In maximal efforts lasting slightly longer (10 to 15 minutes), $\dot{V}O_2$max may also be reached, but it takes a little longer. Traditionally, $\dot{V}O_2$max-pace training is done at the runner's approximate 5K race pace. There's an elite bias in this tradition because $\dot{V}O_2$max pace corresponds more closely to 1,500- to 3,000-meter race pace for most runners, but the difference has no practical significance. The PZI system follows tradition and places $\dot{V}O_2$max pace at roughly 5K race pace. Naturally, $\dot{V}O_2$max pace corresponds to 100 percent $\dot{V}O_2$max (really 98 to 100 percent) and also to 95 to 100 percent HRmax.

Training at $\dot{V}O_2$max pace is the most effective way to increase $\dot{V}O_2$max. It also yields improvement in running economy and better resistance to neuromuscular fatigue. In performance terms, these benefits translate into the ability to run faster at $\dot{V}O_2$max intensity. The ultimate benefit is the ability to run faster at race distances in which oxygen consumption capacity is limiting, or 3,000 meters to 10K for most runners.

$\dot{V}O_2$max pace is typically targeted in workouts featuring intervals of three to five minutes with active recovery periods of equal duration. These intervals may be performed on level terrain or hills. In the early part of the training cycle, $\dot{V}O_2$max pace may also be used in fartlek runs involving shorter intervals.

■ **Pace zone 9: gray zone 4.** Gray zone 4 (pace zone 9) is a narrow gray zone that is just slightly faster than the pace required to reach 100 percent $\dot{V}O_2$max. The reason it is typically not targeted in workouts is that you can't run long enough at pace levels corresponding to 105 to 115 percent of $\dot{V}O_2$max to actually reach 100 percent $\dot{V}O_2$max, because neuromuscular fatigue occurs before your muscles' capacity to consume oxygen has become fully saturated. You can, however, reach $\dot{V}O_2$max at this pace range in nontraditional workouts featuring short intervals (30 to 60 seconds) separated by shorter recoveries (20 to 45 seconds).

On the other hand, gray zone 4 (pace zone 9) is a bit on the slow side for workouts designed to develop stride power and neuromuscular fatigue resistance, which entail very short intervals with longer recovery opportunities. Therefore this pace zone is typically not targeted in workouts.

■ **Pace zone 10: speed.** Speed pace corresponds to roughly 1,500-meter race pace on the high end and a full sprint on the low end. Heart rate and $\dot{V}O_2$max measurements have little relevance to speed pace because speed pace is faster than the pace at which heart rate and oxygen consumption plateau. Training in the speed pace zone increases stride power, running economy, and resistance to neuromuscular fatigue. As mentioned previously, speed pace is typically targeted in workouts featuring short intervals and longer active recovery periods. A typical example is 10 × 300 meters with 3:00 active recoveries.

USING THE PACE ZONE INDEX

There are three steps to using the pace zone index:

1. Determine your current PZI score.
2. Train in your current PZI zones.
3. Adjust your PZI as necessary.

Determine Your PZI Score

To determine your current pace zone index (PZI) score, refer to table 4.1 and simply look up a recent 3K, 5K, or 10K race time in the three columns on the left, or conduct a time trial at one of these distances and look up that time, or just estimate how fast you would run a race at one of these three distances today. Your current PZI score is the number in the fourth column of the row where you find your recent race or time trial result. In all likelihood you won't find your exact time, so just find the range it falls within. For example, if you recently ran a 5K in 22:22, you will find a 5K time range of 22:27 to 22:02 that's on the PZI 34 row of the table.

Table 4.1 Pace Zone Index Scores (English Measurements)

RECENT RACE (MIN:SEC)				TARGET TRAINING PACE ZONES (MIN:SEC PER MILE)					
3K	5K	10K	PZI	2: Low aerobic	3: Moderate aerobic	4: High aerobic	6: Threshold	8: VO$_2$max	10: Speed
18:10-17:41	32:55-32:01	68:04-66:21	50	14:41-13:21	13:20-12:15	12:14-11:37	11:01-10:41	10:08-9:58	9:38-2:40
17:40-17:13	32:00-31:06	66:20-64:37	49	14:22-13:02	13:01-11:57	11:56-11:19	10:44-10:24	9:51-9:41	9:22-2:40
17:12-16:46	31:05-30:15	64:36-62:55	48	14:03-12:43	12:42-11:39	11:38-11:02	10:29-10:09	9:35-9:25	9:06-2:40
16:45-16:21	30:14-29:33	62:54-61:17	47	13:45-12:25	12:24-11:22	11:21-10:45	10:13-9:54	9:19-9:09	8:50-2:40
16:20-15:57	29:32-28:42	61:16-59:40	46	13:27-12:07	12:06-11:05	11:04-10:29	9:57-9:38	9:03-8:53	8:34-2:40
15:56-15:34	28:41-28:00	59:39-58:10	45	13:11-11:51	11:50-10:50	10:49-10:15	9:43-9:24	8:51-8:41	8:22-2:40
15:33-15:12	27:59-27:19	58:09-56:44	44	12:50-11:30	11:29-10:34	10:33-10:00	9:29-9:11	8:39-8:29	8:09-2:40
15:11-14:51	27:18-26:41	56:43-55:23	43	12:41-11:21	11:20-10:21	10:20-9:47	9:17-8:59	8:27-8:18	7:56-2:40
14:50-14:31	26:40-26:04	55:22-54:07	42	12:25-11:05	11:04-10:07	10:06-9:33	9:04-8:46	8:15-8:06	7:42-2:40
14:30-14:12	26:03-25:29	54:06-52:48	41	12:12-10:52	10:51-9:54	9:53-9:21	8:53-8:36	8:03-7:54	7:32-2:40
14:11-13:54	25:28-24:55	52:47-51:43	40	11:59-10:39	10:38-9:41	9:40-9:08	8:42-8:25	7:51-7:42	7:22-2:40
13:53-13:37	24:54-24:24	51:42-50:36	39	11:47-10:27	10:26-9:30	9:29-8:57	8:32-8:15	7:43-7:34	7:14-2:40

RECENT RACE (MIN:SEC)				TARGET TRAINING PACE ZONES (MIN:SEC PER MILE)					
3K	5K	10K	PZI	2: Low aerobic	3: Moderate aerobic	4: High aerobic	6: Threshold	8: $\dot{V}O_2$max	10: Speed
13:36-13:20	24:23-23:53	50:35-49:32	38	11:30-10:15	10:14-9:18	9:17-8:46	8:20-8:04	7:35-7:26	7:06-2:40
13:19-13:03	23:52-23:24	49:31-48:31	37	11:19-10:04	10:03-9:08	9:07-8:36	8:10-7:54	7:27-7:18	6:58-2:40
13:02-12:48	23:23-22:55	48:30-47:33	36	11:07-9:52	9:51-8:57	8:56-8:25	8:00-7:44	7:18-7:10	6:50-2:40
12:47-12:40	22:54-22:28	47:32-46:37	35	10:57-9:42	9:43-8:47	8:46-8:16	7:51-7:36	7:10-7:02	6:42-2:40
12:39-12:19	22:27-22:02	46:36-45:43	34	10:46-9:31	9:30-8:37	8:36-8:06	7:41-7:26	7:02-6:54	6:34-2:40
12:18-12:05	22:01-21:38	45:42-44:50	33	10:37-9:22	9:21-8:28	8:27-7:57	7:33-7:18	6:50-6:42	6:26-2:40
12:04-11:52	21:37-21:13	44:49-44:01	32	10:27-9:12	9:11-8:18	8:17-7:48	7:24-7:10	6:46-6:38	6:18-2:40
11:51-11:39	21:12-20:51	44:00-43:13	31	10:17-9:02	9:01-8:10	8:09-7:40	7:17-7:03	6:38-6:30	6:09-2:40
11:38-11:27	20:50-20:29	43:12-42:27	30	10:08-8:53	8:52-8:02	8:01-7:32	7:09-6:55	6:30-6:22	6:02-2:40
11:26-11:15	20:28-20:07	42:26-41:43	29	10:00-8:45	8:46-7:53	7:52-7:24	7:02-6:49	6:24-6:17	5:56-2:40
11:14-11:04	20:06-19:46	41:42-41:00	28	9:47-8:37	8:36-7:46	7:45-7:17	6:58-6:45	6:18-6:11	5:50-2:40
11:03-10:53	19:45-19:26	40:59-40:19	27	9:40-8:30	8:29-7:38	7:37-7:09	6:51-6:37	6:11-6:04	5:45-2:40
10:52-10:42	19:25-19:08	40:18-39:40	26	9:31-8:21	8:20-7:31	7:30-7:02	6:44-6:32	6:09-6:02	5:41-2:40
10:41-10:32	19:07-18:49	39:39-39:01	25	9:24-8:14	8:13-7:24	7:23-6:56	6:38-6:26	6:03-5:56	5:36-2:40
10:31-10:22	18:48-18:31	39:00-38:24	24	9:17-8:07	8:06-7:17	7:16-6:49	6:32-6:20	5:57-5:50	5:31-2:40
10:21-10:13	18:30-18:13	38:23-37:49	23	9:10-8:00	7:59-7:11	7:10-6:43	6:26-6:15	5:50-5:44	5:26-2:40
10:12-10:03	18:12-17:57	37:48-37:14	22	9:03-7:53	7:52-7:04	7:03-6:37	6:21-6:10	5:44-5:38	5:20-2:40
10:02-9:54	17:56-17:41	37:13-36:41	21	8:56-7:46	7:45-6:58	6:57-6:31	6:15-6:04	5:40-5:34	5:16-2:40
9:53-9:46	17:40-17:25	36:40-36:08	20	8:50-7:40	7:39-6:52	6:51-6:25	6:09-5:59	5:36-5:30	5:09-2:40

(continued)

Table 4.1 Pace Zone Index Scores *(continued)*

RECENT RACE (MIN:SEC)				TARGET TRAINING PACE ZONES (MIN:SEC PER MILE)					
3K	5K	10K	PZI	2: Low aerobic	3: Moderate aerobic	4: High aerobic	6: Threshold	8: $\dot{V}O_2$max	10: Speed
9:45-9:37	17:24-17:10	36:07-35:37	19	8:44-7:34	7:33-6:44	6:43-6:19	6:04-5:54	5:32-5:26	5:05-2:40
9:36-9:29	17:09-16:55	35:36-35:07	18	8:33-7:28	7:27-6:39	6:38-6:14	5:59-5:49	5:28-5:22	5:01-2:40
9:28-9:21	16:54-16:41	35:06-34:38	17	8:26-7:21	7:20-6:35	6:34-6:09	5:55-5:46	5:24-5:19	4:57-2:40
9:20-9:13	16:40-16:27	34:37-34:09	16	8:21-7:16	7:15-6:30	6:29-6:04	5:50-5:41	5:20-5:15	4:53-2:40
9:12-9:06	16:26-16:14	34:08-33:42	15	8:15-7:10	7:09-6:25	6:24-5:59	5:46-5:37	5:16-5:11	4:49-2:40
9:05-8:59	16:13-16:01	33:41-33:15	14	8:10-7:05	7:04-6:20	6:19-5:54	5:40-5:32	5:12-5:07	4:45-2:40
8:58-8:52	16:00-15:48	33:14-32:48	13	8:04-6:59	6:58-6:15	6:14-5:49	5:36-5:28	5:08-5:03	4:41-2:40
8:51-8:45	15:47-15:36	32:47-32:23	12	7:59-6:54	6:53-6:10	6:09-5:45	5:32-5:24	5:04-4:59	4:37-2:40
8:44-8:38	15:35-15:23	32:22-31:59	11	7:53-6:48	6:47-6:05	6:04-5:40	5:28-5:21	4:59-4:55	4:33-2:40
8:37-8:31	15:22-15:12	31:58-31:35	10	7:49-6:44	6:43-6:01	6:00-5:36	5:24-5:17	4:55-4:51	4:29-2:40
8:30-8:25	15:11-15:01	31:34-31:11	9	7:44-6:39	6:38-5:57	5:56-5:32	5:20-5:13	4:51-4:47	4:25-2:40
8:24-8:19	15:00-14:50	31:10-30:49	8	7:35-6:35	6:34-5:53	5:52-5:28	5:16-5:10	4:47-4:43	4:21-2:40
8:18-8:13	14:49-14:39	30:48-30:27	7	7:29-6:29	6:28-5:48	5:47-5:24	5:12-5:06	4:43-4:39	4:17-2:40
8:12-8:07	14:38-14:28	30:26-30:06	6	7:25-6:25	6:24-6:44	6:43-5:20	5:08-5:02	4:40-4:37	4:13-2:40
8:06-8:01	14:27-14:18	30:05-29:46	5	7:21-6:21	6:20-5:40	5:39-5:16	5:05-5:00	4:39-4:36	4:09-2:40
8:00-7:56	14:17-14:08	29:45-29:24	4	7:16-6:16	6:15-5:36	5:35-5:12	5:02-4:57	4:35-4:31	4:08-2:40
7:55-7:51	14:07-13:58	29:23-29:05	3	7:12-6:12	6:11-5:33	5:32-5:09	4:59-4:54	4:31-4:28	4:04-2:40
7:50-7:46	13:57-13:49	29:04-28:45	2	7:08-6:08	6:07-5:29	5:28-5:05	4:54-4:50	4:27-4:24	4:01-2:40
7:45-7:40	13:48-13:40	28:44-28:27	1	7:03-6:03	6:02-5:25	5:24-5:01	4:51-4:47	4:23-4:20	3:58-2:40
7:39-7:35	13:39-13:31	28:26-28:09	0	7:00-6:00	5:59-5:22	5:21-4:58	4:48-4:44	4:22-4:29	3:57-2:40

Courtesy of TrainingPeaks (www.trainingpeaks.com).

Your training pace zones are in the columns on the right side of the table that are in the same row as your current PZI score. You will notice that all PZI scores share the same maximum pace of 2:40 per mile at the top of pace zone 10. This number corresponds to world-class pace for 100 meters and is meant to represent a full sprint. (If you train in metric, see the metric version of the PZI table in the appendix, page 201.)

Training Peaks WKO+ offers another option to establish appropriate training pace zones that uses the pace zone index but skips over the step of assigning an actual PZI score. All you have to do is enter your current functional threshold pace in the pace zone calculator and it will calculate your other pace zones. Your functional threshold pace is the fastest pace you could sustain for one hour. If you're currently not fit enough to run for one hour, or you can't accurately estimate your one-hour pace, use the race or time trial method just described.

Using Training Peaks WKO+ to determine your target pace zones allows for a greater degree of customization. For example, if you use the PZI method and determine that your PZI score is 37, you will be assigned a particular set of target pace zones that correspond to that score in table 4.1. The threshold pace zone associated with PZI 37 happens to be 8:10 to 7:54. Now suppose that you are able to accurately estimate that your true functional threshold pace is 8:04 per mile. If you enter this precise value in the Training Peaks WKO+ training pace zones calculator, you will get a slightly different set of target pace zones.

Even if you determine your training pace zones initially using the PZI method, if you use Training Peaks WKO+ you will have to enter your threshold pace into the pace zone calculator so that the application can calculate accurate training stress scores for each run, create an accurate pace zone distribution chart, and so forth. Figure 4.1 shows a screen shot of the Training Peaks WKO+ pace zone

Pace Training Zones					Options ▼
◀ ▶ Effective	1/25/2009 ▼	and after			
Name	Abbr	From	To	▲	Threshold
Speed	10	4:57	up		5:45
Gray IV	9	5:07	4:58		
VO2max	8	5:14	5:08		
Gray III	7	5:33	5:15		
Thresh	6	5:45	5:34	▼	

Figure 4.1 Training Peaks WKO+ pace zone calculator.
Courtesy of TrainingPeaks (www.trainingpeaks.com).

calculator. (Note that only zones 7 to 10 are visible. You'd have to scroll down to see zones 1 to 6.) The numbers in the table represent paces in minutes and seconds per mile. Note that you will seldom run a full mile in pace zone 8 and never run a full mile in pace zone 10 in workouts, but you can still use your speed and distance device to find the right pace for short intervals in these zones.

Certainly the most precise way to determine your current PZI score is to run a race or time trial at the 3K, 5K, or 10K distance, if you're up for a little suffering. In addition to providing valuable information, a time trial is also a terrific workout that will start you on the road toward lowering your PZI score. There's no best distance to choose. Each of the three options is equally reliable.

Suppose you decide to use a 5K time trial to determine your current PZI score. Plan a route that is free of hills and other annoyances such as traffic lights, or just go to the local high school or university track. Warm up with about a mile (1.5 to 2 km) of easy jogging, then hit the lap button on your speed and distance device and run 3.10 miles, or 12.5 laps, on a standard 400-meter track, as fast as you can. Hit the lap button again and cool down with another mile of slow jogging. When you get home, look up your 5K split time on table 4.1. Let's suppose it's 20:43. This time falls within the range of 20:50 to 20:29 that corresponds to a PZI score of 30. The pace zones associated with this score are as follows:

Pace zone 1: gray zone 1—59:59 to 10:09

Pace zone 2: low aerobic—10:08 to 8:53

Pace zone 3: moderate aerobic—8:52 to 8:02

Pace zone 4: high aerobic—8:01 to 7:32

Pace zone 5: gray zone 2—7:31 to 7:10

Pace zone 6: threshold—7:09 to 6:55

Pace zone 7: gray zone 3—6:54 to 6:31

Pace zone 8: $\dot{V}O_2$max—6:30 to 6:22

Pace zone 9: gray zone 4—6:21 to 6:03

Pace zone 10: speed—6:02 to 2:40

Train in Your PZI Zone

Having established your current PZI score, you may now use your pace zones to control your pace appropriately in workouts. Garmin's speed and distance devices allow you to program all 10 PZI zones into the unit. Other speed and distance devices do not allow you to program multiple target pace zones, but they do allow you to program a single target pace zone for each workout. Most runners find it easiest simply to remember their current pace zones (it doesn't take long to become familiar with them) and control pace simply by checking it periodically during runs.

Naturally, practicing PZI-based training requires that you know which pace zones should be targeted in the various workout types. This information is provided later in the chapter. Runners who are new to the PZI system often wonder exactly how fast they should run—that is, precisely what pace to run within each pace zone. For example, as shown, the threshold pace zone for a PZI score of 30 is 7:09 to 6:55 per mile. When running a threshold workout, precisely how fast should a 30 PZI runner go? Initially, you will simply have to go by feel. If your first threshold workout calls for 3 miles of running in threshold zone (pace zone 6) between a warm-up and a cool-down, just aim to run faster than 7:10 per mile during that 3-mile segment and allow your subjective rating of perceived exertion to determine how much faster. After completing the workout, review it in your performance management software to find your average pace for the threshold portion of the workout. That precise pace—suppose it's 7:04 per mile—becomes your stake in the ground. In subsequent threshold workouts, aim to run 7:04 per mile or slightly faster. Use the same approach with every pace zone except the low aerobic zone, which is used exclusively for active recovery and therefore should be controlled primarily by perceived exertion. It should always feel very comfortable, no matter how slow you have to go to keep it comfortable.

To use heart rate as a secondary metric to monitor and control the intensity of PZI-based runs, wear a heart-rate monitor during all of your workouts and determine the heart-rate range that is associated with each pace range. Once you've established these links, you can use either pace or heart rate to monitor and control your pace in subsequent workouts, depending on which is most convenient or useful at any given time. For example, when running on hilly terrain, you will probably want to use heart rate because hills skew the relationship between pace and physiological intensity.

Adjust Your PZI

As your fitness improves, you will need to make periodic adjustments to your PZI score. Scheduled races provide perfect opportunities to make these adjustments, but you may find that your PZI changes more often than you race, so you should not always wait for races to recalibrate your PZI score. Regularly scheduled time-trial workouts can help you make such adjustments when appropriate between races, but these workouts are very taxing and you don't want to do them too often, either.

A simple and nondisruptive way to adjust your PZI score whenever necessary involves paying attention to the relationship between perceived effort and pace in your workouts. As you run in your various pace zones during the normal course of your training, you will become familiar with how hard each

Briana Boehmer on Coaching Youth Runners With Speed and Distance Devices

Briana Boehmer is a professional triathlete and duathlete whose competitive credentials include a win in the elite division of the 2006 U.S. Duathlon National Championship. She also coaches triathletes and runners with an outfit called Transition, based in Pewaukee, Wisconsin, and the Brookfield East High School girls track and field team.

In 2008 Boehmer acquired five speed and distance devices for use by her distance runners during the fall cross-country season, when they were coached by a teacher who lacked any kind of background as a competitive runner and had no formal training as a distance running coach. Boehmer wanted to test her hypothesis that speed and distance devices and their supporting software could make up for the coach's lack of experience in training. The results of this experiment were mixed.

On the positive side, the devices were well received by the athletes, who genuinely enjoyed using them. "They were superexcited, to the point where they even named their units like pets," says Boehmer. Having grown up with technology, the girls learned to operate the devices quickly and paid almost obsessive attention to the data the devices provided while training.

On the negative side, their coach struggled not only in learning how to operate the devices but also in understanding the concepts used by the training software to analyze training data. As a result, she was not able to use the data to actively guide her runners' fitness development.

Fortunately, Boehmer was there to help, and she feels that in the end the devices made a big difference in the performance of most of the runners. "The devices really helped them with pace recognition—how to manipulate pace to make each workout serve a definite purpose," she says. "They became much better able to make their easy days easy and their hard days hard."

Among the runners was one overachiever who constantly pushed too hard and tried to do too much. Boehmer was able to use the performance management software to show her that she was doing too much and rein her in. At the end of the season, this runner qualified for the sectional championship meet—an achievement that was unexpected and perhaps less likely to have happened without her technological advantage.

Two of the other runners on the team had the opposite problem. "They were talented but a bit lazy," says Boehmer, who used the software to prove that they were not working hard enough. The pair subsequently put more effort into their training and by the end of the season each had significantly improved her personal best times.

Even the two runners on the team who performed below expectations will ultimately be helped by the technology, Boehmer suggests, because it has helped them understand why they underachieved and how to run better in the future.

The conclusion Boehmer reached at the end of her informal study was that speed and distance devices are probably most useful in the coaching of youth runners when training is overseen by a knowledgeable coach. But she remains hopeful that such technology will eventually provide powerful support to the more typical coach, who is just a teacher looking to make a little extra money outside the classroom. "Once the technology gets to the point where the software can reliably tell the coach what to do next with each runner based on the training that's been done already, this thing could really take off," she concludes.

pace zone feels. The more your fitness improves, the easier it will feel to run in each of your pace zones and the faster you will be able to run at the effort level previously associated with each pace zone. Don't hold yourself back when the pace zones associated with your currently established PZI begin to feel too slow. Allow yourself to continue running at a consistent effort level when targeting any given pace zone repeatedly over time, even when it means that you begin to run outside that zone on the fast side.

You will notice this effect especially in the higher pace zones—threshold, $\dot{V}O_2$max, and speed—because these pace zones are narrower and there is less overlap between adjacent PZI scores in these higher pace zones. The lower pace zones—low, moderate, and high aerobic—are broader, and there is more overlap, so you can move up substantially within them without necessarily moving out of them.

When you find yourself consistently running faster than the target pace zones—and especially the faster pace zones—in workouts, even though you're running at the same effort level at which you used to run within the target pace zones, it's time to lower your PZI score one level and begin to use the target pace zones associated with that new level.

TRAINING WITH PACE-BASED WORKOUTS

Run workouts may be classified into 10 types. Table 4.2 lists the 10 types of training runs and the pace zones associated with each type. The far-right column identifies the fitness components that are developed by each workout type. There are four components of running fitness: raw endurance (or the capacity to run far), lactate threshold (or the capacity to run fast for approximately one hour), aerobic capacity (or the capacity to run fast for 15 minutes or so), and speed. We say more about these four components of running fitness in chapter 5.

Some of these workouts, such as base runs, have a single basic format, while others, such as interval runs, may be structured in a variety of ways. All workouts may be performed at a wide range of challenge levels. The challenge level of the workout is determined by its duration and intensity. The most accurate way to quantify the challenge level of a specific format of any given workout type is by training stress score (TSS), which was covered in chapter 3.

Tables 4.3 through 4.13 feature descriptions of each of the 10 workout types and guidelines for their practice. Specific workout examples representing various challenge levels for each workout type are given and ranked according to their approximate TSS. For the purpose of these examples, we have created a hypothetical runner with a current PZI of 26. This means his threshold pace range is 6:44 to 6:32 per mile. Recall that training stress scores are based on the relationships between workout pace and duration and the runner's threshold pace. A one-hour run at threshold pace yields a TSS of 100. Because all of the workout examples that follow are based on distance instead of time, they are

Table 4.2 Training Run Types and Pace Zones

Type of training run	Pace zones	Fitness components trained
Recovery run	Pace zone 2 (low aerobic)	Raw endurance
Base run	Pace zone 3 (moderate aerobic)	
Long run	Pace zone 3 (moderate aerobic)	
Progression run	Start in pace zone 2 (low aerobic) or pace zone 3 (moderate aerobic) and progress to pace zone 4 (high aerobic) or pace zone 6 (threshold)	Raw endurance Lactate threshold
Marathon-pace run	Pace zone 4 (high aerobic)	Raw endurance Lactate threshold
Fartlek run	Start at pace zone 3 (moderate aerobic) and incorporate intervals at pace zone 8 ($\dot{V}O_2$max) or pace zone 10 (speed)	Raw endurance Lactate threshold Aerobic capacity Speed
Hill repetitions	If similar to lactate intervals, start in pace zone 8 ($\dot{V}O_2$max) with active recovery in pace zone 2 (low aerobic); if similar to speed intervals, pace zone 10 (speed)	Aerobic capacity Speed
Threshold run	Pace zone 6 (threshold)	Lactate threshold
Lactate intervals	Start in pace zone 8 ($\dot{V}O_2$max) with active recovery in pace zone 2 (low aerobic)	Aerobic capacity
Speed intervals	Pace zone 10 (speed)	Speed
Mixed intervals	Varies	Lactate threshold Aerobic capacity Speed

accurate only for our hypothetical runner (and any other runner with a PZI of 26). This is because it will take runners with higher and lower PZI scores more or less time to run the same distance at the same relative intensity.

For example, one of the base runs calls for the runner to run 10 miles at moderate aerobic pace (pace zone 3). It would take our hypothetical runner roughly 1 hour 19 minutes to complete this run. Thus, for the purpose of TSS calculation, this workout consists of 79 minutes at moderate aerobic pace (pace zone 2), which yields a TSS of 104. But for a slower runner with a PZI of 30, a 10-mile run at moderate aerobic pace (pace zone 3) would take approximately 1 hour 24 minutes to complete. That's really a different workout, and therefore yields a higher TSS score of 107. To get the same workout and the same TSS score as our hypothetical runner, the runner with a 30 PZI would need to run a shorter distance that would take 1 hour 19 minutes to complete at moderate aerobic pace (pace zone 3).

Table 4.3 Recovery Run

A recovery run is a relatively short and slow run performed at a steady pace in pace zone 2 (low aerobic). The name of this workout is somewhat misleading. A recovery run does not actually promote recovery from a preceding hard workout. Rather, it is simply easy enough so as not to create any additional need for recovery. A properly executed recovery run therefore does not impede recovery from preceding hard training or sabotage performance in the next hard workout. The true purpose of doing recovery runs is to add aerobic volume to your training without limiting the volume or quality of high-intensity running you can do.

Sample recovery runs	TSS
3 mi. at pace zone 2	26.5
3.5 mi. at pace zone 2	31
4 mi. at pace zone 2	36
4.5 mi. at pace zone 2	40
5 mi. at pace zone 2	45
5.5 mi. at pace zone 2	49
6 mi. at pace zone 2	54

Table 4.4 Base Run

A base run is a relatively short- to moderate-length run undertaken at a steady pace in pace zone 3 (moderate aerobic). While individual base runs are not meant to be challenging, they are meant to be done frequently. In the aggregate they stimulate big improvements in aerobic capacity, endurance, and running economy.

Sample base runs	TSS
4 mi. at pace zone 3	40.5
4.5 mi. at pace zone 3	46
5 mi. at pace zone 3	51
5.5 mi. at pace zone 3	56
6 mi. at pace zone 3	61
6.5 mi. at pace zone 3	67
7 mi. at pace zone 3	72
7.5 mi. at pace zone 3	77
8 mi. at pace zone 3	82
8.5 mi. at pace zone 3	88
9 mi. at pace zone 3	93
10 mi. at pace zone 3	104

Table 4.5 Long Run

A long run is simply a base run that lasts long enough to leave you moderately to severely fatigued. The function of a long run is to stimulate physiological adaptations that increase endurance by exposing the body to fatigue in a prolonged moderate-intensity effort. The distance or duration required for this effect depends on your current level of endurance. Somewhat arbitrarily, we define long runs as base runs lasting longer than 10 miles (6.2 km).

Sample long runs	TSS
11 mi. at pace zone 3	114
12 mi. at pace zone 3	125
13 mi. at pace zone 3	135.5
14 mi. at pace zone 3	146
15 mi. at pace zone 3	157
16 mi. at pace zone 3	168
17 mi. at pace zone 3	178
18 mi. at pace zone 3	189
19 mi. at pace zone 3	200
20 mi. at pace zone 3	211
21 mi. at pace zone 3	221.5
22 mi. at pace zone 3	232
23 mi. at pace zone 3	243
24 mi. at pace zone 3	254

Table 4.6 Progression Run

A progression run is a run that begins in pace zone 2 or 3 and ends in pace zone 4 or 6. In general, progression runs are intended to be moderately challenging—harder than base runs but easier than most threshold and interval runs. Progression runs can be very challenging, however, when a pace zone 4 progression is tacked onto the end of a long run (exceeding 10 miles or 6.2 km). Long progression runs are excellent as specific training for half marathons and marathons.

Sample progression runs	TSS
5 mi. at pace zone 3 plus 1 mi. at pace zone 4	64
6 mi. at pace zone 3 plus 1 mi. at pace zone 4	74
5 mi. at pace zone 3 plus 2 mi. at pace zone 4:	77
7 mi. at pace zone 3 plus 1 mi. at pace zone 4	85
8 mi. at pace zone 3 plus 1 mi. at pace zone 4	95.5
7 mi. at pace zone 3 plus 2 mi. at pace zone 4	98
9 mi. at pace zone 3 plus 1 mi. at pace zone 4	106
8 mi. at pace zone 3 plus 2 mi. at pace zone 4	109
9 mi. at pace zone 3 plus 2 mi. at pace zone 4	119
10 mi. at pace zone 3 plus 2 mi. at pace zone 4	130
11 mi. at pace zone 3 plus 2 mi. at pace zone 4	141
10 mi. at pace zone 3 plus 3 mi. at pace zone 4	143
11 mi. at pace zone 3 plus 3 mi. at pace zone 4	154

Table 4.7 Marathon-Pace Run

A marathon-pace run is just that: a prolonged run at marathon pace (i.e., the fast end of pace zone 4). It's a good workout to perform at a very challenging level in the final weeks of preparation for a marathon, after you've established adequate raw endurance with long runs in pace zone 3 and longer progression runs featuring smaller amounts of marathon-pace running.

Sample marathon-pace runs	TSS
1 mi. warm-up at pace zone 2 plus 6 mi. at marathon pace	79
1 mi. warm-up at pace zone 2 plus 7 mi. at marathon pace	91
1 mi. warm-up at pace zone 2 plus 8 mi. at marathon pace	103
1 mi. warm-up at pace zone 2 plus 9 mi. at marathon pace	115
1 mi. warm-up at pace zone 2 plus 10 mi. at marathon pace	126.5
1 mi. warm-up at pace zone 2 plus 11 mi. at marathon pace	138.5
1 mi. warm-up at pace zone 2 plus 12 mi. at marathon pace	150

Table 4.8 Fartlek Run

A fartlek run is a base run sprinkled with short, fast intervals, usually 30 to 60 seconds in pace zone 8 or 10. Think of a fartlek run as a gentle lactate interval or speed interval. It's a good way to begin the process of developing efficiency and fatigue resistance at faster speeds in the early phases of the training cycle.

Sample fartlek runs	TSS
1 mi. at pace zone 3 6 × 30 sec. at pace zone 8 with 2-min. active recoveries at pace zone 2 1 mi. at pace zone 3	35.5
1 mi. at pace zone 3 6 × 30 sec. at pace zone 10 with 2-min. active recoveries at pace zone 2 1 mi. at pace zone 3	33
2 mi. at pace zone 3 8 × 30 sec. at pace zone 8 with 2-min. active recoveries at pace zone 2 2 mi. at pace zone 3	49
2 mi. at pace zone 3 8 × 30 sec. at pace zone 10 with 2-min. active recoveries at pace zone 2 2 mi. at pace zone 3	51
2 mi. at pace zone 3 6 × 45 sec. at pace zone 8 with 2-min. active recoveries at pace zone 2 2 mi. at pace zone 3	50
2 mi. at pace zone 3 6 × 45 sec. at pace zone 10 with 2-min. active recoveries at pace zone 2 2 mi. at pace zone 3	53
2 mi. at pace zone 3 8 × 45 sec. at pace zone 8 with 2-min. active recoveries at pace zone 2 2 mi. at pace zone 3	50
2 mi. at pace zone 3 6 × 60 sec. at pace zone 10 with 2-min. active recoveries at pace zone 2 2 mi. at pace zone 3	57
2 mi. at pace zone 3 8 × 60 sec. at pace zone 10 with 2-min. active recoveries at pace zone 2 2 mi. at pace zone 3	60.5

Table 4.9 Hill Repetitions

Hill repetitions are essentially lactate intervals or speed intervals run uphill. The ideal hill on which to run repetitions features a steady, moderate gradient of 4 to 6 percent. Hill repetitions provide much the same benefits as lactate and speed intervals while also building run-specific strength. They are typically run at the intensity associated with pace zones 8 and 10; however, they will be slower because of the gradient.

Sample hill repetitions	TSS
1 mi. at pace zone 2 4 × (200m uphill at pace zone 10 and 200m downhill at pace zone 2) 1 mi. at pace zone 2	32
1 mi. at pace zone 2 8 × (200m uphill at pace zone 10 and 200m downhill at pace zone 2) 1 mi. at pace zone 2	50
1 mi. at pace zone 2 6 × (400m uphill at pace zone 8 and 400m downhill at pace zone 2) 1 mi. at pace zone 2	60
1 mi. at pace zone 2 9 × (400m uphill at pace zone 8 and 400m downhill at pace zone 2) 1 mi. at pace zone 2	80

Table 4.10   Threshold Run

A threshold run is a workout that features one or two sustained efforts in pace zone 6. Threshold runs increase the pace you can sustain for a prolonged time and increase the time you can sustain a relatively fast pace.

Sample threshold runs	TSS
1 mi. at pace zone 2 1 mi. at pace zone 6 1 mi. at pace zone 2	31
1 mi. at pace zone 2 1 mi. at pace zone 6 0.5 mi. at pace zone 2 1 mi. at pace zone 6 1 mi. at pace zone 2	49
1 mi. at pace zone 2 2 mi. at pace zone 6 1 mi. at pace zone 2	44
1 mi. at pace zone 2 1.5 mi. at pace zone 6 0.5 mi. at pace zone 2 1.5 mi. at pace zone 6 1 mi. at pace zone 2	62
1 mi. at pace zone 2 3 mi. at pace zone 6 1 mi. at pace zone 2	57
1 mi. at pace zone 2 2 mi. at pace zone 6 0.5 mi. at pace zone 2 2 mi. at pace zone 6 1 mi. at pace zone 2	74
1 mi. at pace zone 2 4 mi. at pace zone 6 1 mi. at pace zone 2	70
1 mi. at pace zone 2 2.5 mi. at pace zone 6 0.5 mi. at pace zone 2 2.5 mi. at pace zone 6 1 mi. at pace zone 2	87
1 mi. at pace zone 2 5 mi. at pace zone 6 1 mi. at pace zone 2	82
1 mi. at pace zone 2 3 mi. at pace zone 6 0.5 mi. at pace zone 2 3 mi. at pace zone 6 1 mi. at pace zone 2	100
1 mi. at pace zone 2 6 mi. at pace zone 6 1 mi. at pace zone 2	95

Table 4.11 Lactate Intervals

Lactate intervals take the form of relatively short to moderately long intervals (200 m to 1 km) in pace zone 8 with active recoveries in pace zone 2. They're an excellent means of progressively developing efficiency and fatigue resistance at fast running speeds.

Sample lactate intervals	TSS
1 mi. at pace zone 2 6 × (400 m at pace zone 8 and 400 m at pace zone 2) 1 mi. at pace zone 2	50
1 mi. at pace zone 2 8 × (400 m at pace zone 8 and 400 m at pace zone 2) 1 mi. at pace zone 2	61
1 mi. at pace zone 2 6 × (600 m at pace zone 8 and 400 m at pace zone 2) 1 mi. at pace zone 2	60
1 mi. at pace zone 2 8 × (600 m at pace zone 8 and 400 m at pace zone 2) 1 mi. at pace zone 2	74
1 mi. at pace zone 2 4 × (800 m at pace zone 8 and 400 m at pace zone 2) 1 mi. at pace zone 2	52
1 mi. at pace zone 2 6 × (800 m at pace zone 8 and 400 m at pace zone 2) 1 mi. at pace zone 2	70
1 mi. at pace zone 2 4 × (1 km at pace zone 8 and 400 m at pace zone 2) 1 mi. at pace zone 2	59
1 mi. at pace zone 2 5 × (1 km at pace zone 8 and 400 m at pace zone 2) 1 mi. at pace zone 2	70

Table 4.12 Speed Intervals

Speed intervals are short or relatively short intervals of 100 to 400 meters run in pace zone 10, which ranges from roughly 1,500-meter race pace to a full sprint. Longer speed intervals should be run at 1,500-meter pace, while shorter speed intervals should be run faster, between 800-meter pace and a full sprint, depending on the length of the intervals. (The shorter, the faster.)

Sample speed intervals	TSS
1 mi. at pace zone 2 16 × (100 m at pace zone 10 and 400 m at pace zone 2) 1 mi. at pace zone 2	66
1 mi. at pace zone 2 8 × (200 m at pace zone 10 and 400 m at pace zone 2) 1 mi. at pace zone 2	49
1 mi. at pace zone 2 12 × (200 m at pace zone 10 and 400 m at pace zone 2) 1 mi. at pace zone 2	66
1 mi. at pace zone 2 8 × (300 m at pace zone 10 and 400 m at pace zone 2) 1 mi. at pace zone 2	57
1 mi. at pace zone 2 10 × (300 m at pace zone 10 and 400 m at pace zone 2) 1 mi. at pace zone 2	69
1 mi. at pace zone 2 10 × (400 m at pace zone 10 and 400 m at pace zone 2) 1 mi. at pace zone 2	76.5
1 mi. at pace zone 2 12 × (400 m at pace zone 8 and 400 m at pace zone 2) 1 mi. at pace zone 2	83

Table 4.13 Mixed Intervals

Mixed intervals, as the name suggests, are intervals of various distances run at different pace levels, usually pace zone 6 (threshold), pace zone 8 (VO2max), and pace zone 10 (speed). Mixed-interval runs are an excellent means of including a variety of training stimuli in a single workout.

Format	TSS
1 mi. at pace zone 2 1 min. at pace zone 10 1 min. at pace zone 2 2 min. at pace zone 8 2 min. at pace zone 2 3 min. at pace zone 6 3 min. at pace zone 2 2 min. at pace zone 8 2 min. at pace zone 2 1 min. at pace zone 10 1 min. at pace zone 2 2 min. at pace zone 8 2 min. at pace zone 2 3 min. at pace zone 6 1 mi. at pace zone 2	57
1 mi. at pace zone 2 1 min. at pace zone 10 1 min. at pace zone 2 2 min. at pace zone 8 2 min. at pace zone 2 3 min. at pace zone 6 3 min. at pace zone 2 2 min. at pace zone 8 2 min. at pace zone 2 1 min. at pace zone 10 1 min. at pace zone 2 2 min. at pace zone 8 2 min. at pace zone 2 3 min. at pace zone 6 3 min. at pace zone 2 2 min. at pace zone 8 2 min. at pace zone 2 1 min. at pace zone 10 1 mi. at pace zone 2	68
1 mi. at pace zone 2 1 mi. at pace zone 6 400 m at pace zone 2 800 m at pace zone 8 400 m at pace zone 2 400 m at pace zone 10 1 mi. at pace zone 2	43.5

Format	TSS
1 mi. at pace zone 2	45
1 mi. at pace zone 6	
400 m at pace zone 2	
800 m at pace zone 8	
400 m at pace zone 2	
600 m at pace zone 8	
400 m at pace zone 2	
400 m at pace zone 10	
400 m at pace zone 2	
200 m at pace zone 10	
1 mi. at pace zone 2	

So, then, why do we use distance rather than duration in these examples? First, runners prefer to think and plan in terms of distance instead of duration. Second, races are run by distance, not duration. Therefore, all runners need to prepare themselves to go the distance regardless of their speed and how their speed affects the duration of workouts. A runner with a 30 PZI will take longer to complete a marathon than a runner with a 26 PZI, and for this very reason, his longest training runs had better last longer than the faster runner's longest training runs, although they may be identical in distance.

This does not mean that slower runners have to train more than faster runners. It just means that the most race-specific workouts that slower runners do need to be roughly equivalent in distance, therefore longer in duration, than the most race-specific workouts that faster runners do. Typically, because they are fitter and more competitive, faster runners are able and willing to do more total training than slower runners.

FINDING COMPLETENESS

Step 1 of performance management, monitoring, is a prerequisite to step 2, analyzing, which is the topic of chapter 5. Without a fairly complete record of the training you've done, you won't have sufficient data to provide the basis for definitive conclusions about what's working and what's not working, how much progress you're making, and which needs are unmet.

The importance of consistent data collection to effective performance management cannot be overstated. It's like joining the Rotary Club: Either you're in or you're out, and if you're in, you'd better be all the way in. For example, suppose you forget to take your speed and distance device with you on a four-day business trip during which you manage to squeeze in three runs, and then resume using your device and uploading data upon returning home. The missing data will skew the tables, charts, and graphs in your performance management software, making it less reliable. Or suppose you forget to wear your heart-rate monitor strap occasionally when you run. These lapses will have a similar effect on the tables, charts, and graphs that include heart rate. Although there are ways around missing data, it's always best to have real, complete data from your devices.

CHAPTER

Analyzing Data for Balanced Training

The second step of the performance management system is analysis, which involves connecting cause and effect in your training. It's where you draw conclusions about the impact of your training on your fitness and performance and use these conclusions in planning your future training appropriately, which is the third step of performance management. In chapter 3, which provided a broad overview of the performance management system, we discussed eight ways in which the effects of your training can be quantified. The analysis step of performance management consists of looking at these effects through the prism of specific questions, the answers to which are critical to determining the best course in your future training.

There are numerous ways to analyze your training data. Indeed, we could have written an entire book on this topic alone. But a handful of types of analysis are particularly helpful, and we'd like to focus on those in this chapter. If you master these few types of analysis and never bother to learn or practice any others, you will still make great strides in your development as a self-coached runner. Learning these most helpful types of analysis will give you an excellent foundation of confidence and expertise that will enable you to easily explore other types of analysis in the future. The specific types of training data analysis we discuss here may be formulated as five questions that you should attempt to answer throughout the training process by studying the tables, graphs, and charts in your performance management software:

1. How good was my last workout?
2. Am I training hard enough, or too hard?

3. Do I need a rest?

4. Am I getting fitter?

5. Is my training appropriately balanced?

Consider these questions every time you add new workout data to your performance management software, and make it a habit to upload your workout data to your performance management software after each run. By doing so, you will be able to keep your finger on the pulse of your fitness development with minimal time and effort. Some specific ways of answering the questions do require a special initiative, such as a test workout, but need not be performed as often. Let's now take a close look at each of the five types of analysis that are entailed in answering these questions.

HOW GOOD WAS MY LAST WORKOUT?

Running performance does not improve in a linear fashion from workout to workout. When you're training properly, there is an overall trend toward better performance, but from day to day there are good runs, bad runs, and average runs. Every time you complete a run, you have some sense of how good it was. Either you feel better than usual, worse than usual, or about the same as usual for the type of workout you're doing. And if you monitor your pace or record your split times, then you have some sense of how your performance compares to your performance in recent workouts of the same type.

Performance in Similar Key Workouts

Such informal ratings of your workouts may bolster your confidence when your training is going well and may set you on a course of troubleshooting when it's not going so well, but a more formal rating of your workouts using performance management software carries greater benefits. By using performance management tools to quantify your performance in each workout, you can also determine exactly how strong a training stimulus you achieved in the workout, how close you are to reaching the level of fitness required to attain your race goals, and whether you need to adjust your training pace targets to take advantage of recent progress and initiate further progress.

Your hardest workouts are the easiest ones to rate. Because you push your performance limits in these workouts, they provide the best indication of where your limits are—relative to your expectations and recent performance in similar workouts—at the time you tackle each of them. In most interval runs, hill repetition runs, and marathon-pace runs, and in some threshold runs, progression runs, and long runs, your objective is to perform better than you have in recent runs of the same type, whether it's by maintaining a faster average pace over a given distance, by covering more distance at a given pace, by completing more intervals at the same pace, or by completing longer intervals at the same pace. When you meet this objective, you've had a good run. When you fail to meet it, you've had a bad run.

Let's look at an example of this type of comparison from Matt Fitzgerald's own marathon training. In the sixth week of a ramp-up for the Boston Marathon, using the pace zone index system of pacing, Matt completed a progression run consisting of 9.5 miles in pace zone 3 (moderate aerobic pace) plus 4.5 miles in pace zone 6 (threshold pace). Because he wore a Garmin Forerunner 405, he was able to perform this run on an unmeasured road course. Three weeks later Matt completed a slightly more challenging progression run. The total distance was the same, but this time the first 9 miles were run in pace zone 3 and the last 5 miles in pace zone 6. Matt's exact pace for the 4.5-mile threshold-pace progression in the first run was 5:34 per mile. Three weeks later, Matt ran the slightly longer 5-mile progression at the same perceived effort level as in the first workout and his pace was 5:33 per mile. Because he ran a bit faster over a longer distance in the second workout, Matt judged it a good workout that indicated his training was on track.

Running Index

The limitation of using pace to rate workouts is that, again, it's useful only for hard workouts in which you push your performance limits. But every workout is important. Even base runs and recovery runs matter in the big picture. So it would be nice if there were a way that you could assess your performance in workouts in which you're not pushing yourself to the point of significant fatigue. Polar's running index, described in detail in chapter 3, rates runs through a complex analysis of the relationship between pace and heart rate in a given run. Essentially, the feature calculates the physiological stress of running at any pace, a value that is determined by your aerobic fitness and your running economy, both of which slowly improve with training, but may be slightly compromised by fatigue from day to day. Running economy is analogous to fuel economy in a car; it refers to how much energy it costs to go a given speed or distance. In running, we generally measure economy as the rate of oxygen consumption at a given pace. Since heart rate is closely correlated to the rate of oxygen consumption, the heart rate–running pace relationship is a proxy for running economy.

When you have a lousy run because you are carrying fatigue from recent training, this fatigue often will manifest itself in the form of reduced aerobic power and running economy, which in turn will likely reveal themselves through changes in the way your heart rate responds to the challenge of running at any pace, even if the pace is not very challenging. Alternatively, even if running economy (oxygen consumption and running pace) is not directly affected, often the heart rate–pace relationship may be altered because the body's fight of flight system is activated to a greater extent during submaximal runs when the runner is fatigued. This results in an elevated heart rate at a given pace, which would appear as a change in the running index, although not really a change in running economy. Regardless, Polar argues the running index is sensitive enough to measure these changes in a meaningful way.

A Polar device will automatically calculate running index after 12 minutes of running at a pace associated with a heart rate that is at least 40 percent of your maximum. It will continuously recalculate running index from that point until you stop running or surpass 60 minutes of running, at which point it will show your final running index score for the run.

Polar provides the following rankings for use with the running index:

$\leq$30: very poor
31–37: poor
38–44: fair
45–51: average
52–58: good
59–65: very good
>65: excellent

You can ignore the qualitative ratings very poor, poor, and so forth. These designations are not helpful, because your running index is determined by your natural, genetically based running ability more than anything else, such that many runners cannot ever exceed the "fair" range regardless of how hard and how well they train. It's best just to note your running index number after each run and compare it to past runs. This use of the tool gives you a reliable quantitative assessment of the quality of each run, whether it's a punishing marathon-pace run or a short, slow recovery run.

As you track your running index over time, you will develop a feel for the optimal rate of running index improvement in response to training. You can then use this knowledge in troubleshooting when your running index fails to improve at the expected rate.

Figure 5.1 is a graph that shows the relationship between running index and race performance for an individual runner—our friend Roberto Veneziani, whom you met in chapter 3—over a two-year period. It clearly demonstrates that running index was strongly predictive of racing performance. It also shows that this particular runner is able to raise his running index at an average rate of 1.0 to 1.3 per week during periods of consistent, progressive training.

You may recall from chapter 3 that if you do not use a Polar speed and distance device, you can manually calculate an approximate running index value for a run. Refer to page 48 in chapter 3 for instructions.

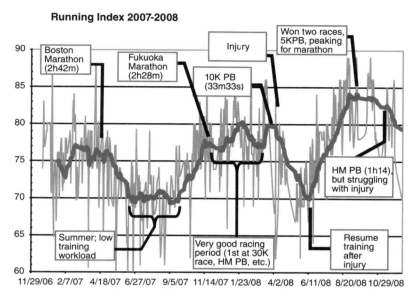

Figure 5.1 Relationship between running index and race performance over a two-year period.
Courtesy of Roberto Veneziani.

AM I TRAINING HARD ENOUGH, OR TOO HARD?

One of the most challenging and most important types of analysis you can perform is determining whether you are training not hard enough, hard enough, or too hard. The consequences of training even slightly too hard can be significant. You will begin to feel persistently flat in workouts and your performance eventually will deteriorate. The obvious way to prevent these consequences is to consciously train well within your limits. But if you're too conservative, then you will sacrifice fitness and will not perform as well as you would like to. Therefore, the goal of every competitive runner is to train as hard as possible without training too hard, which is easier said than done.

Interpreting TSB, CTL, and ATL

Your speed and distance device and performance management software can make training workload optimization much easier. The concept of training stress balance (TSB) is particularly useful in this regard. As first mentioned in chapter 3, training stress balance (TSB) is simply the difference between your chronic training load (how hard you've been training over the past six weeks, or fitness) and your acute training load (how hard you've been training within the past week, or fatigue). In colloquial terms, TSB represents form, or how well you can expect to perform given your current fitness and fatigue levels.

When your recent training workload is greater than your average training workload (that is, your ATL is greater than your CTL), your training stress balance will be negative. On a graph, the line representing your current TSB will dip below 0 and the line representing your ATL will be above the line representing your CTL, as in figure 5.2, where the dashed line on top represents the ATL, the solid line in middle represents the CTL, and the dotted line on the bottom represents the TSB.

A negative training stress balance indicates that you are probably less than fully recovered from your most recent training. In other words, you are fatigued. Therefore, you will tend not to have your best running performances when your TSB is negative, although there can be exceptions to this pattern, especially when your TSB is only slightly negative (–1 to –10).

On the other hand, when your recent training workload is less than your average training workload over the past several weeks (that is, your ATL is less than your CTL), your TSB will be positive (figure 5.3). On a graph, the line representing your current TSB will be above 0 and the line representing your ATL will be below the line representing your CTL. A slightly positive TSB indicates that your body is well recovered from recent training. In other words, you are fresh. When your TSB is slightly positive, you will tend to have some of your better running performances—but again, this rule is not absolute. However, a large positive TSB indicates that you are losing fitness, because it results from a

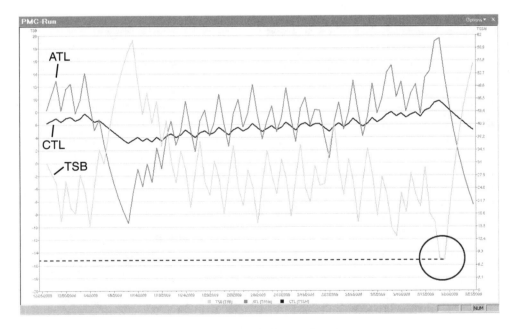

Figure 5.2   Negative training stress balance (TSB).
Courtesy of TrainingPeaks (www.trainingpeaks.com).

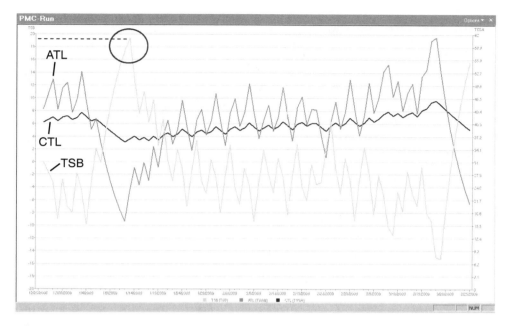

Figure 5.3 Positive training stress balance (TSB).
Courtesy of TrainingPeaks (www.trainingpeaks.com).

marked or extended reduction in training. When your TSB is strongly positive (10+), you will not feel fatigued but you will tend to perform poorly because you have lost fitness as the result of reduced training.

Based on our analysis of TSB data provided by numerous runners, we have concluded that the two best predictors of performance are a slightly positive TSB (between 1 and 10) and a very high CTL (relative to your experience level, your level of competitiveness, and your race distance, as suggested in table 5.1). In plain English, this means that your very best race performances will result when you first build your chronic training load, or fitness, to the highest level possible and then reduce your acute training load, or fatigue, until your body is fresh, but still fit.

Naturally, individual runners differ in the amount of training they can handle, by which we mean the maximum training workload the body can absorb without a negative impact on performance. Experienced runners can handle a greater training workload than beginners. Because of genetic factors, some experienced runners can handle harder training than others, and even some beginners can increase their training workload faster than others. Of course, appropriate workloads are event specific. Marathon runners need to achieve a higher peak training workload than track runners. Table 5.1 presents peak CTL ranges that runners of various categories may use as targets. These targets serve only as general guidelines because an individual runner in any given category is unique in terms of the actual maximum training workload capacity.

Table 5.1 Suggested Peak Chronic Training Loads for Various Runners

The peak CTL that is most appropriate for you depends on how competitive you are and the distance of your next peak race. Use the numbers in this table as general targets.

	Beginner	Low-key competitive	Competitive	Highly competitive	Elite
5K	20–30	25–35	40–50	50–60	90–110
10K	25–35	30–40	45–55	60–70	95–115
Half marathon	35–40	35–45	50–60	70–80	100–120
Marathon	35–50	50–60	60–80	85–105	110–150

We have also observed that performance tends to suffer and injuries tend to occur when runners try to increase their workload at a rate that causes their CTL to increase by more than 5 points per week. An increase in CTL of 2 or 3 points per week works best for most runners. That said, your average daily TSS should not increase every week. Put another way, your total TSS for the week should not increase every week, because you must reduce your training workload for a few days once every few weeks to give your body a chance to recover from and adapt to all of your hard training. These recovery periods may be brief and infrequent enough so that they have no real effect on your CTL. Indeed, the CTL line on your TSB should seldom dip downward or even flatline during periods of focused preparation for a peak race. It should come down only during prerace taper periods and planned regeneration periods between peak races.

Finding Training Patterns Through TSB Tracking

These general guidelines will get you started. The real value of tracking these variables becomes manifest when you study them for patterns that help you to determine how much training in terms of both volume and intensity is not enough, how much is enough, and how much is too much for you. To find these patterns, it is helpful to plot some performance benchmarks, such as test workout results, against the ATL, CTL, and TSB lines of a graph.

A good example of the sort of learning you can do through this process comes from a study that Stephen McGregor did with Kevin Sullivan, a world-class miler from Canada. Stephen analyzed seven years of Kevin's training and race performances by converting raw training log data into training stress scores and graphing fluctuations in ATL, CTL, and TSB. He then plotted Kevin's race performances on the graph.

Stephen saw the same pattern repeated each year for all seven years analyzed. Figure 5.4 represents the 2000 competitive year, which is typical of the others. At the beginning of the year, Kevin steadily increased his training workload at

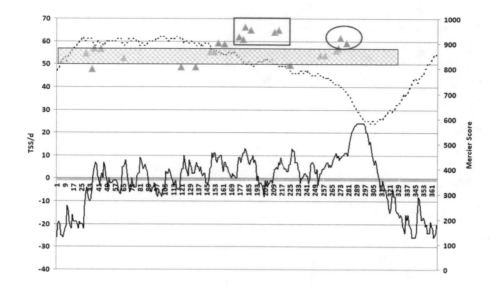

Figure 5.4 Kevin Sullivan's race performances for the 2000 competitive year compared with his TSS, ATL, CTL, and TSB.

Reprinted, with permission, from S.J. McGregor, R.K. Weese, and I.K. Ratz, "Peformance modeling in an Olympic 1500 m finalist: A practical approach. *"Journal of Strength and Conditioning Research,* in press.

an aggressive rate (but seldom exceeded 5 points per week) as he focused on developing base fitness after coming off an autumn break. Then his workload leveled off and even began to dip slightly as he entered the competitive season and prioritized being fresh for races. Kevin recorded some excellent race results at this time. His very best performance occurred at the end of June, where he ran a national record in the 1500 m at the Golden League in Rome. In July, he ran a national record in the mile in Oslo, and also won the Canadian National Championships/Olympic Qualifier handily. Kevin's training workload then continued to slowly decline over the next couple of months as he continued racing and tapering in the run-up to the Plympics, which were in September. Unfortunately, while he did well enough to qualify for the Olympic finals of the 1,500-meter, his best race performances occurred in the first half of the season.

Stephen concluded that Kevin was not managing his workload properly. He clearly raced best when his CTL was quite high—between 49 and 55 TSS—and he tapered just enough to reduce his ATL sufficiently to make his TSB slightly positive. He did not race as well when trying to maintain a slightly lower CTL in order to be fresh for races. When you race as often as a miler does over such a long season, it's not possible to have your best race every time. But you do want to race best in your most important races, and this is what Kevin failed to do. He raced better in the Olympic Trials than in the Olympic Games. Based on

© Michael Steele/Getty Images Sport

Kevin Sullivan of Canada and Carsten Schlangen of Germany during a heat for the men's 1500m race at the Beijing Olympics.

his analysis, Stephen suggested to Kevin that he would be better off training through the first half of the competitive season—that is, maintaining a very high CTL at the expense of some freshness—and putting up with suboptimal performance in these races. Only at the end of the season should he taper to lower his ATL (fatigue) and make his TSB positive at a higher CTL (fitness level) so that he could produce his peak performances in championship races.

The use of training stress balance to analyze the effects of training workload has one important limitation. It does not distinguish the individual effects of various types of training, and changes in the individual types of training you emphasize and deemphasize are likely to have a big impact on your performance independent of your overall training workload. For example, suppose you are training for a 5K race and you start your training by doing a steadily increasing volume of mostly moderate-pace running. After increasing your volume to the highest level you can handle, you begin to gradually decrease your overall distance from week to week while gradually increasing the average intensity of your training until, in the last few weeks before your 5K race, your training volume is quite moderate but you're doing frequent hard workouts at and near 5K pace. In this scenario, the CTL line may look relatively flat between the point where your initial volume ramp-up ends and your 5K race take place, but your race-specific fitness is likely to continuously improve as you combine increasingly challenging race-specific workouts with adequate recovery.

In the majority of realistic scenarios, your CTL will not hold steady for an extended period if you're training appropriately. However, we present this hypothetical case to underscore the point that analysis of your training workload does not tell the whole story of your fitness and performance.

DO I NEED A REST?

Managing fatigue by reducing your training as necessary is one of your most important responsibilities as a competitive runner. Fatigue is a symptom of incomplete physiological adaptation to recently completed training. When fatigue persists, it means that your body is not benefiting from the hard training that is causing your fatigue. A day or two of soreness and low energy after hard workouts is normal and indeed much preferable to never feeling fatigued, which would indicate that you weren't training hard enough to stimulate positive fitness adaptations. Extended recovery deficits, however, must be avoided at all costs.

You can minimize the need for spontaneous training reductions simply by training appropriately. Don't ramp up your training workload too quickly (obey the guideline of 5 CTL points per week), don't try to do more than three hard workouts per week, follow each hard day with an easy day (featuring an easy run, an easy cross-training workout, or complete rest), and plan reduced-workload recovery weeks into your training every few weeks. Even if you take these measures, however, you will, assuming you train as hard as you can within these parameters, find yourself sometimes feeling flat on days when you had hoped and expected to feel strong for a harder workout, or find your fatigue level building and building over several days. At these times it's important that you listen to your body and reduce your training for a day or two or three to put your body back on track.

Technology is no substitute for your own perceptions in these cases. No device can measure your recovery status and readiness to train hard any better than your own body can. When your body is poorly recovered from recent hard training, you can always feel it. And when factors outside of your training, such as lack of sleep or job stress, compromise your capacity to perform, you can always feel that. Before you even lace up your shoes, you know that you're not going to have a good day because of the heaviness, sluggishness, soreness, or low motivation you feel. Your body itself is an exquisitely crafted piece of technology whose primary function is self-preservation. One of the most important mechanisms that your body uses to preserve your health through hard training is a set of symptoms of poor recovery (those just named) that encourage you to take it easy when that's what your body needs most. It's important that you learn to recognize these symptoms and get in the habit of obeying them. Pay attention to how your body feels before each workout and then note how you perform in the run so that you can discern patterns. Through this habit you will develop the ability to anticipate when it's best to reduce workouts or take a day off and when to go through with planned training.

Technology can be an adjunct to listening to your body in making such decisions. We recommend three specific practices: monitoring your resting pulse, correlating poor workout performances with training stress balance, and performing a neuromuscular power test.

Resting Pulse

The first practice is monitoring your resting pulse, or performing orthostatic testing, as described in chapter 1. Look for patterns in the relationship between the numbers observed in orthostatic testing and how you perform in your workouts. (It will take at least three weeks for such patterns to become observable.) If, for example, you always perform poorly in workouts on days when your morning pulse is at least four beats per minute higher than normal, you can use this information to change your workout plans as soon as you observe a high morning pulse reading instead of waiting to find out the hard way that you need a recovery day (that is, by feeling lousy in the planned run).

Training Stress Balance

A second way to use technology in determining whether and when you need a rest is to note where especially poor workouts and stale patches of training tend to fall in relation to your ATL, CTL, and TSB. Specifically, on days when you have a harder run planned and you expect to feel ready to perform well but instead you feel fatigued and have a subpar performance, note your present ATL, CTL, and TSB. The next time these variables line up in a similar way, you will know to expect lingering fatigue and can alter your training accordingly. Don't expect to find 100 percent predictability through this exercise, however, because many other variables factor into your daily running performance that these variables do not capture.

These variables may be somewhat more reliable in predicting the multiday stale patches that sometimes occur during periods of hard training. For example, you might find that you always hit a stale patch when your CTL exceeds 50, or when your TSB drops below –20, or when these two things happen simultaneously. Again, once you have observed such a pattern, you can take future actions to reduce the frequency of those stale patches.

Neuromuscular Power Test

Finally, you can use a neuromuscular power test to assess your recovery status. Research has shown that when the body is carrying lingering fatigue from endurance training, maximal power performance is compromised. Your maximum sprint speed is one good indicator of your current neuromuscular power. Running a set of short sprints once a week is a good way to increase and then maintain your stride power, but it also serves as a reliable recovery status indicator. For example, each Monday, after completing a short, easy recovery run, you might run 4 to 10 × 10 seconds uphill on the same hill each time at maximum speed. After completing the sprints, note the highest speed achieved. Pay attention to how you perform in the next hard workout that follows a sprint set in which your maximum speed is lower than normal. Through this process you might locate a maximum speed threshold that indicates the need to alter your training plans for additional recovery.

AM I GETTING FITTER?

The whole point of training is to increase your running fitness. More exactly, the point is to gradually increase your race-specific fitness until it reaches a peak level at the time of your most important race. So the one question you want to answer more than any other throughout the training process is this: Am I getting fitter?

When your fitness level is increasing, it's usually rather obvious even if you do not use a speed and distance device and performance management software. You feel stronger in most of your workouts, you are able to run longer before you begin to show signs of fatigue, and you achieve faster split times on measured courses. But when you do use a speed and distance device and performance management software, you can measure your fitness gains in more sophisticated ways.

Chronic Training Load

Perhaps the simplest way to monitor your fitness is to monitor your chronic training load, because CTL is intended specifically to quantitatively represent fitness. It is essentially the average of the work you have done over the past six weeks. But that is only one way to represent fitness. There is an argument to be made for defining fitness in terms of performance rather than in terms of work accomplished. After all, fitness is relative. For example, optimal marathon fitness is different from optimal 1,500-meter fitness. When you are in peak shape for 1,500-meter racing, your CTL may be only 50, because volume contributes heavily to CTL and in 1,500-meter training you necessarily limit your running volume in favor of high-intensity running. But when you are in peak shape for a marathon, your CTL might be 70 because of all the extra miles you're running. It would be a mistake to assume that you could run a better 1,500 meters at this time simply because your CTL is higher. You are fitter for the marathon, less fit for the 1,500 meters.

Weekly Average Pace

Another simple way to monitor your running fitness, which is slightly more performance based, is to track your average pace in all of your running week by week. As we become fitter, we generally tend to run faster in each type of workout. Perhaps this basic truth has been overlooked in the past because it was not easy to monitor average pace accurately. But speed and distance devices make it easy. At the end of each week, just divide your total training distance by your total training time. For example, if your total training distance was 36.16 miles and your total training time was 5 hours 7 minutes 21 seconds, you know your average pace for the week was 8:30. Look for that pace to come down slowly in subsequent weeks. If you're using a performance analysis software package such as WKO+, you can simply plot weekly average pace or NGP and follow it over time. If you're not using such a package and don't want to calculate on your own, you can use online pace calculators such as http://www.coolrunning.com/engine/4/4_1/96.shtml or http://www.runnersworld.com/cda/pacecalculator/.

Races, Time Trials, and Key Workouts

The most familiar way to measure fitness gains is to compare performances in tune-up races, time trials, and other hard training sessions of similar structure. If you run a 5K tune-up race today and your time is 25 seconds faster than your time in a 5K tune-up race run five weeks ago, you know that you have gained a significant amount of fitness in that period. You can race only so often, however, and you will certainly want to see proof of progress more often than you race. In a well-designed training program, you will perform two or three challenging workouts per week, each of a different type. Comparing performances in hard workouts of the same type undertaken in consecutive weeks gives you a basis for measuring fitness gains on a smaller time scale. For example, you might perform a set of 1-kilometer intervals in an average time of 3:43 this week and again in an average time of 3:41 next week.

Test Workouts

Formal test workouts are a more exact way to quantify fitness in performance terms. But because fitness is task specific, no single test gives you a complete picture of your running fitness. Instead, different test protocols are required for assessing different components of running fitness. For example, French exercise physiologist Veronique Billat developed a simple test workout that determines a runner's current velocity at $\dot{V}O_2max$, or $v\dot{V}O_2max$, which is the speed at which the runner's maximum rate of oxygen consumption is reached. The original test uses metric measurements; an English system equivalent is described here. With a speed and distance device you can perform it in any environment that's conducive to fast running.

Through her research, Billat discovered that the average runner is able to sustain $v\dot{V}O_2max$ for approximately six minutes. Therefore, you can get a rough estimate of your current $v\dot{V}O_2max$ by warming up and running as far as you can in six minutes. Set the timer on your speed and distance device for six minutes so that you can ignore it during the effort and just concentrate on running hard.

When the chime sounds, cool down and then review your workout to find your average pace for the six-minute effort. That pace is your current $v\dot{V}O_2$max.

Perform a $v\dot{V}O_2$max test every four to six weeks throughout the training process. You should see gradual improvement. This improvement indicates either that your aerobic capacity is increasing, or your running economy is improving, or both. But it doesn't really matter how your $v\dot{V}O_2$max improves. What matters is that it improves, because again, it is one of the best predictors of performance in running races. We describe some tests for other components of running fitness later in this chapter.

Running Index

The Polar running index, discussed earlier in the chapter, enables you to track changes in your fitness level on a day-to-day timescale. It takes more than 24 hours for your body to fully adapt to the stimulus of a single workout so that your fitness level does not change from day to day. But keep in mind that you are not the same runner every day. Both your short-term adaptations to workouts and the level of fatigue you carry as a result of incomplete adaptation to recent training will have small, day-to-day effects on your aerobic power and efficiency that the running index can measure. Some days, when you are more fatigued, your running index will be lower than it was the previous day. More often, assuming you're training appropriately, your running index will be slightly higher than it was yesterday. It is not necessary to note your running index every day, but if you own a Polar speed and distance device you might as well, because the device records the running index automatically, and it can be interesting and instructive to see the pattern of change in your running index unfold as you train for an event.

Polar Fit Test

Polar devices have another interesting feature called the fit test, which you can use as a supplementary tool to measure fitness changes. The fit test measures heart-rate variability, or the degree to which your actual heart rate deviates from its average resting rate. Contrary to what most people believe, the heart never beats with a perfectly steady rhythm; in fact, it's been argued that the healthiest hearts have the most variability in rhythm. This is still a controversial area in the research world, but Polar has exploited one approach to the determination of heart rate variability as a means of assessing your fitness level and especially of marking changes in your fitness.

To do the test, simply strap on the heart rate monitor strap, put the device into the proper mode, and lie down quietly for one to three minutes. Then press the Start button and lie still for another three to five minutes. The device is now measuring your heart rate variability. In periods when your fitness is increasing

Greg McMillan on Training Your Inner GPS

A speed and distance device is meant to be a tool, not a crutch. But this type of technology does become a crutch for some runners at times. Renowned running coach Greg McMillan is as aware of this risk as anyone, and he has come up with an effective strategy to prevent it, which he calls training your inner GPS.

Unlike some old-school running coaches, McMillan is not against the use of speed and distance devices altogether. "Over the last few decades, remarkable advances such as heart-rate and speed and distance monitors have enhanced our ability to better prescribe and monitor training for a variety of runners," says McMillan, who coaches a group of elite runners in Flagstaff, Arizona, and is a *Running Times* senior writer. "The problem is that we are at risk of becoming too dependent on the technology—so dependent that we forget the art of learning our bodies. And learning our bodies is what this sport is about."

The reason such overdependence is dangerous is that racing is inherently unpredictable. You never know ahead of time exactly how your body will be able to perform on any given race day. Thus, to perform to your potential in each race, you must be able to read your body and pace yourself correctly based on what your body tells you. That's where training your inner GPS comes in. "The crux of inner GPS training is that it reconnects your body and your mind," McMillan says. "You use workouts that help you better judge race pace internally, allowing you to adapt to myriad factors that can affect race performance."

Inner GPS training is simply a matter of running by effort instead of by pace and heart rate in fast-pace workouts. The idea is to develop a better feel for how fast you can run for various distances and times by forcing yourself to guide your effort by body sensations only. McMillan recommends that you do these workouts primarily in the early part of the training cycle and then graduate to workouts in which you use pace and distance feedback to provide precise information about your performance level and to ensure that you hit specific pace targets.

One example of an inner GPS training session is a progression run in which you run the first few miles easy and the last 2 miles at half-marathon pace. Hit the Lap button on your speed and distance device at the beginning of the 2-mile progression but don't look at it again until you complete it. Your goal is to run as close to your half-marathon pace as possible by feel.

You can turn any form of interval workout into an inner GPS training session as well by ignoring the crutch of your speed and distance device. For example, run 5 × 1-mile intervals at 10K pace by feel with 3-minute jogging recoveries between intervals.

Effective communication between your mind and body is critical to racing success. Your speed and distance device could limit this communication if you allowed it to. Using Greg McMillan's system of calibrating your inner GPS will ensure that this doesn't happen.

becuase of progressive training, it will take a few weeks for your fit test score to increase to a meaningful degree, so don't bother doing the test more often. Because this test is not done on the run, it is less valuable than those that are, but it still may be a good secondary means of measuring the effects of all the hard work you're doing out there on the roads and tracks.

IS MY TRAINING APPROPRIATELY BALANCED?

Running fitness has a few components. Developing the various components in the proper balance is essential to achieving peak race-specific fitness. Running fitness is made up of raw endurance (or the ability to run far at a moderate to moderately fast pace), lactate threshold (the ability to sustain a fast pace for one hour), aerobic capacity (the ability to resist fatigue at paces exceeding your threshold pace), and speed (the ability to run very fast over short distances). They are all related, but at the same time they are distinct. Thus, if you fail to develop any single one of these fitness components adequately, its weakness will hinder your development of peak race-specific fitness.

It is not necessary to improve in every facet of running fitness throughout the training process. In fact, it can even be counterproductive. Sometimes it is best to merely maintain your current level of development in a specific fitness component. For example, your speed should not increase in the final weeks of preparation for a marathon, because the only way it could increase at this point is if you were failing to train adequately for raw endurance and lactate threshold, the two most important components of running fitness for marathon performance. Table 5.2 shows the proper objectives for the four components of running fitness in three phases of training for each of the most popular road racing distances.

Because it's important that the various components of your running fitness be moving in the right direction—or at least not moving in the wrong direction—as you train for an event, it's also important that you know which direction each component is going throughout the process. Framed more narrowly, you need to know whether any single component of your running fitness is weaker than it should be and therefore holding back your development of peak race-specific fitness. This requires that you consistently measure your performance in each fitness component. Following are some ways of doing so.

Raw Endurance

During prolonged running at any steady pace, your heart rate will hold steady for a while and then begin to slowly increase, possibly because of decreasing mechanical efficiency or increasing fight or flight activation. This phenomenon,

Table 5.2 Fitness Objectives in Three Phases of Training for Four Race Distances

The guidelines in this table are not intended to be scientifically precise. They serve as a general map for the course that your fitness development should take as you prepare for a peak race at one of these four distances.

	Base phase	Build phase	Peak phase
5K	• Increase raw endurance • Maintain lactate threshold • Maintain anaerobic capacity • Increase speed	• Maintain raw endurance • Increase lactate threshold • Increase anaerobic capacity • Increase speed	• Maintain raw endurance • Maintain lactate threshold • Increase anaerobic capacity • Maintain speed
10K	• Increase raw endurance • Maintain lactate threshold • Maintain anaerobic capacity • Increase speed	• Maintain raw endurance • Increase lactate threshold • Increase anaerobic capacity • Increase speed	• Maintain raw endurance • Increase lactate threshold • Increase anaerobic capacity • Maintain speed
Half marathon	• Increase raw endurance • Maintain lactate threshold • Maintain anaerobic capacity • Increase speed	• Increase raw endurance • Increase lactate threshold • Increase anaerobic capacity • Maintain speed	• Maintain raw endurance • Increase lactate threshold • Maintain anaerobic capacity • Maintain speed
Marathon	• Increase raw endurance • Maintain lactate threshold • Increase anaerobic capacity • Increase speed	• Increase raw endurance • Increase lactate threshold • Increase anaerobic capacity • Increase speed	• Increase raw endurance • Increase lactate threshold • Maintain anaerobic capacity • Maintain speed

first mentioned in chapter 1, has been termed *decoupling* by triathlon coach Joe Friel, and can be indicative of raw endurance. Friel has observed in runners he works with that as their endurance increases, they are able to go longer at a given pace before their heart rate and pace become decoupled, and the degree of decoupling will decrease.

If you want to take advantage of this approach, make a habit of measuring your decoupling in each of your long runs exceeding one hour in duration. Joe Friel suggests the following protocol: Hit the Split button on your speed and distance device when you reach the halfway point of a long run. Upon returning home, determine your average speed and average heart rate for each half. Divide the first-half speed by the first-half heart rate to determine your speed-to-heart-rate ratio for that half of the run and then do the same thing for the second half. Finally, subtract the second-half ratio from the first and divide the remainder by the first-half ratio. This yields a decoupling ratio for the workout. Here's an example

First-half speed (8.1 mph) ÷ first-half heart rate (140 bpm) = first-half speed-to-heart-rate ratio (0.058)

Second-half speed (8.0 mph) ÷ second-half heart rate (145 bpm) = second-half speed-to-heart-rate ratio (0.055)

[First-half speed-to-heart-rate ratio (0.58) − second-half speed-to-heart-rate ratio (0.55)] ÷ first half ratio (0.58) = 0.052, or 5.2%

According to Friel, well-trained endurance athletes are typically able to keep their decoupling ratios below 5 percent. If yours is above 5 percent, as in this example, put greater emphasis on endurance training until it falls below the 5 percent threshold.

A second type of decoupling test will give you additional information for assessing your raw endurance. Hit the Split button on your speed and distance device at every 5 km (or 3-mile) point throughout a long run, or set your device to record an autosplit at these intervals. When you get home, calculate your speed-to-heart-rate ratio for each segment and look for the point where a decoupling trend originates. (You can skip this calculation if your pace is perfectly steady throughout the run, in which case it is sufficient simply to note the point where your heart rate begins to rise.) If you're training for shorter races, you should be able to run for at least one hour in the moderate aerobic pace zone before your heart rate begins to become decoupled from your pace. If you're training for longer races, decoupling should not begin until you're at least two hours into a run.

Lactate Threshold

A lactate profile is a graph that plots running pace against blood lactate concentration. These graphs always have the same basic shape: Beginning from the left, the line representing the blood lactate concentration at increasing running speeds shows a shallow upward slope and then abruptly becomes much steeper, as shown in figure 5.5.

The lactate profile of every runner looks similar, regardless of his or her ability level. The abrupt switch from a gradual, apparently linear increase to a very steep exponential rise, which represents the lactate threshold, occurs, on average, at a blood lactate concentration of approximately 4 millimoles per liter, or mmol/L, although the actual value at which it occurs could vary greatly on an individual basis. The important difference between runners is the pace at

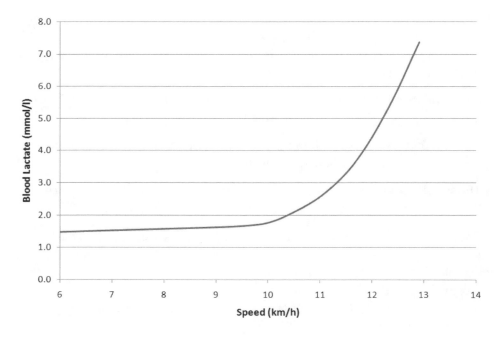

Figure 5.5 Sample blood lactate curve.
Courtesy of TrainingPeaks (www.trainingpeaks.com).

which this transition occurs. Naturally gifted and highly fit runners are able to attain a much faster speed than less gifted and less trained runners before their blood lactate concentration rises exponentially.

With proper training, your lactate threshold pace will gradually increase. The duration for which you can sustain a given pace will increase with lactate threshold pace to an even greater degree. For example, a beginner might be able to sustain an 8:00 pace for only 20 minutes. But after four or five months of training, this beginner likely will be able to sustain an 8:00 pace for an hour. Most trained runners of every ability level can sustain their lactate threshold pace four about an hour. But again, that pace is significantly faster for some runners than for others.

Aerobic Capacity

We have seen one way of measuring and tracking aerobic capacity already in this chapter: the $v\dot{V}O_2max$ test described on page 94. But there are other ways. Workouts that test and increase aerobic capacity typically target pace zone 8 ($\dot{V}O_2max$ pace), which for most runners is a little slower than $v\dot{V}O_2max$. This is the narrowest pace zone in the PZI system because it corresponds very closely to 5K race pace. Try to run the $\dot{V}O_2max$ pace segments of workouts at your true current 5K race pace. When you complete these workouts, determine your average pace for these segments and compare it against your official 5K race pace associated with your current PZI score. Naturally, you'll want to see your true 5K pace improve during periods when you are actively working to increase your aerobic capacity.

To determine whether your aerobic capacity is in line with, ahead of, or lagging behind the other components of your fitness, compare your average time in the pace zone 8 segments of workouts against your average time in long runs targeting pace zone 3, threshold runs targeting pace zone 6, and interval workouts targeting 1,500-meter pace (the upper limit of pace zone 10) with a view toward ranking them within your current PZI level. For example, suppose you are currently training at PZI level 17. Your average pace in a recent lactate interval workout targeting pace zone 8 was 5:25 per mile, your average pace in a recent long run targeting pace zone 3 was 7:04 per mile, your average pace in a recent tempo run targeting pace zone 6 was 5:46 per mile, and your average pace in a recent speed interval workout targeting pace zone 10 was 5:02 per mile. Compare these numbers against the target zones for your PZI level (table 5.3).

As you can see, the actual pace zone 3 pace was smack in the middle of the target zone, and the actual pace zone 6 pace was at the fast end of the target zone, but the pace zone 8 pace was just outside the target zone on the slow end and the pace zone 10 pace was even further off the mark. Assuming you performed appropriately structured workouts in all cases, this comparison suggests that your endurance fitness and threshold fitness are ahead of your aerobic capacity and speed. Therefore, you probably need to work harder to develop your aerobic capacity and speed.

Speed

In the pace zone index, the speed pace (pace zone 10) range extends from 1,500-meter race pace on the slow end to a full sprint on the fast end. The simplest way to measure your speed is to record your top speed in a full sprint. As mentioned previously, we recommend that all runners perform a small number of maximum sprints, ideally on a hill, every week to boost and then maintain stride power. One set of 4 to 10 hill sprints per week is plenty. When you analyze your workout

Table 5.3 Target Zones for PZI Level 17

Pace zone	Average pace levels in recent workouts	PZI 17 target ranges
Pace zone 3 (moderate aerobic)	7:04 per mi.	7:20–6:35 per mi.
Pace zone 6 (threshold)	5:46 per mi.	5:55–5:46 per mi.
Pace zone 8 ($\dot{V}O_2$max)	5:25 per mi.	5:24–5:19 per mi.
Pace zone 10 (speed)	5:02 per mi.	4:57–2:40 per mi.

after completing it, note the fastest speed you achieved. During periods when you're trying to increase your speed, this value should gradually increase from session to session. During periods when you are trying to maintain speed, this value should not decrease from one session to the next.

Polar's running index offers another way to diagnose relative strength and weakness in the various components of running fitness. All you have to do is note your running index in workouts focused on each of the four components of running fitness just discussed. If your running index scores in one of these types of workouts is typically lower than they are in workouts that test the other components, you have pretty good evidence that your fitness is lagging in that outlying component and deserves more attention.

NO NAVEL GAZING

The term *navel gazing* is used to mock the habit of analyzing things just to analyze them. There is no navel gazing in the performance management system. The types of training data analysis described in this chapter are done with a specific purpose in mind: to plan your future training in the most informed way possible. The third step in the performance management system, planning, is the topic of chapter 6.

6

Planning for More Productive Training

You are probably accustomed to thinking of planning as the first step of the training process. After all, very few competitive runners lace up their shoes and just wing it every day. They plan workouts before they do them—often many weeks in advance. However, your planning has to be based on something, and the best basis for the planning of your future training is the monitoring and analysis of training you've already done. That is why planning is the third step of the performance management process.

There are really two types of planning you do as a competitive runner. One type of planning involves creating long-term training plans that prepare you for maximum performance in peak races. The design of such plans is based largely on the tried-and-true periodization practices that countless runners and coaches collectively have developed over many decades. This type of planning is the subject of chapter 7, where we present a new way to approach training periodization with digital technologies.

The second type of planning entails tweaking, adjusting, and fine-tuning your long-term plan each day based on how your body has responded to the training you've completed so far. This is the type of planning that constitutes the third step of performance management, and it's really more important than the first type because it's impossible to predict exactly how your body will respond to planned training. If optimal training consists of doing the right workout each day, then long-term planning represents perhaps 25 percent of the optimal training equation; short-term planning is the other 75 percent.

PLANNING DAY TO DAY

Weekly workout cycles are a very old convention in running. In the typical runner's training week, one day is set aside for a long run, two other days feature some type of higher-intensity work, and the remaining four days are easy days. But if your objective is to do the right workout every day, and your body's current state of fitness and fatigue determines what the right workout is, then wouldn't it be best to scrap the weekly workout cycle and take each day as it comes?

We don't think so. There are two reasons why seven-day training cycles are valuable. First, effective training requires that you expose your body to the various types of training stimuli in the right proportions. Weekly training cycles help to ensure that this requirement is met. It would be much harder to ensure that you do neither too little nor too much raw endurance, threshold, aerobic capacity, and speed training if you trained completely without structure. The truth is that, on any given day when your fatigue level is relatively low, you can benefit from any of several types of challenging workouts. Your choice should be made in consideration of which specific type of training you're most due for. Weekly workout cycles take much of the guesswork out of this process by scheduling the various workout types in a recurring rotation.

A second reason why weekly workout cycles are valuable is that they make the flux between fatigue and freshness predictable, so you generally know when you'll need recovery and when you'll be ready for hard work and can plan accordingly. This way you are spared the hassle of having to spontaneously come up with the right workout to do except on those days when you are unexpectedly fatigued.

No single weekly workout cycle works best for every runner. Nor is it necessary that you use precisely the same routine every week. But some elements should be incorporated into your standard weekly training cycle. First, the weekly training cycle should have three hard workouts. Each of these workouts should have a distinct primary training objective: raw endurance, lactate threshold, aerobic capacity, or speed. These three workouts should fall on nonconsecutive days. You should exercise at least six days per week, although it is not necessary to run every day. For example, you might choose to do a recovery workout in a nonimpact modality such as bicycling once a week. Speaking of which, one day per week should be set aside as a recovery day, when your exercise load is lighter than on any other day. Your recovery day may be a day of total rest, if you prefer. We also recommend that you perform one set of sprints (ideally hill sprints) per week as a speed-development stimulus and recovery status indicator. Table 6.1 shows an example of a weekly workout cycle that works well for many runners.

Your weekly workout cycle should feature a high degree of intensity and workload modulation. Intensity modulation refers to changing the pace zones you target from one day to the next. Each pace zone stimulates fitness benefits in a slightly different way than the others, so it's important to regularly experience

Table 6.1 Sample Weekly Workout Cycle

Mon.	Tues.	Wed.	Thurs.	Fri.	Sat.	Sun.
Easy run (recovery day)	High-intensity run (intervals, threshold, hills)	Easy run plus hill sprints	Moderate run (progression run, fartlek run)	High-intensity run (intervals, threshold, hills)	Easy run	Long run

all six of them. Weekly workout cycles ensure that you do. Table 6.2 shows how the suggested weekly workout cycle presented in table 6.1 looks when we replace the suggested workout types with the primary pace zones targeted in each.

The intensity factor (IF) variable that you learned how to calculate in chapter 3 provides a simple means of tracking your intensity modulation. Recall that intensity factor is a measure of your normalized graded pace in a given run relative to your current threshold pace. If your normalized graded pace for an entire workout is equal to your threshold pace, the intensity factor will be 1.0. If your normalized graded pace is slower than your threshold pace, the intensity factor will be a fraction, such as 0.656 or 0.903. It is rare but possible to record an intensity factor greater than 1.0, such as in a short race or time trial. One reason why such scores are rare, even in very high-intensity workouts, is that warm-ups, cool-downs, and active recoveries tend to slow the overall pace of a workout. Even so, different types of workouts predictably produce different intensity factors. Seeing a good degree of variation in your intensity factors in a week of training indicates that you are modulating your running intensity appropriately. Table 6.3 shows an example of a week of workouts and intensity factors.

Table 6.2 Sample Weekly Workout With Pace Zones

Mon.	Tues.	Wed.	Thurs.	Fri.	Sat.	Sun.
PZ 2 or 3 plus PZ 10	PZ 6, 8, or 10	PZ 2 or 3	PZ 3 plus PZ 6, 8, or 10	PZ 6, 8, or 10	PZ 2 or 3	PZ 3 or 4

Table 6.3 Sample Weekly Workout With Intensity Factors

Mon.	Tues.	Wed.	Thurs.	Fri.	Sat.	Sun.
5 mi. at PZ 2 plus 6 hill sprints	1 mi. warm-up at PZ 1 6 × 800 m at PZ 8 with 400 m active recoveries 1 mi. cool-down at PZ 2	4 mi. at PZ 3 plus 1 mi. at PZ 4	1 mi. at PZ 3 10K at PZ 6 0.5 mi. at PZ 2	6 mi. at PZ 3	20 mi. at PZ 3	6 mi. at PZ 3
IF: 0.707	IF: 0.919	IF: 0.807	IF: 0.967	IF: 0.761	IF: 0.818	IF: 0.770

As in this example, in a typical week you should have two runs with intensity factors above 0.9, two or three runs with intensity factors between 0.7 and 0.8, and the rest between 0.8 and 0.9.

Training workload modulation refers to varying your training stress from day to day throughout the week. Typically, you should have three days with relatively high training stress, two or three days with relatively low training stress, and one or two days with moderate training stress. Remember that workload and intensity are not the same. Your high-intensity workouts will typically be among your high-training-stress workouts, but your long, moderate-intensity runs will often entail the greatest workload. Use training stress score (TSS) to monitor your workload modulation throughout the week. Table 6.4 shows the TSS for the week of training presented in table 6.3.

Table 6.4 Training Stress Scores for Sample Training Week

Mon.	Tues.	Wed.	Thurs.	Fri.	Sat.	Sun.
5 mi. at PZ 2 plus 6 hill sprints	1 mi. warm-up at PZ 1 6 × 800 m at PZ 8 with 400 m active recoveries 1 mi. cool-down at PZ 2	4 mi. at PZ 3 plus 1 mi. at PZ 4	1 mi. at PZ 3 10K at PZ 6 0.5 mi. at PZ 2	6 mi. at PZ 3	20 mi. at PZ 3	6 mi. at PZ 3
TSS: 38.7	TSS: 69.4	TSS: 33.1	TSS: 86.6	TSS: 48.9	TSS: 183.0	TSS: 49.2

Whether a given TSS counts as a light, moderate, or heavy training stress depends on your fitness level, but all runners should distribute their total weekly training stress similarly. In this example, the total training stress for the week is 508.9. Together, the two high-intensity workout days account for a little less than a third of the total TSS for the week. The long run accounts for another third, and the remaining four easy to moderate days account for the final third. This is a good balance for a long-distance runner (half marathon and marathon). If your race distance is 10K or less, aim for a distribution that's closer to 50 percent of total weekly TSS on your two high-intensity days, 25 percent in your long run, and 25 percent in your easy runs.

Suunto speed and distance devices have a proprietary feature called training effect (first described in chapter 3) that is also useful for modulation of training workload. Similar to TSS, training effect rates the relative physiological stress level of each workout on a five-point scale. Training effect is determined by calculating excess postexercise oxygen consumption, or EPOC (which is essentially how long it takes for your breathing rate to decrease to normal resting levels after a run is completed), and comparing this value to your current performance level. The result is a number that indicates the strength of the cardiorespiratory fitness stimulus provided by the workout. Suunto suggests the following interpretations for training effect values:

1: minor or recovering effect

2: maintaining effect

3: improving effect

4: highly improving effect

5: overreaching

Table 6.5 shows an example of sensible modulation in training workload in a weekly training cycle as represented in training effect values.

Table 6.5 Sample Weekly Training Cycle With Training Effect Values

Mon.	Tues.	Wed.	Thurs.	Fri.	Sat.	Sun.
2 or 3	4 or 5	1 or 2	4 or 5	1 or 2	2 or 3	4 or 5

MANAGING YOUR TRAINING STRESS BALANCE

One way to look at short-term planning is as a process of managing your training stress balance (TSB) or controlling your workload throughout the training process in ways that ultimately maximize your performance in a peak race. To achieve this objective, you will need to manage your training stress balance to achieve the following results:

■ Your training stress balance is slightly positive (+5 or so) on race day. Past monitoring of TSB by thousands of endurance athletes has shown that most competitors perform best with a slightly positive TSB.

■ Your chronic training load (CTL) reaches its highest level two to three weeks before race day. CTL is a measure of fitness level, and you want your fitness level to peak close to your peak race, but not so close that you don't have time to reduce your fatigue level with a proper taper.

■ Your chronic training load never decreases for two consecutive weeks (when your CTL is averaged over a full week) after you begin focused preparation for a peak race. A declining CTL indicates declining fitness. It's okay and even necessary for your CTL to decline slightly when you reduce your training to promote recovery once every few weeks, but if you reduce your training enough to see your CTL decline for two straight weeks, you're going beyond recovery and entering the realm of detraining.

Asker Jeukendrup on Using Science and Technology to Diagnose Overreaching and Overtraining

Asker Jeukendrup, PhD, is the director of the human performance laboratory at the University of Birmingham, England. He also is an accomplished endurance athlete with 16 Ironman finishes, including three Hawaii Ironman Triathlon World Championship finishes. He coaches and advises athletes ranging from beginning triathletes to marathon world record-holder Haile Gebrselassie of Ethiopia.

Jeukendrup uses his scientific knowledge and expertise with digital training technologies to diagnose overtraining and, more often, overreaching in himself and the athletes he coaches. Overtraining is a severe disturbance of the immune, nervous, and endocrine systems that is caused by training at an extremely high level without adequate rest for a long period. The condition is rarely seen outside of the elite echelons of running and other endurance sports. Many weeks, even months, of relative rest are needed in order to overcome this downward spiral. More common is overreaching, which is a period of performance decline, fatigue, mood disturbance, and other symptoms caused by a short-term recovery deficit. Overreaching usually can be corrected with just a few days of reduced training.

According to Jeukendrup, the clearest early sign of overreaching is a drop in performance, which is easy to detect with regular use of a speed and distance device. He advises, "First you must establish a baseline by using the device in the full range of workout types in your regimen and noting your normal performance level in each in terms of pace." When your pace is slower than normal for more than three or four consecutive days, you likely are overreaching and in need of additional rest.

Overreaching affects the sympathetic nervous system, which regulates the heart rate. Therefore you can look to your heart rate for signs that you are overreaching. "When an athlete is in a state of overreaching, the maximum heart rate is reduced," says Jeukendrup. You will notice during periods of overreaching that you are unable to elevate your heart rate to normal levels in familiar workouts. This is essentially your body's way of trying to force you to take it easy.

Jeukendrup also recommends wearing a heart-rate monitor at night while you sleep, when you are concerned about overreaching. First, to establish a baseline, you need to wear it when you are certain that you are not overreaching. Your overnight heart rate should show a wavelike pattern of gentle increases and decreases throughout the night. When you are overreaching, your heart rate also will fluctuate, but its high points will be significantly higher and its low points not as low.

You can also use standardized questionnaires to diagnose overreaching through other symptoms such as mood state. (Irritability and loss of training motivation are hallmark psychological signs of overreaching.) Jeukendrup relies on these questionnaires as a secondary tool for monitoring recovery status. Among the most sophisticated of these questionnaires is the Recover-Stress Questionnaire for Athletes developed by *Michael Kellmann, PhD, and K. Wolfgang Kallus, PhD.* The much simpler questionnaire that follows was developed by sport psychologist Jack Raglin, PhD. Take it once a week throughout training and as often as once daily during peak periods. A score of 40 or higher indicates you need to rest.

1. How is your mood today?
    Very, very good (−2 points)
    Very good (−1 point)
    Good (0 points)
    Average (1 point)
    Bad (3 points)
    Very bad (5 points)
    Very, very bad (7 points)
2. How many hours did you sleep last night?
    More than nine (−1 point)
    Eight or nine (0 points)
    Seven (1 point)
    Five to six (3 points)
    Less than five (5 points)
3. How did you sleep last night?
    Same as normal (0 points)
    One hour more than normal (1 point)
    Two or more hours more than normal (3 points)
    One hour less than normal (1 point)
    Two hours less than normal (3 points)
    Three or more hours less than normal (5 points)
4. Have you been sick the past week?
    Yes (5 points)
    No (0 points)
5. How would you rate yesterday's workout?
    Very, very easy (−3 points)
    Very easy (−1 point)
    Easy (0 points)
    Average (1 point)
    Hard (3 points)
    Very hard (5 points)
    Very, very hard (7 points)
6. How do your muscles feel?
    Very, very good (−3 points)
    Very good (−1 point)
    Good (0 points)
    Tender, but not sore (1 point)
    Sore (3 points)
    Very sore (5 points)
    Very, very sore (7 points)
7. Do your legs feel heavy?
    No (0 points)
    A little (1 point)
    Somewhat (3 points)
    Very (7 points)

■ Your chronic training load never increases at a rate exceeding 5 TSS points per week. Past monitoring of TSB by thousands of endurance athletes has shown that increasing the chronic training load faster than 5 TSS points per week typically results in performance decline or injury.

■ Your TSB does not drop below –20 more than once every 10 days. A TSB of –20 indicates a severe level of fatigue that runners cannot experience frequently without negatively affecting their performance in workouts and potentially risking injury.

Note that in managing your training stress balance according to these parameters, you might not have a positive TSB at any point in the training process until you taper for your peak race. In other words, since a negative TSB indicates a state of fatigue, you could be at least slightly fatigued throughout the entire training process. This might seem counterintuitive, but it's nothing to worry about. The fact is that you can carry a small to moderate fatigue deficit resulting from a gradually and steadily increasing training load for weeks on end without negative consequences. One of the cool things about the process of monitoring your TSB is that it clearly quantifies such mysterious realities of exercise physiology.

On the other hand, it is certainly not necessary to maintain a negative TSB throughout the training process, and for some athletes it might not be ideal. And if you do any tune-up races before your peak race, you likely will want to bring your TSB up to a slightly positive level for these.

Managing your training stress balance is essentially a three-step process. Step 1 is to create a sensible training plan that promises to keep your ATL, CTL, and TSB within the five parameters given previously. This is easier to do if you have completed at least one full training cycle (a multiweek period of training that culminates in a race undertaken at peak fitness) with monitoring of these variables already, because you can look back at your records and see exactly how particular workout sequences affected your ATL (fatigue), CTL (fitness), and TSB (form). But any well-designed training plan should at least come close to heeding the five parameters.

In any case, schedule your highest-workload training week as the third-to-last or next-to-last week of your training before your next peak race. Choose a formal start date that allows you to ramp up your training at a rate that takes you to the level of your peak training week without transgressing the five parameters. Make each week between your first week and your peak training week more challenging than the previous one, except every third or fourth week when you should reduce the workload to promote recovery.

Step 2 is to pay close attention to how your ATL, CTL, and TSB develop as the training process unfolds and make adjustments as necessary to stay within the five parameters. If, for example, you find that your TSB falls lower than –20 in a given week and your next week of planned workouts is even harder than the last, consider scaling down the next week's workload slightly. Let your body have the last word, however. If you find that you are able to sometimes sail through several weeks of training with a TSB that dips below –20 more often than once every 10 days, then don't hesitate to do so again periodically in the future.

This point leads to step 3 of managing your training stress balance, which is to study the relevant variables in search of your personal parameters and use these custom parameters to steer your short-term workout planning. Each athlete responds to training in a unique way, with individual limitations in terms of rate of increase in training load, maximum toler-

Kara Goucher runs in the New York Marathon. Use technology to guide your training for your most important races.

able negative training stress balance, and so forth. Your personal optimal training parameters are sure to look something like the five general ones given previously, but the small differences could be important for you.

Again, be aware that only after you have compiled a complete training cycle's worth of workout data will these patterns begin to take a definite form. So use the general guidelines provided to manage your training stress balance in your first digitally supported training cycle and then use what you learn from the first in managing the second, and so forth.

ADDRESSING WEAKNESSES

If you have a good training plan, stick to it as much as you reasonably can. But when your analysis of training data reveals that it is more reasonable to depart from your plan, be ready to do so. One of the most important types of analysis you can do is to look for indications that any components of your running fitness are lagging. In the previous chapter we discussed some ways of doing this. Naturally, when you do determine that a particular fitness component is lagging,

Dean Karnazes on Mapping Your Runs

Dean Karnazes is the real Forrest Gump. His memoir, *Ultramarathon Man,* became a surprise bestseller in 2005 and has inspired tens of thousands of men, women, and kids around the world to start running and to run farther. Karnazes won the 2004 Badwater Ultramarathon and a 2007 ESPY Award for running a marathon in each of the 50 United States in 50 days. He wore a Timex Ironman Bodylink throughout the Endurance 50 and now uses a Garmin Forerunner 405 in races such as the Atacama Desert six-day stage race in Chile.

"Wearing the Bodylink during the Endurance 50 created an interesting record of that challenge," says Karnazes. The device recorded 1,310 total miles, 160,355 calories burned, 1,374,721 heartbeats, and an average pace of 8:53 per mile. In multiday races, Karnazes puts the device to more serious use. "There are no mile markers in those events," he says. "When I'm bushwhacking through a wilderness like the Atacama Desert, I rely on my speed and distance device to tell me how far I've gone and what my pace is. Karnazes is most excited about the capacity to couple GPS with cell technology to provide real-time mapping and tracking capabilities during running. "With this combination your data can be pushed onto the Internet so that others can see where you are and how you're doing," he explains. For example, runnersworld.com put a "Where's Dean?" section on its Web site that allowed other runners to locate him and then physically find and run with him as he ran from New York City, site of his last marathon, to St. Charles, Missouri, after completing the Endurance 50. He uses a similar setup to enable his family to keep tabs on him from their home in northern California while he's racing in remote environments.

Karnazes has plans to put these technologies to an even more advanced use. "I want to start working with a coach who can advise me remotely while I'm out there running," he says. His coach will log onto a Web site that provides data from Karnazes' speed and distance device in real time. The coach will use this data to give Karnazes verbal instructions through an earbud he wears. "It'll be like a super-high-tech version of what they do in the Tour de France," he says.

The real Forrest Gump encourages all runners with GPS-based speed and distance devices to explore their more advanced mapping capabilities. He specifically recommends the Web sites mapmyrun.com and bonesinmotion.com.

the appropriate response is to increase your commitment to that component. The specific nature of your response should depend on several factors, including your current phase of training and your peak race goal. For example, if you're in the late build phase of training for a marathon and you determine that your speed is lagging, your response should be conservative. Speed is not the most important component of marathon fitness and it's fairly late in the game, so there's not a lot of opportunity to make significant gains. On the other hand, if you're at the same point in your marathon training and you determine that your raw endurance is lagging, then a more aggressive response is appropriate.

The word *aggressive* is relative, however. It's important to maintain balance in your training at all times by including some amount of training in each target pace zone every week. In modifying your planned training to address a weakness, you should not risk creating a new weakness by too sharply reducing your training for one of your stronger fitness components to make room for additional training for your weakest one. Simply adding training for your weakest fitness component without reducing your training for one or more other components is not a good idea, either, because it risks increasing your overall workload too suddenly.

There are two basic ways to increase your training for a weak fitness component without upsetting your overall training balance. The first is to increase the challenge of your primary workout for that component. The second is to add a secondary workout for that training component to your weekly workout cycle. You may choose to do both. Whatever you do to increase your training stimulus for your fitness weakness, scale back your workload in other workouts so that your overall training workload for the week stays the same or increases only slightly.

When addressing a weakness, your objective is to increase the amount of time you spend in the training zones associated with your weakness. In most cases, you will achieve this objective at least in part by increasing the training stress score (TSS) of your primary workout targeting that limiter.

Let's look at a few specific examples of how to modify your planned training to address a weakness. Following are five one-week workout cycles. The first represents a planned week of training for a hypothetical runner. The second cycle represents how this planned training might be modified to address a perceived lack of raw endurance. The next three cycles represent how the original week of planned training might be modified to address a perceived lack of threshold fitness, aerobic capacity, and speed, respectively.

Originally Planned Week

In the sample training week shown in table 6.6, the most challenging workouts are Tuesday's threshold run and Friday's $\dot{V}O_2$max intervals. Speed training is limited, and the long run is moderate in length. This workout mix would be most appropriate for a runner in the late build phase of training for a half marathon.

Table 6.6 Sample One-Week Workout Cycle

Mon.	Tues.	Wed.	Thurs.	Fri.	Sat.	Sun.
Base run and hill sprints 4 mi. at PZ 3 6 × 10 sec. hill sprints at PZ 10	Threshold run 1 mi. at PZ 2 5 mi. at PZ 6 1 mi. at PZ 2	Base run 5 mi. at PZ 3	Base run 5 mi. at PZ 3	$\dot{V}O_2$max intervals 1 mi. at PZ 2 8 × 600 m at PZ 8 with 400 m recoveries at PZ 2 1 mi. at PZ 2	Rest	Long run 12 mi. at PZ 3

Modified Week: Addressing a Raw Endurance Limiter

Raw endurance comes from running long and running often. To boost his lagging raw endurance, our hypothetical runner replaces Saturday's rest with a recovery run and adds 2 miles to Sunday's long run (table 6.7). To prevent overtraining from occurring as a result of these changes, the pace and distance of Wednesday's run are slightly reduced and Thursday's base run is also shortened by 1 mile.

Table 6.7 Sample One-Week Workout Cycle Modified for Raw Endurance

Mon.	Tues.	Wed.	Thurs.	Fri.	Sat.	Sun.
Base run plus hill sprints 4 mi. at PZ 3 6 × 10 sec. hill sprints at PZ 10	Threshold run 1 mi. at PZ 2 5 mi. at PZ 6 1 mi. at PZ 2	Recovery run 4 mi. at PZ 2	Base run 4 mi. at PZ 3	$\dot{V}O_2max$ intervals 1 mi. at PZ 2 8 × 600 m at PZ 8 with 400 m recoveries at PZ 2 1 mi. at PZ 2	Recovery run 5 mi. at PZ 2	Long run 14 mi. at PZ 3

Modified Week: Addressing a Threshold Fitness Limiter

Running in pace zone 6 provides the primary stimulus for increased threshold fitness. To boost his limiting threshold fitness, our hypothetical athlete transforms Thursday's base run into a progression run with 2 miles in pace zone 6 (table 6.8). Wednesday's base run is turned into a shorter recovery run to accommodate the additional threshold-pace running.

Table 6.8 Sample One-Week Workout Cycle Modified for Threshold Fitness

Mon.	Tues.	Wed.	Thurs.	Fri.	Sat.	Sun.
Base run and hill sprints 4 mi. at PZ 3 6 × 10 sec. hill sprints at PZ 10	Threshold run 1 mi. at PZ 2 5 mi. at PZ 6 1 mi. at PZ 2	Recovery run 4 mi. at PZ 3	Progression run 4 mi. at PZ 3 2 mi. at PZ 6	$\dot{V}O_2max$ intervals 1 mi. at PZ 2 8 × 600 m at PZ 8 with 400 m recoveries at PZ 2 1 mi. at PZ 2	Rest	Long run 12 mi. at PZ 3

Modified Week: Addressing an Aerobic Capacity Limiter

Running in pace zone 8 is the primary stimulus for increased aerobic capacity. To boost his aerobic capacity, our hypothetical runner transforms Sunday's long run into a long fartlek run featuring roughly 1.5 miles of running in pace zone 8 (table 6.9). Because this run is 1 mile shorter than the originally planned long run, its TSS will be only marginally higher.

Table 6.9   Sample One-Week Workout Cycle Modified for Aerobic Capacity

Mon.	Tues.	Wed.	Thurs.	Fri.	Sat.	Sun.
Base run and hill sprints 4 mi. at PZ 3 6 × 10 sec. hill sprints at PZ 10	Threshold run 1 mi. at PZ 2 5 mi. at PZ 6 1 mi. at PZ 2	Base run 5 mi. at PZ 3	Base run 5 mi. at PZ 3	$\dot{V}O_2$max intervals 1 mi. at PZ 2 8 × 600 m at PZ 8 with 400 m recoveries at PZ 2 1 mi. at PZ 2	Rest	Fartlek run 11 mi. at PZ 3 with 6 × 400 m at PZ 6

Modified Week: Addressing a Speed Limiter

To address a perceived lack of speed, our hypothetical runner replaces Friday's aerobic-capacity interval workout with a mixed-interval workout that includes 1,200 meters of running in pace zone 10 (table 6.10), which is, of course, the primary stimulus for speed gains.

Table 6.10   Sample One-Week Workout Cycle Modified for Speed

Mon.	Tues.	Wed.	Thurs.	Fri.	Sat.	Sun.
Base run and hill sprints 4 mi. at PZ 3 6 × 10 sec. hill sprints at PZ 10	Threshold run 1 mi. at PZ 2 5 mi. at PZ 6 1 mi. at PZ 2	Base run 5 mi. at PZ 3	Base run 5 mi. at PZ 3	Mixed intervals 1 mi. at PZ 2 4 × 600 m at PZ 8 with 400 m recoveries at PZ 2 4 × 300 m at PZ 10 with 400 m recoveries at PZ 2 1 mi. at PZ 2	Rest	Long run 12 mi. at PZ 3

MANAGING SETBACKS

Injuries are all too common in the sport of distance running. When you miss planned runs because of an injury, you will probably have to adjust your planned workouts even after you return to running to account for lost fitness and possibly also for lingering limitations imposed by the injury. For example, when you resume running after suffering from a hamstring strain, you should avoid fast running for at least a couple of weeks to minimize the risk of reinjury. The extent of the adjustments that are required depends on how much fitness you've lost and the nature of the injury.

You can minimize the amount of fitness you lose when injured by cross-training in an activity that you can perform pain free. The best cross-training options for runners are bicycling, elliptical training, slideboarding, steep uphill walking, and deep-water running. When cross-training through an injury, do workouts in your chosen alternative activity that mimic the duration and intensity of your planned runs as closely as possible. You won't maintain 100 percent of your preinjury running fitness, but it's a lot better than not exercising at all.

Be cautious when returning from an injury-imposed running layoff of more than a few days. Your first two or three runs should be moderate in duration and intensity. Their main purpose is to reacquaint your bones, muscles, and connective tissues with repetitive impact; to restore some of the neuromuscular coordination you have lost; and to prevent your running fitness from deteriorating any further. After completing two or three base runs, do a PZI test workout to determine precisely how much fitness you have lost.

If your peak race is a 5K, do the following test: After a thorough warm-up, run 5K at 95 percent of maximum effort. After finishing, estimate how much faster you could have run at maximum effort. Look up this time on table 4.1 (page 60) to determine your current PZI. If you're training for a 10K, half marathon, or marathon, do this test instead: After a thorough warm-up, run 10K at 95 percent of maximum effort. After finishing, estimate how much faster you could have run at maximum effort. Look up this time on table 4.1 (page 60) to determine your current PZI.

Once you have determined your current PZI level, open your performance management software and go back to the most recent point in your past training when your fitness was at the same level. Modify your planned training so that the challenge level of individual workouts and the overall training workload match those of the training you did previously at that fitness level. The specific mix of training stimuli should be appropriate for your current phase of training, however.

Another, complementary way to assess how much fitness you've lost during an injury layoff is to manipulate your performance management chart to reflect changes in your training. Do this by manually entering any and all cross-training workouts you did while unable to run and assigning a training stress score (TSS) to each. We recommend that you assign values that are equivalent to 80 percent of the TSS for a run of comparable duration and intensity. As a result of this exercise, your acute training load (fatigue) most likely will decrease significantly, your chronic training load (fitness) will decrease somewhat less, and your training stress balance (form) will markedly increase. After updating your performance management chart, go back to the last time your CTL, or fitness, was at the same level and note the challenge level (the TSS) of the workouts you were doing back then. Resume your run training with workouts of a similar challenge level. Use the training stress balance management guidelines discussed in chapter 5 to plan and execute workouts that steadily restore your fitness without making you overfatigued.

Major disruptions in your training might require that you change your race goal or even postpone your peak race. To help make these decisions, compare your current PZI level with the PZI level associated with your race goal time. Also compare your current CTL with the CTL you had hoped to achieve in the peak phase of your training. Now look at past training cycles and note your rate of PZI improvement and your rate of CTL increase. If, after coming off an injury, you cannot achieve your goal PZI or CTL at the same rate in the time remaining before your next peak race, then scale down your goal race time or choose a later peak race that affords you enough time to reach a true fitness peak.

Mastering Periodization for Peak Performance

So far, the new running technologies have not drastically altered the way runners train—and they probably never will. After all, the modern sport of distance running has been around for well over 100 years. During that time, training methods evolved extensively as athletes and coaches tried new workouts and programs and retained and shared those that worked while discarding those that did not. The standard training methods used by most runners today are a refined collection of best practices that are proven to work from the highest levels of the sport on down. These methods are unlikely to change significantly under any new influence, technology included.

Nevertheless, speed and distance devices and their associated software have brought about a modest but important shift in how runners periodize their training. Specifically, these technologies are shifting runners away from a traditional approach called linear periodization toward a newer approach called nonlinear periodization.

Linear periodization was developed by Romanian exercise physiologist Tudor Bompa and legendary Australian coach Arthur Lydiard, among others, in the 1950s and '60s. In this system, the training process is divided into distinct phases with a distinct fitness objective and type of training prioritized in each phase. Lydiard's periodization model begins with a base phase focused on building basic aerobic fitness and raw endurance followed by a strength phase, a speed phase, and a tapering period. A typical week's workouts look quite different in each of these different phases, with lots of long, slow workouts in the base phase, an emphasis on hills and fartlek intervals in the strength phase, and so forth.

Linear periodization works much better than the intuitive approaches to workout sequencing that preceded it, and that's why it became almost universally practiced by endurance athletes in the last third of the 20th century and remains highly influential today. More recently, however, elite endurance athletes have begun to move away from linear periodization because of practical pressures. It is not uncommon for a professional runner to race at least once in nine different months of the year. Because prize money and sponsor expectations are on the line at each event, a pro racer must be at or near peak fitness for each of them. Linear periodization does not bend to such constraints, because race-specific training is emphasized in only the last of several phases, and each preceding phase establishes a needed piece of the foundation for peak performance. An athlete who has just completed a race at peak fitness and wants to race again at the same level in six weeks cannot possibly squeeze a complete, four-phase linear periodization cycle between these events.

Nonlinear periodization evolved as a solution to this problem. In this method of sequencing workouts, the various fitness objectives and types of workouts are blended more evenly throughout the training cycle. No single piece of the peak performance puzzle—aerobic fitness, endurance, strength, speed, and anaerobic threshold—is ever neglected. Consequently, athletes who practice this approach are able to pop off a good race almost anytime. The most they ever need is a few weeks of sharpening.

You don't have to be a professional runner to benefit from nonlinear periodization. In fact, it's the best approach to fitness development for every competitive runner. That's because with nonlinear periodization your base fitness level is both higher and broader than it is in linear periodization, because you always include a variety of training stimuli (breadth) and some challenging workouts (height) in your training, even when your next race is far off. The greater height of this fitness foundation enables you to peak at a higher level of fitness, and the greater breadth of this fitness foundation reduces the likelihood that you will be slowed down by specific limiters as you go through the process of developing race-specific fitness.

The risk associated with nonlinear periodization is that, if you're not careful, you might lose the directionality of training that is the great virtue of the linear models. If you train too consistently throughout the training cycle, you will never truly peak. Either you will consistently train at the level required in order to achieve peak fitness and burn out well before your target race or you will train at a sustainable workload and wind up no fitter at the end of the training cycle than you were at the beginning. You can easily avoid both of these scenarios, however, by incorporating a little bit of the linear into your nonlinear periodization—specifically, by changing your primary training emphasis (albeit less drastically than in conventional linear periodization models) as you approach each race and by saving your hardest training for the last few weeks before your taper.

Speed and distance devices and performance management software applications facilitate nonlinear periodization by making it easier to manage your fitness over a prolonged period—to take a seasonal approach to your training instead of a race-to-race approach. When your primary metric for quantifying your training is miles per week, as it is for most runners, it is very difficult to plan for and predict your fitness level many months in the future. But with digital tools such as acute training load (ATL), chronic training load (CTL), and training stress balance (TSB), you can plan entire annual training cycles easily and effectively.

To illustrate how, let's return to the example of Kevin Sullivan, the elite miler discussed in chapter 5. You will recall that this runner had his best race performance at the Olympic Trials at the beginning of the summer instead of at the Olympic Games themselves, when he would have preferred to have his best performance. This pattern of achieving his annual peak performance at the beginning of the racing season was also seen in other years. By translating the runner's training log information into training stress scores and using these to create a yearlong performance management chart, Stephen was able to isolate the cause of this pattern. Sullivan achieved his highest fitness level (that is, his highest chronic training load) in the late spring and early summer, when his training was interrupted by few races. But through the summer, during which he raced frequently, he reduced his training load to boost freshness for races and consequently sacrificed too much fitness. This phenomenon is often referred to as a period of race and recovery. Often it results in reduced fitness due to the lack of long, middle-intensity runs that build the lactate threshold and generate the highest training stress scores. Even a middle-distance runner, whose efforts last only a few minutes, needs a high lactate threshold pace so she doesn't fade at the end of the race. Once runners, even middle-distance runners, shift into race and recovery mode, their performances will suffer down the road as fitness (as represented by the CTL) declines over time. This is why a peak cannot be maintained indefinitely and needs to be planned to arrive at the optimal place in the season.

Now it so happens that Kevin Sullivan kept a meticulous training log. But a paper training log does not afford the big-picture perspective on training and fitness that he would have needed in order to make the same deduction on his own. A performance management chart, like the one that can be created with Training Peaks WKO+, made it easy for Stephen to gain this perspective. Granted,

Joe Friel on Working With a Coach

Joe Friel is among the world's leading practitioners of computer-assisted coaching for endurance athletes. Perhaps best known as the author of *The Triathlete's Training Bible,* Friel is also the founder of Training Peaks and Training Bible Coaching, an online coaching group.

Although Friel began his coaching career as a running coach (having been a competitive runner throughout the 1970s and opening a running store in 1978), none of his current athlete clients are runners. The reason is simple, according to Friel. "Runners are tight with their money," he says with a laugh. It's a shame, really, because runners can get the same benefits from working with a coach that cyclists and triathletes get.

Specifically, "A coach can help a runner avoid making some of the most common training errors," says Friel. These errors include training with too little specificity to their goals, paying too much attention to mileage and not enough attention to pace, not targeting the right paces in workouts, pacing ineffectively in races, and failing to adjust future training based on the results of past training.

While granting that a speed and distance device can help runners overcome these errors, Friel believes that most runners could still get more out of their speed and distance devices with the help of a coach. When asked how the advent of speed and distance devices and power meters (which he uses to analyze the bike workouts of his cyclist and triathlete clients) has changed how he coaches athletes, Friel doesn't hold back:

"The data that I get out of a power meter and a speed and distance device has revolutionized the way I coach athletes," he says. "It's dramatically different than it was even two years ago—much more effective. At the end of every week, I go back and pick out workouts for my athletes that were important and I grab the graphs of those workouts and show what we accomplished or didn't accomplish. I take a screen shot of the graph and then annotate it with my own notes. On Sunday I send the graphs to them through the Internet. I also summarize graphically how they're coming along in terms of fatigue, fitness, and form. And if there's any other data I believe they can benefit from seeing, I make a screen shot of that, annotate it, and send that as well. So at the end of the week they'll get two, three, four, sometimes half a dozen charts from me. After they get all of that, I call them and we talk about all the things I'm seeing. Having seen all of the charts and talked about them, athletes not only have a better idea of what we're trying to accomplish and can therefore be more purposeful in their training, but they also have greater motivation to do workouts designed to accomplish things that we've agreed are necessary in order for them to achieve their goals."

Athletes can do all of this for themselves, according to Friel, and many do. But the learning curve is very steep at first. By working with a coach, you can compress that learning curve substantially. And if, after a few months, you think that you have mastered the process, you can go back to self-coaching, having spent only the equivalent of the cost of a few pairs of running shoes.

© PCN Photography/Aurora Photos

Plan training around your most important races. Deena Kastor runs with the Boston skyline in the background.

it required a tedious process of plugging handwritten workout data into a formula that generated TSS, but if he had used a speed and distance device in his training, he could have identified the cause of his late-season slumps without any help and planned his future training accordingly.

You can avoid making similar training errors by using your speed and distance device and performance management software to facilitate a nonlinear approach to periodizing your training. The next section presents some guidelines to follow.

PLANNING A RACING SEASON

At the end of each year, professional runners typically take some time to look ahead to the next year and create a racing plan. Most commonly, they select two specific events as peak events—that is, races for which they wish to achieve the best form possible—because it is generally believed that 12 months is enough time to peak more than once but not more than twice. For example, one runner might choose to peak for a spring marathon and a fall marathon, while another might choose to peak for a summer track event and a winter cross-country race. Professional runners race more than twice a year, of course, but races other than the two chosen peak races are given somewhat lower priority, if only slightly.

It will be beneficial for you to plan ahead in a similar way. Selecting your two most important races for the next year before the year even begins will enable you to plan your training—with the help of your digital tools—in a manner that all but ensures you peak when you want to and at the level you desire. You are free to choose any two events you like, but they should be at least 16 weeks apart. It generally takes a good 16 weeks to reach peak fitness for a race of any distance if you're starting the training process after a short break following your previous peak race.

Always plan to begin a new training cycle in a state of restedness. Total freedom from residual fatigue from previous training is the true foundation for building peak fitness. The concepts of chronic and acute training load and training stress balance are useful in making sense of this need. A positive training stress balance indicates that you are relatively rested, or fresh. But a positive TSB alone may not indicate that you're ready to begin a new training cycle if you've only recently completed a peak race. When this is the case, you should also make sure your CTL, or fitness, is at least 20 percent lower than its highest level in the preceding training cycle. Getting to this point may require that you train very lightly for a week or two after completing your first peak race of the year and only then start training for the second one.

Naturally, the more fitness you give up after a peak race, the more time you need to prepare for the next one, so it's best not to give up much more than 20 percent. Thus, if you're starting at a lower fitness level after an off-season break, you'll need more than 16 weeks to reach peak fitness again. The maximum amount of time you should devote to focused preparation for a peak race is 24 weeks. Focused preparation means you are increasing your weekly training load by an average of five TSS per day for the week, or 35 total TSS per week. Few runners are able to increase their training workload at this optimal rate for more than 24 weeks without becoming overtrained or injured.

After selecting your peak races, you'll want to determine how fit you'll need to be to achieve your event goals, plan your peak training weeks, plan your training phases, and sketch out key workout progressions.

DETERMINING YOUR FITNESS GOALS

Another great thing about a performance management chart, like the one in Training Peaks WKO+, is that it can help you determine how fit you need to be to achieve your race goals. Remember, the chronic training load variable is essentially a measure of your fitness level. The longer you use a performance management chart, the more reliably you will be able to equate specific fitness levels with specific levels of performance.

For example, suppose that after 10 weeks of progressive training your CTL reaches 45 before you taper a bit and run a 5K in 19:29. Based on your chart, you can see that, at this stage in your development as a runner, a CTL (or fitness level) of 45 is associated with approximately a 19:30 5K. So you also know that if you want to run a 19:30 5K again in the future, you probably want to achieve a 45 CTL first. After you've captured one fitness peak in your performance management chart, you probably will have enough information to determine how fit you will have to be to achieve your goals for your next peak races. For example, if your 19:30 5K at CTL 45 was a tune-up race en route to a 10K peak race, which you ran in 39:55 at a 52 CTL, then you might aim for a 55 CTL for your next 10K peak race, in which your goal is to run 39:30.

Obviously, you won't be able to plan your fitness peak in this manner if you have just begun using a performance management chart or if your next peak race is at an unfamiliar distance (perhaps your first marathon). In this case what you can do is jump to the next step in the planning process—planning your peak training week—and use this information to determine the corresponding fitness level.

In any case, it's important to recognize that using the performance management chart to determine a fitness goal is an inexact method even in the best of circumstances. There are several complicating factors. First of all, training harder is not the only way to get faster. Training more efficiently and effectively, such as by modifying your training to better address your weaknesses, will enable you to achieve higher levels of performance at any given level of fitness as measured in CTL terms. In addition, as you develop as a runner you will also tend to achieve better race performances at any given CTL.

PLANNING YOUR PEAK WEEKS

To achieve your peak race goals, not only must you reach the requisite training load but you also must complete appropriate peak-level workouts right before you start your taper. Thus, when planning a season you need to go beyond setting a general training load target and also plan the specific workouts you will do in your hardest week of training. This week should contain three highly challenging, race-specific workouts that will put the finishing touches on your fitness development and, supposing you meet your pace targets in each of them, demonstrate that you are ready to achieve the race goal you've set.

Tables 7.1 through 7.12 present suggested peak training weeks for 12 categories of runner. At each level (beginner, competitive, and highly competitive), the training is fairly similar across distances. This is consistent with the balanced, nonlinear approach to periodization and also reflects the fact that the fitness recipe for success in the 5K is not all that different from the fitness recipe for success in the 10K, half marathon, and marathon. You just need more endurance to succeed in the longer races. The key difference in these sample peak training weeks for various distances is that the hardest workout emphasizes the target pace zone that is closest to race pace for the relevant race distance: $\dot{V}O_2$max pace for the 5K, threshold pace for the 10K and half marathon, and the fast end of high aerobic pace for the marathon.

Table 7.1 Beginner: 5K

Mon.	Tues.	Wed.	Thurs.	Fri.	Sat.	Sun.
Base run 3 mi. at PZ 3 6 × 10 sec. hill sprints at PZ 10	Threshold run 1 mi. at PZ 2 20 min. at PZ 6 1 mi. at PZ 2	Recovery run 3 mi. at PZ 2	Rest	Lactate intervals 1 mi. at PZ 2 5 × 1K at goal race pace (PZ 8) with 400 m active recoveries at PZ 2 1 mi. at PZ 2	Recovery run 3 mi. at PZ 2	Long run 6 mi. at PZ 3

Table 7.2 Competitive: 5K

Mon.	Tues.	Wed.	Thurs.	Fri.	Sat.	Sun.
Base run 6 mi. at PZ 3 10 × 10 sec. hill sprints at PZ 10	Threshold run 1 mi. at PZ 2 30 min. at PZ 6 1 mi. at PZ 2	Recovery run 6 mi. at PZ 2	Fartlek run 6 mi. at PZ 3 with 6 × 30 sec. at PZ 10 sprinkled in	Lactate intervals 1.5 mi. at PZ 2 5 × 1K at goal race pace (PZ 8) with 300 m active recoveries at PZ 2 1.5 mi. at PZ 2	Recovery run 6 mi. at PZ 2	Long pro-gression run 9 mi. at PZ 3 1 mi. at PZ 4

Table 7.3 Highly Competitive: 5K

Mon.	Tues.	Wed.	Thurs.	Fri.	Sat.	Sun.
Base run 8 mi. at PZ 3 10 × 10 sec. hill sprints at PZ 10	Threshold run 1.5 mi. at PZ 2 2 × 20 min. at PZ 6 with 0.5 mi. active recovery at PZ 2 1.5 mi. at PZ 2	Recovery run 8 mi. at PZ 2	Fartlek run 8 mi. at PZ 3 with 10 × 30 sec. at PZ 10 sprin-kled in	Lactate intervals 2 mi. at PZ 2 5 × 1K at goal race pace (PZ 8) with 200 m active recoveries at PZ 2 2 mi. at PZ 2	Recovery run 6 mi. at PZ 2	Long pro-gression run 12 mi. at PZ 3 2 mi. at PZ 4

Table 7.4 Beginner: 10K

Mon.	Tues.	Wed.	Thurs.	Fri.	Sat.	Sun.
Base run 4 mi. at PZ 3 6 × 10 sec. hill sprints at PZ 10	Threshold run 1 mi. at PZ 2 24 min. at PZ 6 1 mi. at PZ 2	Recovery run 4 mi. at PZ 2	Rest	Mixed intervals 1 mi. at PZ 2 1 mi. at PZ 6 400 m at PZ 2 1K at PZ 8 400 m at PZ 2 600 m at PZ 10 1 mi. at PZ 2	Recovery run 4 mi. at PZ 2	Long run 8 mi. at PZ 3

Table 7.5 Competitive: 10K

Mon.	Tues.	Wed.	Thurs.	Fri.	Sat.	Sun.
Base run 6 mi. at PZ 3 8 × 10 sec. hill sprints at PZ 10	Threshold run 1 mile at PZ 2 2 × 16 min. at PZ 6 with 0.5 mi. active recovery at PZ 2 1 mi. at PZ 2	Recovery run 6 mi. at PZ 2	Fartlek run 6 mi. at PZ 3 with 6 × 45 sec. at PZ 8 sprinkled in	Mixed intervals 1 mi. at PZ 2 2 × (1 mi. at PZ 6, 400 m at PZ 2, 1K at PZ 8, 400 m at PZ 2, 600 m at PZ 10) 1 mi. at PZ 2	Recovery run 6 mi. at PZ 2	Long progression run 10 mi. at PZ 3 2 mi. at PZ 4

Table 7.6 Highly Competitive: 10K

Mon.	Tues.	Wed.	Thurs.	Fri.	Sat.	Sun.
Base run 8 mi. at PZ 3 10 × 10 sec. hill sprints at PZ 10	Threshold run 1.5 mi. at PZ 2 2 × 20 min. at PZ 6 with 0.5 mi. active recovery at PZ 2 1.5 mi. at PZ 2	Recovery run 8 mi. at PZ 2	Fartlek run 10 mi. at PZ 3 with 10 × 45 sec. at PZ 8 sprinkled in	Mixed intervals 1 mi. at PZ 2 3 × (1 mi. at PZ 6, 400 m at PZ 2, 1K at PZ 8, 400 m at PZ 2, 600 m at PZ 10) 1 mi. at PZ 2	Recovery run 8 mi. at PZ 2	Long progression run 13 mi. at PZ 3 3 mi. at PZ 4

Table 7.7 Beginner: Half Marathon

Mon.	Tues.	Wed.	Thurs.	Fri.	Sat.	Sun.
Base run 5 mi. at PZ 3 6 × 10 sec. hill sprints at PZ 10	Threshold run 1 mi. at PZ 2 24 min. at PZ 6 1 mi. at PZ 2	Recovery run 4 mi. at PZ 2	Rest	Mixed intervals 1 mi. at PZ 2 1 mi. at PZ 6 400m at PZ 2 1K at PZ 8 400 m at PZ 2 600 m at PZ 10 1 mi. at PZ 2	Recovery run 4 mi. at PZ 2	Long run 12 mi. at PZ 3

Table 7.8 Competitive: Half Marathon

Mon.	Tues.	Wed.	Thurs.	Fri.	Sat.	Sun.
Base run 6 mi. at PZ 3 8 × 10 sec. hill sprints at PZ 10	Threshold run 1 mi. at PZ 2 2 × 16 min. at PZ 6 with 0.5 mi. active recovery at PZ 2 1 mi. at PZ 2	Recovery run 6 mi. at PZ 2	Fartlek run 8 mi. at PZ 3 with 6 × 45 sec. at PZ 8 sprinkled in	Mixed intervals 1 mi. at PZ 2 2 × (1 mi. at PZ 6, 400 m at PZ 2, 1K at PZ 8, 400 m at PZ 2, 600 m at PZ 10) 1 mi. at PZ 2	Recovery run 6 mi. at PZ 2	Long progression run 12 mi. at PZ 3 2 mi. at PZ 4

Table 7.9 Highly Competitive: Half Marathon

Mon.	Tues.	Wed.	Thurs.	Fri.	Sat.	Sun.
Base run 10 mi. at PZ 3 10 × 10 sec. hill sprints at PZ 10	Threshold run 1.5 mi. at PZ 2 2 × 20 min. at PZ 6 with 0.5 mi. active recovery at PZ 2 1.5 mi. at PZ 2	Recovery run 8 mi. at PZ 2	Fartlek run 10 mi. at PZ 3 with 10 × 45 sec. at PZ 8 sprinkled in	Mixed intervals 1 mi. at PZ 2 3 × (1 mi. at PZ 6, 400 m at PZ 2, 1K at PZ 8, 400 m at PZ 2, 600 m at PZ 10) 1 mi. at PZ 2	Recovery run 8 mi. at PZ 2	Long progression run 15 mi. at PZ 3 3 mi. at PZ 4

Table 7.10 Beginner: Marathon

Mon.	Tues.	Wed.	Thurs.	Fri.	Sat.	Sun.
Base run 6 mi. at PZ 3 6 × 10 sec. hill sprints at PZ 10	Threshold run 1 mi. at PZ 2 24 min. at PZ 6 1 mi. at PZ 2	Recovery run 4 mi. at PZ 2	Rest	Fartlek run 6 mi. at PZ 3 with 6 × 45 sec. at PZ 8 sprinkled in	Recovery run 4 mi. at PZ 2	Long run 20 mi. at PZ 3

Table 7.11 Competitive: Marathon

Mon.	Tues.	Wed.	Thurs.	Fri.	Sat.	Sun.
Base run 6 mi. at PZ 3 8 × 10 sec. hill sprints at PZ 10	Threshold run 1 mi. at PZ 2 2 × 16 min. at PZ 6 with 0.5 mi. active recovery at PZ 2 1 mi. at PZ 2	Recovery run 6 mi. at PZ 2	Fartlek run 6 mi. at PZ 3 with 6 × 45 sec. at PZ 8 sprinkled in	Progression run 8 mi. at PZ 3 4 mi. at PZ 4	Recovery run 6 mi. at PZ 2	Marathon pace run 1 mi. at PZ 2 14 mi. at PZ 4

Table 7.12 Highly Competitive: Marathon

Mon.	Tues.	Wed.	Thurs.	Fri.	Sat.	Sun.
Base run 10 mi. at PZ 3 10 × 10 sec. hill sprints at PZ 10	Threshold run 1.5 mi. at PZ 2 2 × 20 min. at PZ 6 with 0.5 mi. active recovery at PZ 2 1.5 mi. at PZ 2	Recovery run 8 mi. at PZ 2	Fartlek run 10 mi. at PZ 3 with 10 × 45 sec. at PZ 8 sprinkled in	Progression run 10 mi. at PZ 3 4 mi. at PZ 4	Recovery run 8 mi. at PZ 2	Marathon pace run 4 mi. at PZ 2 14 mi. at PZ 4

PLANNING YOUR TRAINING PHASES

Some runners who practice nonlinear periodization do away with training phases entirely. Others still find it helpful to divide the training process into separate phases, even if these phases are much less distinct than the phases employed in old-school linear periodization models. One advantage of retaining separate phases is that it encourages runners to develop their fitness in a rational sequence of steps. Although nonlinear periodization is different from linear periodization in that the former includes a healthy variety of training stimuli in every phase of training, not every training stimulus is given equal emphasis in every phase. The order in which the various training stimuli are emphasized and deemphasized is important. Specifically, the training pace zone that is closest to your peak race goal pace should be least emphasized in the early base phase of training and most emphasized in the peak phase. Pace zones that are significantly faster and slower should be emphasized earlier in the training process and deemphasized later.

The pace zone distribution graph in Training Peaks WKO+ can be used in planning the appropriate level of emphasis for each pace zone in each phase. This graph shows you the percentage of your total running time within the past 28 days or any other time range that was spent in each of the six target pace zones used in the pace zone index (PZI). Essentially, it shows you how balanced your training is in the intensity dimension and helps you plan your training for optimal intensity balance and improve this balance when you find that it's not as it should be.

The appropriate distribution of your weekly training among the six target pace zones depends on your goal race distance and how far along you are in the training process. Tables 7.13 through 7.16 present suggested running pace zone distributions for various phases of training for each of four race distances: 5K, 10K, half marathon, and marathon. In comparing them, bear in mind that greater total volume is assumed for the 10K plan than for the 5K plan, and so forth.

Table 7.13 5K Pace Zone Distribution

Pace zone	Early base phase	Late base phase	Early build phase	Late build phase	Early peak phase	Late peak phase
2	5%	7%	10%	12%	12%	10%
3	80%	69%	63%	60%	58%	63%
4	5%	10%	5%	5%	5%	5%
6	5%	7%	10%	12%	15%	12%
8	2%	3%	5%	6%	6%	7%
10	3%	4%	7%	5%	4%	3%

Table 7.14   10K Pace Zone Distribution

Pace zone	Early base phase	Late base phase	Early build phase	Late build phase	Early peak phase	Late peak phase
2	5%	6%	8%	12%	10%	8%
3	80%	69%	63%	60%	62%	64%
4	5%	10%	12%	10%	8%	6%
6	5%	5%	7%	10%	12%	15%
8	2%	5%	7%	5%	5%	4%
10	3%	5%	3%	3%	3%	3%

Table 7.15   Half-Marathon Pace Zone Distribution

Pace zone	Early base phase	Late base phase	Early build phase	Late build phase	Early peak phase	Late peak phase
2	5%	3%	5%	9%	8%	7%
3	73%	73%	70%	60%	60%	64%
4	7%	10%	10%	12%	12%	9%
6	5%	5%	7%	10%	12%	14%
8	3%	4%	5%	6%	5%	3%
10	7%	5%	3%	3%	3%	3%

Table 7.16   Marathon Pace Zone Distribution

Pace zone	Early base phase	Late base phase	Early build phase	Late build phase	Early peak phase	Late peak phase
2	5%	3%	5%	7%	6%	5%
3	73%	71%	63%	56%	57%	58%
4	7%	10%	12%	15%	17%	20%
6	5%	7%	12%	15%	14%	12%
8	3%	4%	5%	4%	3%	3%
10	7%	5%	3%	3%	3%	2%

When planning your training, calculate the pace zone distribution of selected weeks of scheduled training; in other words, figure out how much time you will spend running within each pace zone. Check the pace zone distribution against the suggested distribution for each race distance and phase and then adjust your workouts as necessary. Absolute precision is not necessary. The goal of this exercise is to help you divide your training into phases that emphasize the various training stimuli in their proper order.

In addition to planning, you can use the tables in quickly assessing whether you are actually dividing your running as planned in your targeted zones. Once a week or so, look at your pace zone distribution graph and see how closely your actual pace zone distribution matches the planned distribution for your current phase of training. If you find any significant discrepancies, consider tweaking your future training to bring it in line with your plan, especially if these discrepancies appear to have given rise to a weakness in your fitness.

Note that you will never be able to actually get 100 percent of your running time to fall within these six target pace zones. There are four nontargeted gray zones in the PZI that are impossible to avoid completely. But if you divvy the time you do spend in these gray zones equally into the adjoining target pace zones, you should be able to get your pace zone distribution percentages to match up fairly closely to the values recommended in these tables. For example, if your pace zone distribution graph says you spent 2 percent of your total running time within the past 28 days in pace zone 5 (gray zone 2), then add 1 percent to time spent in pace zone 4 (high aerobic) and 1 percent to time spent in pace zone 6 (threshold).

MAPPING KEY WORKOUT PROGRESSIONS

The final step in planning a yearlong nonlinear periodization cycle is to map out key workout progressions. Recall that key workouts are the most challenging runs in your weekly training cycle—usually two high-intensity runs during the week and a long run on the weekend. It will help you get where you want to go in your training if you at least decide what the toughest key workout of each type will look like and when you will do it in the process of ramping up toward a peak race. Putting these benchmarks in place will give you a good sense of how to progressively approach them in the key workouts of the same type that you do in proceeding weeks.

If you are a natural-born planner, you may choose to plan all of your key workouts for the entire training cycle in detail, but be prepared to modify them as necessary as you execute the plan. If you're more spontaneous by nature, you can do just as well with a freer approach. Just introduce each key workout type at the appropriate point in the training process with a moderately challenging version of the workout and then make each subsequent workout of the same type a little more challenging (except in recovery weeks) until you reach the benchmark you planned in advance.

Remember that the key workout type whose target pace is closest to the goal pace of your peak race should reach its peak level closest to the peak race itself. Key workouts targeting faster and slower paces should reach their peak level earlier. Your most challenging workout of any type also should be of the type whose target pace is closest to the goal pace of your peak race. Your other workouts generally should peak at slightly lower levels. For example, threshold runs targeting threshold pace are the most race-specific key workouts for both 10K and half-marathon races. Thus, if you're training for a 10K or a half marathon, your toughest threshold run should occur no more than 18 days before your peak race to ensure that on race day your body still holds the fitness stimulated by that workout, and it should be more challenging than the toughest threshold workout you would do if you were training for a 5K or a marathon.

Tables 7.17, 7.18, and 7.19 show examples of progressions for three types of key workouts: lactate intervals, threshold runs, and long runs. They show how far a runner might want to develop each of them in training for a 5K, a 10K, a half marathon, and a marathon. These examples are not appropriate for every runner, nor do they necessarily represent complete progressions. In some cases you might want to insert additional workouts between contiguous workouts in these tables to make the progressions more gradual. In short, these tables are presented merely as illustrations.

Table 7.17 shows a sequence of six lactate interval runs. Runners training for races of all distances from the 5K to the marathon should do the first four, but only runners training for a 5K peak race should go on to complete the last two. Table 7.18 shows a sequence of eight threshold runs with two versions of each of the last two. Runners training for peak races of all distances should complete the first six. Only runners training for a 10K peak race should go on to do the A-version of the last two threshold runs. Only runners training for a half-marathon peak race should go on to do the B-version of the last two threshold runs. Table 7.19 shows a sequence of 11 long runs. Runners training for peak races of all distances should do the first three. Only runners training for 10K, half-marathon, and marathon peak races should go on to do the next long run. Only runners training for half-marathon and marathon peak races should then go on to do the next two long runs. And only runners training for a marathon peak race should go on to do the last five long runs.

Table 7.17 Lactate Interval Run Progression

5K 10K Half marathon Marathon	12 × 400 m at PZ 8 with 400 m active recoveries at PZ 2
	8 × 600 m at PZ 8 with 400 m active recoveries at PZ 2
	6 × 800 m at PZ 8 with 400 m active recoveries at PZ 2
	5 × 1K at PZ 8 with 400 m active recoveries at PZ 2
5K only	5 × 1K at goal race pace with 300 m active recoveries at PZ 2
	5 × 1K at goal race pace with 200 m active recoveries at PZ 2

Table 7.18 Threshold Run Progression

5K 10K Half marathon Marathon	4 mi. at PZ 6	
	4.5 mi. at PZ 6	
	5 mi. at PZ 6	
	5.5 mi. at PZ 6	
	6 mi. at PZ 6	
	10K at PZ 6	
A		**B**
5 × 1 mi. at goal 10K race pace* with 400 m active recoveries at PZ 2	⊠10K only	8 × 1 mi. at goal half-marathon race pace** with 400 m active recoveries at PZ 2
6 × 1 mi. at goal 10K race pace with 400 m active recoveries at PZ 2	Half marathon only⊠	4 × 2 mi. at goal half-marathon race pace with 400 m active recoveries at PZ 2

* This may fall in gray zone 3 for some runners.

** This may fall in gray zone 2 for some runners.

Table 7.19 Long Run Progression

5K 10K Half marathon Marathon	8 mi. at PZ 3
	8 mi. at PZ 3 plus 2 mi. at PZ 4
	10 mi. at PZ 3 plus 2 mi. at PZ 4
10K Half marathon Marathon	12 mi. at PZ 3 plus 2 mi. at PZ 4
Half marathon Marathon	12 mi. at PZ 3 plus 3 mi. at PZ 4
	13 mi. at PZ 3 plus 3 mi. at PZ 4
Marathon	16 mi. at PZ 3 plus 2 mi. at PZ 4
	1 mi. at PZ 3 10 mi. at PZ 4 1 mi. at PZ 3
	18 mi. at PZ 3 plus 2 mi. at PZ 4
	1 mi. at PZ 3 13.1 mi. at PZ 4 1 mi. at PZ 3
	18 mi. at PZ 3 plus 4 mi. at PZ 4

BEST-LAID PLANS

You might finish far behind the professional runners in big road races, but that doesn't mean you cannot borrow a few cues from their training. Most of today's elites have abandoned the traditional linear, race-by-race approach to periodization in favor of a multirace, seasonal approach in which they maintain a consistently high level of fitness by including a variety of training stimuli and challenging workouts in their regimens.

The few steps to planning a yearlong training cycle that we discussed in this chapter are a simple method of practicing the nonlinear approach to periodization. These steps provide a solid but flexible framework to guide your training, which is different from the rigid, detailed training plans used in traditional linear training plans. Speed and distance devices and performance management software can help you practice this method by making it easy to quantify your training in both the big picture and the small so that you always know whether you're on track even without a detailed map.

Traditional training plans have their place, however. They help runners avoid making all kinds of common training errors, such as failing to vary their training adequately, increasing their training workload too quickly, and not incorporating adequate recovery into the training process. Regardless of which specific plan is chosen, runners who have never previously followed a formal, expert-designed training plan almost always improve markedly when they make the commitment to use such a plan for the first time.

Many runners simply aren't ready to walk the tightrope of loosely planning their own yearlong training cycles without the net of a detailed, day-by-day map of workouts. Often runners need to follow a few ready-made training plans before they feel ready to train like the pros. For those runners, chapter 8 provides a sampling of ready-made plans that incorporate some of the principles of nonlinear periodization discussed here, but they have a focused timeline and aim toward a single peak race.

Building Training Plans on Race Goals

In this chapter you will find sample training plans that illustrate the periodization guidelines presented in chapter 7. There are three plans for each of four peak race distances: 5K, 10K, half marathon, and marathon. The level 1 plans are for beginners and others who need or prefer a low-mileage training approach. The level 2 plans are moderate-mileage plans for competitive runners. The level 3 plans are high-mileage plans for highly competitive and experienced runners. Choose the plan that's the best fit for you and adjust it as necessary to make it fit your needs even better. Refer to the last section of this chapter for guidelines on customizing training plans.

Table 8.1 presents the peak chronic training load (CTL) score for each of the 12 plans. Recall that a CTL score is a rolling average of your daily training stress score over the past 42 days. Your peak CTL is the highest CTL you achieve in a period of training and falls at the end of the next-to-last week in these plans. The peak CTL numbers in this table will help you select your training plan after you've accumulated enough workout data to know the CTL range that is best for you.

Hal Higdon on Choosing an Online Training Plan

Using an Internet search engine, type in a phrase such as "marathon training plans" and you will find dozens of purveyors of online training plans for runners. Some are better than others. What can you do to ensure that you choose a plan that you're happy with? Simple: Follow the advice of Hal Higdon, the undisputed king of online training plans for runners. For more than a decade, Higdon, a four-time Olympic Trials qualifier and author of more than 30 books on running, has been the most popular source of running workout schedules. Here are Higdon's shopping tips:

■ **Seek referrals.** "The better online coaches have good word of mouth," says Higdon. "If you talk to other runners, it won't take long to find out which ones have the strongest reputation." He suggests querying the staff of your local running specialty shop, running club members, and online running message board users.

■ **Kick the tires.** "Some coaches let you preview plans before you buy one," says Higdon. "Others don't. Obviously, you have a better chance of getting a plan that you're comfortable with if you're able to look at it first." When previewing plans, Higdon suggests, check out whether they provide only a bare-bones schedule or whether there is additional information to ensure you perform workouts correctly and other tips to make the process of using the plan more like having a coach.

■ **Consider the platform.** The technologies used in delivering online training plans are as widely varying as the plans themselves. Some popular features include nutrition tracking tools, the ability to upload workout data from training devices, and automatic e-mail delivery of each day's workout to the runner's inbox. Some platforms offer none of these features, while others have different sets of bells and whistles. Inspect these as closely as you inspect the plan itself before you buy.

■ **Join a community.** With some online services, you buy a plan, receive it, and then you're more or less on your own. With others you have the ability to communicate with the coach who created the plan—or at least with other runners who are following the coach's plans—as you follow it. This is definitely the way to go, according to Higdon. "My Web site has a very lively message board with a lot of activity," says Higdon. He personally answers six or seven questions each day and there is also a good deal of communication between runners. "It not only helps them get more out of their plans but it also helps with motivation, which is just as important," he adds.

Table 8.1 Peak Chronic Training Load (CTL) Scores for Training Plans

Plan	Peak CTL
5K level 1	34
5K level 2	46
5K level 3	64
10K level 1	39
10K level 2	56
10K level 3	70
Half marathon level 1	48
Half marathon level 2	58
Half marathon level 3	79
Marathon level 1	53
Marathon level 2	66
Marathon level 3	88

Key to Abbreviations

AR = active recovery; jog in pace zone 2 to recover between high-intensity efforts

base = base run

fartlek = fartlek run

HMP = half-marathon pace

hills = hill repetitions

HS = hill sprints; run 10 seconds up a steep hill at maximum speed and then walk back down the hill for recovery between sprints

lactate = lactate intervals

mixed = mixed-interval run

MP = marathon-pace run

progression = progression run

PZ3 = pace zone 3*

recovery = recovery run

speed = speed intervals

threshold = threshold run

X-train = cross-train by doing a nonimpact cardiorespiratory activity such as bicycling

* Example: 3 mi. PZ3 with 4 × 30 sec. PZ8 means run 3 miles in pace zone 3 and scatter four intervals of 30 seconds in pace zone 8 throughout the run.

Table 8.2 5K Level 1 Training Plan

Week	Mon.	Tues.	Wed.	Thurs.	Fri.	Sat.	Sun.
1	Base 3 mi. PZ3	Fartlek 3 mi. PZ3 with 4 × 30 sec. PZ8	Off	Progression 2 mi. PZ3 1 mi. PZ4	Off	Base 3 mi. PZ3	Off
2	Base 3 mi. PZ3 plus 1 × 10 sec. HS PZ10	Fartlek 3 mi. PZ3 with 4 × 30 sec. PZ8	Off	Progression 3 mi. PZ3 1 mi. PZ4	Base 3 mi. PZ3	Off	Base 4 mi. PZ3
3	Base 3 mi. PZ3 plus 2 × 10 sec. HS PZ10	Fartlek 4 mi. PZ3 with 6 × 30 sec. PZ8	Off	Progression 3 mi. PZ3 1 mi. PZ6	Base 3 mi. PZ3	Off	Base 5 mi. PZ3
4	Base 4 mi. PZ3 plus 3 × 10 sec. HS PZ10	Fartlek 4 mi. PZ3 with 8 × 30 sec. PZ8	Off	Progression 3.5 mi. PZ3 1.5 mi. PZ6	Base 4 mi. PZ3	Off	Base 6 mi. PZ3
5	Base 4 mi. PZ3 plus 4 × 10 sec. HS PZ10	Hills 1 mi. PZ2 4 × 400 m hills PZ10 (AR = 400 m PZ2) 1 mi. PZ2	Off	Base 4 mi. PZ3	Threshold 1 mi. PZ2 2 mi. PZ6 1 mi. PZ2	Off	Base 5 mi. PZ3
6	Base 4 mi. PZ3 plus 5 × 10 sec. HS PZ10	Speed 1 mi. PZ2 6 × 400 m PZ10 (AR = 400 m PZ2) 1 mi. PZ2	Off	Progression 2 mi. PZ3 2 mi. PZ6	Lactate 1 mi. PZ2 12 × 400 m PZ8 (AR = 400 m PZ2) 1 mi. PZ2	Off	Progression 4 mi. PZ3 1 mi. PZ6
7	Base 4 mi. PZ3 plus 6 × 10 sec. HS PZ10	Lactate 1 mi. PZ2 12 × 400 m PZ8 (AR = 400 m PZ2) 1 mi. PZ2	Off	Progression 3 mi. PZ3 1 mi. PZ4	Threshold 1 mi. PZ2 3 mi. PZ6 1 mi. PZ2	Off	Base 6 mi. PZ3
8	Base 4 mi. PZ3 plus 6 × 10 sec. HS PZ10	Lactate 1 mi. PZ2 8 × 600 m PZ8 (AR = 400 m PZ2) 1 mi. PZ2	Off	Base 4 mi. PZ3	Mixed 1 mi. PZ2 1 mi. PZ6 400 m PZ2 1K mi. PZ8 400 m PZ2 600 m PZ10 1 mi. PZ2	Off	Progression 5 mi. PZ3 1 mi. PZ6

Week	Mon.	Tues.	Wed.	Thurs.	Fri.	Sat.	Sun.
9	Base 4 mi. PZ3 plus 6 × 10 sec. HS PZ10	Lactate 1 mi. PZ2 6 × 800 m PZ8 (AR = 400 m PZ2) 1 mi. PZ2	Off	Progression 3 mi. PZ3 1 mi. PZ4	Threshold 1 mi. PZ2 4 mi. PZ6 1 mi. PZ2	Off	Base 6 mi. PZ3
10	Base 4 mi. PZ3 plus 6 × 10 sec. HS PZ10	Hills 1 mi. PZ2 8 × 600 m uphill PZ8 (AR = 400 m PZ2) 1 mi. PZ2	Off	Progression 3 mi. PZ3 1 mi. PZ6	Mixed 1 mi. PZ2 400 m PZ10 400 m PZ2 600 m PZ8 400 m PZ2 1 mi. PZ6 400 m PZ2 1K PZ8 400 m PZ2 600 m PZ10 1 mi. PZ2	Off	Progression 5 mi. PZ3 1.5 mi. PZ6
11	Base 4 mi. PZ3 plus 6 × 10 sec. HS PZ10	Lactate 1 mi. PZ2 5 × 1K goal 5K race pace (AR = 400 m PZ2) 1 mi. PZ2	Off	Progression 3 mi. PZ3 1 mi. PZ4	Threshold 1 mi. PZ2 5 mi. PZ6 1 mi. PZ2	Off	Base 6 mi. PZ3
12	Base 4 mi. PZ3 plus 4 × 10 sec. HS PZ10	Lactate 1 mi. PZ2 2 × 800 m goal 5K race pace (AR = 400 m PZ2) 1 mi. PZ2	Off	Threshold 1 mi. PZ2 1.5 mi. PZ6 1 mi. PZ2	Base 3 mi. PZ3 plus 4 × 100 m strides goal 5K race pace	Off	Race 5K

Table 8.3 5K Level 2 Training Plan

Week	Mon.	Tues.	Wed.	Thurs.	Fri.	Sat.	Sun.
1	Base 4 mi. PZ3 plus 1 × 10 sec. HS PZ10	Fartlek 4 mi. PZ3 with 4 × 30 sec. PZ8	Off	Progression 3 mi. PZ3 1 mi. PZ4	Off	Base 4 mi. PZ3	Base 5 mi. PZ3
2	Base 4 mi. PZ3 plus 2 × 10 sec. HS PZ10	Fartlek 4 mi. PZ3 with 6 × 30 sec. PZ8	Off	Progression 3 mi. PZ3 1 mi. PZ6	Base 4 mi. PZ3	Base 4 mi. PZ3	Base 6 mi. PZ3
3	Base 5 mi. PZ3 plus 3 × 10 sec. HS PZ10	Fartlek 5 mi. PZ3 with 8 × 30 sec. PZ8	Off	Progression 3 mi. PZ3 1.5 mi. PZ6	Base 4 mi. PZ3	Base 4 mi. PZ3	Base 7 mi. PZ3
4	Base 5 mi. PZ3 plus 4 × 10 sec. HS PZ10	Fartlek 5 mi. PZ3 with 10 × 30 sec. PZ8	Off	Progression 4 mi. PZ3 2 mi. PZ6	Progression 3 mi. PZ3 1 mi. PZ4	Base 4 mi. PZ3	Base 8 mi. PZ3
5	Base 5 mi. PZ3 plus 5 × 10 sec. HS PZ10	Hills 1 mi. PZ2 6 × 400 m hills PZ10 (AR = 400 m PZ2) 1 mi. PZ2	Off	Progression 3 mi. PZ3 1 mi. PZ4	Threshold 1 mi. PZ2 3 mi. PZ6 1 mi. PZ2	Base 4 mi. PZ3	Base 7 mi. PZ3
6	Base 5 mi. PZ3 plus 6 × 10 sec. HS PZ10	Speed 1 mi. PZ2 9 × 400 m hills PZ10 (AR = 400 m PZ2) 1 mi. PZ2	Off	Progression 3 mi. PZ3 2 mi. PZ6	Lactate 1 mi. PZ2 12 × 400 m PZ8 (AR = 400 m PZ2) 1 mi. PZ2	Base 4 mi. PZ3	Progression 5.5 mi. PZ3 1.5 mi. PZ6
7	Base 6 mi. PZ3 plus 7 × 10 sec. HS PZ10	Lactate 1 mi. PZ2 12 × 400 m PZ8 (AR = 400 m PZ2) 1 mi. PZ2	Off	Progression 4 mi. PZ3 2 mi. PZ4	Threshold 1 mi. PZ2 4 mi. PZ6 1 mi. PZ2	Base 4 mi. PZ3	Base 8 mi. PZ3
8	Base 6 mi. PZ3 plus 7 × 10 sec. HS PZ10	Lactate 1 mi. PZ2 8 × 600 m PZ8 (AR = 400 m PZ2) 1 mi. PZ2	Off	Base 6 mi. PZ3	Mixed 1 mi. PZ2 400 m PZ10 400 m PZ2 600 m PZ8 400 m PZ2 1 mi. PZ6 400 m PZ2 1K PZ8 400 m PZ2 600 m PZ10 1 mi. PZ2	Recovery 4 mi. PZ2	Progression 6.5 mi. PZ3 1.5 mi. PZ6

Week	Mon.	Tues.	Wed.	Thurs.	Fri.	Sat.	Sun.
9	Base 6 mi. PZ3 plus 8 × 10 sec. HS PZ10	Lactate 1 mi. PZ2 6 × 800 m PZ8 (AR = 400 m PZ2) 1 mi. PZ2	Off	Progression 4 mi. PZ3 2 mi. PZ4	Threshold 1 mi. PZ2 5 mi. PZ6 1 mi. PZ2	Base 5 mi. PZ3	Base 9 mi. PZ3
10	Base 6 mi. PZ3 plus 8 × 10 sec. HS PZ10	Hills 1 mi. PZ2 8 × 600 m uphill PZ8 (AR = 400 m PZ2) 1 mi. PZ2	Off	Progression 4 mi. PZ3 2 mi. PZ6	Mixed 1 mi. PZ2 2 × (1 mi. PZ6, 400 m PZ2, 1K PZ8, 400 m PZ2, 600 m PZ10) 1 mi. PZ2	Recovery 4 mi. PZ2	Progression 7 mi. PZ3 1.5 mi. PZ6
11	Base 6 mi. PZ3 plus 8 × 10 sec. HS PZ10	Lactate 1 mi. PZ2 5 × 1K goal 5K race pace (AR = 400 m PZ2) 1 mi. PZ2	Off	Progression 5 mi. PZ3 1 mi. PZ4	Threshold 1 mi. PZ2 6 mi. PZ6 1 mi. PZ2	Base 5 mi. PZ3	Base 10 mi. PZ3
12	Base 6 mi. PZ3 plus 5 × 10 sec. HS PZ10	Lactate 1 mi. PZ2 1 mi. goal 5K race pace 1 mi. PZ2	Off	Threshold 1 mi. PZ2 2 mi. PZ6 1 mi. PZ2	Base 4 mi. PZ3	Base 2 mi. PZ3 plus 4 × 100 m strides goal 5K race pace	Race 5K

Table 8.4 5K Level 3 Training Plan

Week	Mon.	Tues.	Wed.	Thurs.	Fri.	Sat.	Sun.
1	Base 4 mi. PZ3 plus 1 × 10 sec. HS PZ10	Fartlek 6 mi. PZ3 with 6 × 30 sec. PZ8	Off	Progression 3 mi. PZ3 1 mi. PZ4	Progression 3 mi. PZ3 1 mi. PZ4	Base 4 mi. PZ3	Base 7 mi. PZ3
2	Base 4 mi. PZ3 plus 2 × 10 sec. HS PZ10	Fartlek 6 mi. PZ3 with 8 × 30 sec. PZ8	Off	Progression 4 mi. PZ3 1 mi. PZ6	Progression 3 mi. PZ3 1 mi. PZ4	Base 6 mi. PZ3	Base 8 mi. PZ3
3	Base 4 mi. PZ3 plus 3 × 10 sec. HS PZ10	Fartlek 6 mi. PZ3 with 12 × 30 sec. PZ8	Base 6 mi. PZ3	Progression 4.5 mi. PZ3 1.5 mi. PZ6	Progression 4 mi. PZ3 1 mi. PZ4	Base 6 mi. PZ3	Base 9 mi. PZ3
4	Base 6 mi. PZ3 plus 4 × 10 sec. HS PZ10	Fartlek 7 mi. PZ3 with 12 × 45 sec. PZ8	Base 6 mi. PZ3	Progression 5 mi. PZ3 2 mi. PZ6	Progression 4 mi. PZ3 1 mi. PZ4	Base 6 mi. PZ3	Base 10 mi. PZ3
5	Base 6 mi. PZ3 plus 5 × 10 sec. HS PZ10	Hills 1.5 mi. PZ2 8 × 400 m hills PZ10 (AR = 400 m PZ2) 1.5 mi. PZ2	Off	Progression 5 mi. PZ3 1 mi. PZ4	Threshold 1.5 mi. PZ2 4 mi. PZ6 1.5 mi. PZ2	Base 6 mi. PZ3	Base 9 mi. PZ3
6	Base 6 mi. PZ3 plus 6 × 10 sec. HS PZ10	Speed 1.5 mi. PZ2 12 × 400 m PZ10 (AR = 400 m PZ2) 1.5 mi. PZ2	Base 6 mi. PZ3	Progression 5 mi. PZ3 2 mi. PZ6	Lactate 1.5 mi. PZ2 13 × 400 m PZ8 (AR = 400 m PZ2) 1.5 mi. PZ2	Recovery 6 mi. PZ2	Progression 6.5 mi. PZ3 1.5 mi. PZ6
7	Base 6 mi. PZ3 plus 7 × 10 sec. HS PZ10	Lactate 1.5 mi. PZ2 13 × 400 m PZ8 (AR = 400 m PZ2) 1.5 mi. PZ2	Base 6 mi. PZ3	Progression 6 mi. PZ3 2 mi. PZ4	Threshold 1.5 mi. PZ2 5 mi. PZ6 1.5 mi. PZ2	Recovery 6 mi. PZ2	Base 10 mi. PZ3
8	Base 6 mi. PZ3 plus 7 × 10 sec. HS PZ10	Lactate 1.5 mi. PZ2 9 × 600 m PZ8 (AR = 400 m PZ2) 1.5 mi. PZ2	Off	Base 8 mi. PZ3	Mixed 1 mi. PZ2 2 × (1 mi. PZ6, 400 m PZ2, 1K PZ8, 400 m PZ2, 600 m PZ10) 1 mi. PZ2	Recovery 6 mi. PZ2	Progression 7.5 mi. PZ3 1.5 mi. PZ6

Week	Mon.	Tues.	Wed.	Thurs.	Fri.	Sat.	Sun.
9	Base 6 mi. PZ3 plus 8 × 10 sec. HS PZ10	Lactate 1.5 mi. PZ2 7 × 800 m PZ8 (AR = 400 m PZ2) 1.5 mi. PZ2	Base 6 mi. PZ3	Progression 6 mi. PZ3 2 mi. PZ4	Threshold 1.5 mi. PZ2 6 mi. PZ6 1.5 mi. PZ2	Recovery 7 mi. PZ2	Base 11 mi. PZ3
10	Base 6 mi. PZ3 plus 9 × 10 sec. HS PZ10	Hills 1.5 mi. PZ2 9 × 600 m uphill PZ8 (AR = 400 m PZ2) 1.5 mi. PZ2	Off	Progression 6 mi. PZ3 2 mi. PZ6	Mixed 1 mi. PZ2 2 × (400 m PZ10, 400 m PZ2, 600 m PZ8, 400 m PZ2, 1 mi. PZ6, 400 m PZ2, 1K PZ8, 400 m PZ2, 600 m PZ10) 1 mi. PZ2	Recovery 6 mi. PZ2	Progression 8.5 mi. PZ3 1.5 mi. PZ6
11	Base 6 mi. PZ3 plus 8 × 10 sec. HS PZ10	Lactate 1.5 mi. PZ2 5 × 1K goal 5K race pace (AR = 400 m PZ2) 1.5 mi. PZ2	Base 6 mi. PZ3	Progression 7 mi. PZ3 1 mi. PZ4	Threshold 1.5 mi. PZ2 7 mi. PZ6 1.5 mi. PZ2	Recovery 8 mi. PZ2	Base 12 mi. PZ3
12	Base 6 mi. PZ3 plus 6 × 10 sec. HS PZ10	Lactate 1.5 mi. PZ2 2 × 1K goal 5K race pace (AR = 400 m PZ2) 1.5 mi. PZ2	Off	Threshold 1.5 mi. PZ2 2 mi. PZ6 1.5 mi. PZ2	Base 5 mi. PZ3	Base 3 mi. PZ3 plus 4 × 100 m strides goal 5K race pace	Race 5K

Table 8.5 10K Level 1 Training Plan

Week	Mon.	Tues.	Wed.	Thurs.	Fri.	Sat.	Sun.
1	Base 3 mi. PZ3	Fartlek 3 mi. PZ3 with 4 × 30 sec. PZ8	Off	Progression 2 mi. PZ3 1 mi. PZ4	Off	Base 3 mi. PZ3	Off
2	Base 3 mi. PZ3 plus 1 × 10 sec. HS PZ10	Fartlek 3 mi. PZ3 with 4 × 30 sec. PZ8	Off	Progression 3 mi. PZ3 1 mi. PZ4	Base 3 mi. PZ3	Off	Base 4 mi. PZ3
3	Base 3 mi. PZ3 plus 2 × 10 sec. HS PZ10	Fartlek 4 mi. PZ3 with 6 × 30 sec. PZ8	Off	Progression 3 mi. PZ3 1 mi. PZ6	Base 3 mi. PZ3	Off	Base 5 mi. PZ3
4	Base 4 mi. PZ3 plus 3 × 10 sec. HS PZ10	Fartlek 4 mi. PZ3 with 8 × 30 sec. PZ8	Off	Progression 3.5 mi. PZ3 1.5 mi. PZ6	Base 4 mi. PZ3	Off	Base 6 mi. PZ3
5	Base 4 mi. PZ3 plus 4 × 10 sec. HS PZ10	Hills 1 mi. PZ2 4 × 400 m hills PZ10 (AR = 400 m PZ2) 1 mi. PZ2	Off	Base 4 mi. PZ3	Threshold 1 mi. PZ2 2 mi. PZ6 1 mi. PZ2	Off	Base 5 mi. PZ3
6	Base 4 mi. PZ3 plus 5 × 10 sec. HS PZ10	Speed 1 mi. PZ2 6 × 300 m PZ10 (AR = 400 m PZ2) 1 mi. PZ2	Off	Progression 3 mi. PZ3 1 mi. PZ4	Threshold 1 mi. PZ2 2.5 mi. PZ6 1 mi. PZ2	Off	Fartlek 6 mi. PZ3 with 6 × 1 min. PZ8
7	Base 4 mi. PZ3 plus 6 × 10 sec. HS PZ10	Hills 1 mi. PZ2 8 × 600 m uphill PZ8 (AR = 400 m PZ2) 1 mi. PZ2	Off	Progression 3 mi. PZ3 1 mi. PZ4	Threshold 1 mi. PZ2 3 mi. PZ6 1 mi. PZ2	Off	Base 6.5 mi. PZ3
8	Base 4 mi. PZ3 plus 6 × 10 sec. HS PZ10	Speed 1 mi. PZ2 6 × 400 m PZ10 (AR = 400 m PZ2) 1 mi. PZ2	Off	Base 4 mi. PZ3	Mixed 1 mi. PZ2 1 mi. PZ6 400 m PZ2 1K PZ8 400 m PZ2 600 m PZ10 1 mi. PZ2	Off	Progression 5 mi. PZ3 1 mi. PZ6

Week	Mon.	Tues.	Wed.	Thurs.	Fri.	Sat.	Sun.
9	Base 4 mi. PZ3 plus 6 × 10 sec. HS PZ10	Lactate 1 mi. PZ2 6 × 800 m PZ8 (AR = 400 m PZ2) 1 mi. PZ2	Off	Progression 3 mi. PZ3 1 mi. PZ4	Threshold 1 mi. PZ2 4.5 mi. PZ6 1 mi. PZ2	Off	Base 7 mi. PZ3
10	Base 4 mi. PZ3 plus 6 × 10 sec. HS PZ10	Lactate 1 mi. PZ2 5 × 1K PZ8 (AR = 400 m PZ2) 1 mi. PZ2	Off	Progression 4 mi. PZ3 1 mi. PZ6	Mixed 1 mi. PZ2 400 m PZ10 400 m PZ2 600 m PZ8 400 m PZ2 1 mi. PZ6 400 m PZ2 1K PZ8 400 m PZ2 600 m PZ10 1 mi. PZ2	Off	Progression 5.5 mi. PZ3 1.5 mi. PZ6
11	Base 4 mi. PZ3 plus 4 × 10 sec. HS PZ10	Fartlek 4 mi. PZ3 with 8 × 45 sec. PZ8 or PZ10	Off	Progression 4 mi. PZ3 1 mi. PZ4	Threshold 1 mi. PZ2 4 mi. PZ6 1 mi. PZ2	Off	Base 7.5 mi. PZ3
12	Base 4 mi. PZ3 plus 6 × 10 sec. HS PZ10	Mixed 1 mi. PZ2 200 m/400 m/ 800 m/400 m/ 200 m PZ8 or PZ10 (AR = 400 m PZ 2) 1 mi. PZ2	Off	Progression 4 mi. PZ3 1 mi. PZ4	Threshold 1 mi. PZ2 5 × 1 mi. goal 10K pace (AR = 400 m PZ2) 1 mi. PZ2	Off	Progression 6 mi. PZ3 2 mi. PZ4
13	Base 4 mi. PZ3 plus 6 × 10 sec. HS PZ10	Mixed 1 mi. PZ2 300 m/600 m/ 1K/600 m/ 300 m PZ8 or PZ10 (AR = 400 m PZ2) 1 mi. PZ2	Off	Progression 4 mi. PZ3 1 mi. PZ4	Threshold 1 mi. PZ2 6 × 1 mi. goal 10K pace (AR = 400 m PZ2) 1 mi. PZ2	Base 5 mi. PZ3	Base 8 mi. PZ3
14	Base 4 mi. PZ3 plus 4 × 10 sec. HS PZ10	Lactate 1 mi. PZ2 3 × 800 m PZ8 (AR = 400 m PZ2) 1 mi. PZ2	Off	Base 3 mi. PZ3	Threshold 1 mi. PZ2 1 mi. goal 10K pace (AR = 400 m PZ2) 1 mi. PZ2	Off	Race 10K

Table 8.6 10K Level 2 Training Plan

Week	Mon.	Tues.	Wed.	Thurs.	Fri.	Sat.	Sun.
1	Base 4 mi. PZ3 plus 1 × 10 sec. HS PZ10	Fartlek 4 mi. PZ3 with 4 × 30 sec. PZ8	Off	Progression 3 mi. PZ3 1 mi. PZ4	Off	Base 4 mi. PZ3	Base 5 mi. PZ3
2	Base 4 mi. PZ3 plus 2 × 10 sec. HS PZ10	Fartlek 4 mi. PZ3 with 6 × 30 sec. PZ8	Off	Progression 3 mi. PZ3 1 mi. PZ6	Base 4 mi. PZ3	Base 4 mi. PZ3	Base 6 mi. PZ3
3	Base 5 mi. PZ3 plus 3 × 10 sec. HS PZ10	Fartlek 5 mi. PZ3 with 8 × 30 sec. PZ8	Off	Progression 3 mi. PZ3 1.5 mi. PZ6	Base 4 mi. PZ3	Base 4 mi. PZ3	Base 7 mi. PZ3
4	Base 5 mi. PZ3 plus 4 × 10 sec. HS PZ10	Fartlek 5 mi. PZ3 with 10 × 30 sec. PZ8	Off	Progression 4 mi. PZ3 2 mi. PZ6	Progression 3 mi. PZ3 1 mi. PZ4	Base 4 mi. PZ3	Base 8 mi. PZ3
5	Base 5 mi. PZ3 plus 5 × 10 sec. HS PZ10	Hills 1 mi. PZ2 6 × 400 m hills PZ10 (AR = 400 m PZ2) 1 mi. PZ2	Off	Progression 3 mi. PZ3 1 mi. PZ4	Threshold 1 mi. PZ2 3 mi. PZ6 1 mi. PZ2	Base 4 mi. PZ3	Base 7 mi. PZ3
6	Base 5 mi. PZ3 plus 6 × 10 sec. HS PZ10	Speed 1 mi. PZ2 9 × 300 m hills PZ10 (AR = 400 m PZ2) 1 mi. PZ2	Off	Progression 4 mi. PZ3 1 mi. PZ4	Threshold 1 mi. PZ2 3.5 mi. PZ6 1 mi. PZ2	Base 4 mi. PZ3	Base 8 mi. PZ3 with 8 × 1 min. PZ8
7	Base 6 mi. PZ3 plus 7 × 10 sec. HS PZ10	Hills 1 mi. PZ2 8 × 600 m uphill PZ8 (AR = 400 m PZ2) 1 mi. PZ2	Off	Progression 4 mi. PZ3 2 mi. PZ4	Threshold 1 mi. PZ2 4 mi. PZ6 1 mi. PZ2	Base 4 mi. PZ3	Base 9 mi. PZ3
8	Base 6 mi. PZ3 plus 7 × 10 sec. HS PZ10	Speed 1 mi. PZ2 9 × 400 m hills PZ10 (AR = 400 m PZ2) 1 mi. PZ2	Off	Base 6 mi. PZ3	Mixed 1 mi. PZ2 400 m PZ10 400 m PZ2 600 m PZ8 400 m PZ2 1 mi. PZ6 400 m PZ2 1K PZ8 400 m PZ2 600 m PZ10 1 mi. PZ2	Recovery 4 mi. PZ2	Progression 6.5 mi. PZ3 1.5 mi. PZ6

Week	Mon.	Tues.	Wed.	Thurs.	Fri.	Sat.	Sun.
9	Base 6 mi. PZ3 plus 8 × 10 sec. HS PZ10	Lactate 1 mi. PZ2 6 × 800 m PZ8 (AR = 400 m PZ2) 1 mi. PZ2	Off	Progression 4 mi. PZ3 2 mi. PZ4	Threshold 1 mi. PZ2 5.5 mi. PZ6 1 mi. PZ2	Base 5 mi. PZ3	Base 10 mi. PZ3
10	Base 6 mi. PZ3 plus 8 × 10 sec. HS PZ10	Lactate 1 mi. PZ2 5 × 1K PZ8 (AR = 400 m PZ2) 1 mi. PZ2	Off	Progression 5 mi. PZ3 2 mi. PZ6	Mixed 1 mi. PZ2 2 × (1 mi. PZ6, 400 m PZ2, 1K PZ8, 400 m PZ2, 600 m PZ10) 1 mi. PZ2	Recovery 4 mi. PZ2	Progression 7.5 mi. PZ3 1.5 mi. PZ6
11	Base 6 mi. PZ3 plus 6 × 10 sec. HS PZ10	Fartlek 6 mi. PZ3 with 10 × 45 sec. PZ8 or PZ10	Off	Progression 5 mi. PZ3 1 mi. PZ4	Threshold 1 mi. PZ2 5 mi. PZ6 1 mi. PZ2	Base 5 mi. PZ3	Base 10.5 mi. PZ3
12	Base 6 mi. PZ3 plus 8 × 10 sec. HS PZ10	Mixed 1 mi. PZ2 200 m/400 m/ 600 m/800 m/ 600 m/400 m/ 200 m PZ8 or PZ10 (AR = 400 m PZ2) 1 mi. PZ2	Off	Progression 6 mi. PZ3 1 mi. PZ4	Threshold 1 mi. PZ2 6 x 1 mi. goal 10K pace (AR = 400) 1 mi. PZ2	Base 5 mi. PZ3	Progression 8 mi. PZ3 2 mi. PZ4
13	Base 6 mi. PZ3 plus 8 × 10 sec. HS PZ10	Mixed 1 mi. PZ2 300 m/600 m/ 1K/1K/ 600 m/300 m PZ8 or PZ10 (AR = 400 m PZ2) 1 mi. PZ2	Off	Progression 6 mi. PZ3 1 mi. PZ4	Threshold 1 mi. PZ2 5 x 2K goal 10K pace (AR = 400 m PZ2) 1 mi. PZ2	Base 7 mi. PZ3	Base 11 mi. PZ3
14	Base 6 mi. PZ3 plus 5 × 10 sec. HS PZ10	Lactate 1 mi. PZ2 4 × 800 m PZ8 (AR = 400 m PZ2) 1 mi. PZ2	Off	Base 5 mi. PZ3	Threshold 1 mi. PZ2 1.5 mi. goal 10K pace (AR = 400 m PZ2) 1 mi. PZ2	Base 3 mi. PZ3 plus 4 × 100 m strides PZ10	Race 10K

Table 8.7 10K Level 3 Training Plan

Week	Mon.	Tues.	Wed.	Thurs.	Fri.	Sat.	Sun.
1	Base 4 mi. PZ3 plus 1 × 10 sec. hill sprint PZ10	Fartlek 6 mi. PZ3 with 6 × 30 sec. PZ8	Off	Progression 3 mi. PZ3 1 mi. PZ4	Progression 3 mi. PZ3 1 mi. PZ4	Base 4 mi. PZ3	Base 7 mi. PZ3
2	Base 4 mi. PZ3 plus 2 × 10 sec. HS PZ10	Fartlek 6 mi. PZ3 with 8 × 30 sec. PZ8	Off	Progression 4 mi. PZ3 1 mi. PZ6	Progression 3 mi. PZ3 1 mi. PZ4	Base 6 mi. PZ3	Base 8 mi. PZ3
3	Base 4 mi. PZ3 plus 3 × 10 sec. HS PZ10	Fartlek 6 mi. PZ3 with 12 × 30 sec. PZ8	Base 6 mi. PZ3	Progression 4.5 mi. PZ3 1.5 mi. PZ6	Progression 4 mi. PZ3 1 mi. PZ4	Base 6 mi. PZ3	Base 9 mi. PZ3
4	Base 6 mi. PZ3 plus 4 × 10 sec. HS PZ10	Fartlek 7 mi. PZ3 with 12 × 45 sec. PZ8	Base 6 mi. PZ3	Progression 5 mi. PZ3 2 mi. PZ6	Progression 4 mi. PZ3 1 mi. PZ4	Base 6 mi. PZ3	Base 10 mi. PZ3
5	Base 6 mi. PZ3 plus 5 × 10 sec. HS PZ10	Hills 1.5 mi. PZ2 8 × 400 m hills PZ10 (AR = 400 m PZ2) 1.5 mi. PZ2	Off	Progression 5 mi. PZ3 1 mi. PZ4	Threshold 1.5 mi. PZ2 4 mi. PZ6 1.5 mi. PZ2	Base 6 mi. PZ3	Base 9 mi. PZ3
6	Base 6 mi. PZ3 plus 6 × 10 sec. HS PZ10	Speed 1.5 mi. PZ2 12 × 300 m PZ10 (AR = 400 m PZ2) 1.5 mi. PZ2	Base 6 mi. PZ3	Progression 5 mi. PZ3 2 mi. PZ6	Threshold 1.5 mi. PZ2 4.5 mi. PZ6 1.5 mi. PZ2	Recovery 6 mi. PZ2	Base 10 mi. PZ3 with 10 × 1 min. PZ8
7	Base 6 mi. PZ3 plus 7 × 10 sec. HS PZ10	Hills 1.5 mi. PZ2 9 × 600 m uphill PZ8 (AR = 400 m PZ2) 1.5 mi. PZ2	Base 6 mi. PZ3	Progression 6 mi. PZ3 2 mi. PZ4	Threshold 1.5 mi. PZ2 5 mi. PZ6 1.5 mi. PZ2	Recovery 6 mi. PZ2	Base 11 mi. PZ3
8	Base 6 mi. PZ3 plus 7 × 10 sec. HS PZ10	Speed 1.5 mi. PZ2 12 × 400 m PZ10 (AR = 400 m PZ2) 1.5 mi. PZ2	Off	Base 8 mi. PZ3	Mixed 1 mi. PZ2 2 × (1 mi. PZ6, 400 m PZ2, 1K PZ8, 400 m PZ2, 600 m PZ10) 1 mi. PZ2	Rec 6 mi. PZ2	Progression 7.5 mi. PZ3 1.5 mi. PZ6

Week	Mon.	Tues.	Wed.	Thurs.	Fri.	Sat.	Sun.
9	Base 6 mi. PZ3 plus 8 × 10 sec. HS PZ10	Lactate 1.5 mi. PZ2 7 × 800 m PZ8 (AR = 400 m PZ2) 1.5 mi. PZ2	Base 6 mi. PZ3	Progression 6 mi. PZ3 2 mi. PZ4	Threshold 1.5 mi. PZ2 6.5 mi. PZ6 1.5 mi. PZ2	Recovery 7 mi. PZ2	Base 12 mi. PZ3
10	Base 6 mi. PZ3 plus 9 × 10 sec. HS PZ10	Lactate 1.5 mi. PZ2 5 × 1K PZ8 (AR = 400 m PZ2) 1.5 mi. PZ2	Off	Progression 7 mi. PZ3 2 mi. PZ6	Mixed 1 mi. PZ2 2 × (400 m PZ10, 400 m PZ2, 600 m PZ8, 400 m PZ2, 1 mi. PZ6, 400 m PZ2, 1K PZ8, 400 m PZ2, 600 m PZ10) 1 mi. PZ2	Recovery 6 mi. PZ2	Progression 9 mi. PZ3 1.5 mi. PZ6
11	Base 6 mi. PZ3 plus 8 × 10 sec. HS PZ10	Fartlek 8 mi. PZ3 with 12 × 45 sec. PZ8 or PZ10	Base 6 mi. PZ3	Progression 7 mi. PZ3 1 mi. PZ4	Threshold 1.5 mi. PZ2 6 mi. PZ6 1.5 mi. PZ2	Recovery 8 mi. PZ2	Base 12.5 mi. PZ3
12	Base 6 mi. PZ3 plus 10 × 10 sec. HS PZ10	Mixed 1 mi. PZ2 200 m/400 m/ 800 m/400 m/ 200 m PZ8 or PZ10 (AR = 400 m PZ2) 1 mi. PZ2	Base 6 mi. PZ3	Progression 8 mi. PZ3 1 mi. PZ4	Threshold 1.5 mi. PZ2 6 × 1 mi. goal 10K pace (AR = 400 m PZ2) 1.5 mi. PZ2	Base 8 mi. PZ3	Progression 10 mi. PZ3 2 mi. PZ4
13	Base 6 mi. PZ3 plus 10 × 10 sec. HS PZ10	Mixed 1 mi. PZ2 2 × (300 m/ 600 m/1K/ 600 m/300 m PZ8 or PZ10) (AR = 400 m PZ2) 1 mi. PZ2	Base 6 mi. PZ3	Progression 8 mi. PZ3 1 mi. PZ4	Threshold 1.5 mi. PZ2 5 × 2K goal 10K pace (AR = 400 m PZ2) 1 mi. PZ2	Base 9 mi. PZ3	Base 13 mi. PZ3
14	Base 6 mi. PZ3 plus 6 × 10 sec. HS PZ10	Lactate 1 mi. PZ2 5 × 800 m PZ8 (AR = 400 m PZ2) 1 mi. PZ2	Base 6 mi. PZ3	Base 5 mi. PZ3	Threshold 1.5 mi. PZ2 2 mi. goal 10K pace (AR = 400 m PZ2) 1 mi. PZ2	Base 3 mi. PZ3 plus 4 × 100 m strides PZ10	Race 10K

Table 8.8 Half Marathon Level 1 Training Plan

Week	Mon.	Tues.	Wed.	Thurs.	Fri.	Sat.	Sun.
1	Off	Base 3 mi. PZ3	Hills 1 mi. PZ2 2 × 400 m PZ8 (AR = 400 m PZ2) 1 mi. PZ2	X-train 20 to 30 min. PZ2 (optional) or rest	Fartlek 3 mi. PZ3 with 4 × 30 sec. PZ10	X-train 20 to 30 min. PZ2 (optional) or rest	Base 4 mi. PZ3
2	Off	Base 3.5 mi. PZ3 plus 1 × 10 sec. HS PZ10	Hills 1 mi. PZ2 4 × 400 m PZ8 (AR = 400 m PZ2) 1 mi. PZ2	X-train 20 to 30 min. PZ2 (optional) or rest	Fartlek 3.5 mi. PZ3 with 6 × 30 sec. PZ10	X-train 20 to 30 min. PZ2 (optional) or rest	Base 5 mi. PZ3
3	Off	Base 4 mi. PZ3 plus 2 × 10 sec. HS PZ10	Hills 1 mi. PZ2 5 × 400 m PZ8 (AR = 400 m PZ2) 1 mi. PZ2	X-train 20 to 30 min. PZ2 (optional) or rest	Fartlek 4 mi. PZ3 with 5 × 45 sec. PZ10	X-train 20 to 30 min. PZ2 (optional) or rest	Progression 5 mi. PZ3 1 mi. PZ4
4	Off	Base 4.5 mi. PZ3 plus 3 × 10 sec. HS PZ10	Hills 1 mi. PZ2 4 × 600 m PZ8 (AR = 600 m PZ2) 1 mi. PZ2	X-train 20 to 30 min. PZ2 (optional) or rest	Fartlek 4.5 mi. PZ3 w/ 4 x 1 min. PZ10	X-train 20 to 30 min. PZ2 (optional) or rest	Progression 5 mi. PZ3 1 mi. PZ4
5	Off	Base 5 mi. PZ3 plus 4 × 10 sec. HS PZ10	Hills 1 mi. PZ2 5 × 600 m PZ8 (AR = 600 m PZ2) 1 mi. PZ2	X-train 20 to 30 min. PZ2 (optional) or rest	Fartlek 4.5 mi. PZ3 with 5 × 1 min. PZ10	X-train 20 to 30 min. PZ2 (optional) or rest	Progression 6 mi. PZ3 1 mi. PZ6
6	Off	Base 5.5 mi. PZ3 plus 5 × 10 sec. HS PZ10	Speed 1 mi. PZ2 6 × 400 m PZ10 (AR = 400 m PZ2) 1 mi. PZ2	X-train 20 to 30 min. PZ2 (optional) or rest	Threshold 1 mi. PZ3 2 × 1 mi. PZ6 (AR = 400 m PZ2) 1 mi. PZ3	X-train 20 to 30 min. PZ2 (optional) or rest	Fartlek 8 mi. PZ3 with 4 × 45 sec. PZ8
7	Off	Base 6 mi. PZ3 plus 6 × 10 sec. HS PZ10	Speed 1 mi. PZ2 7 × 400 m PZ10 (AR = 400 m PZ2) 1 mi. PZ2	X-train 20 to 30 min. PZ2 (optional) or rest	Threshold 1 mi. PZ3 3 x 1 mi. PZ6 (AR = 400 m PZ2) 1 mi. PZ3	X-train 20 to 30 min. PZ2 (optional) or rest	Fartlek 9 mi. PZ3 with 4 × 45 sec. PZ8
8	Off	Base 5 mi. PZ3 plus 4 × 10 sec. HS PZ10	Speed 1 mi. PZ2 4 × 400 m PZ10 (AR = 400 m PZ2) 1 mi. PZ2	X-train 20 to 30 min. PZ2 (optional) or rest	Threshold 1 mi. PZ3 2 × 1 mi. PZ6 (AR = 400 m PZ2) 1 mi. PZ3	X-train 20 to 30 min. PZ2 (optional) or rest	Fartlek 9 mi. PZ3 with 4 × 45 sec. PZ8

Week	Mon.	Tues.	Wed.	Thurs.	Fri.	Sat.	Sun.
9	Off	Base 5.5 mi. PZ3 plus 6 × 10 sec. HS PZ10	Speed 1 mi. PZ2 8 × 400 m PZ10 (AR = 400 m PZ2) 1 mi. PZ2	X-train 20 to 30 min. PZ2 (optional) or rest	Threshold 1 mi. PZ3 3 × 1 mi. PZ6 (AR = 400 m PZ2) 1 mi. PZ3	X-train 20 to 30 min. PZ2 (optional) or rest	Fartlek 9 mi. PZ3 with 4 × 1 min. PZ8
10	Off	Base 6 mi. PZ3 plus 6 × 10 sec. HS PZ10	Lactate 1 mi. PZ2 4 × 800 m PZ8 (AR = 400 m PZ2) 1 mi. PZ2	X-train 20 to 30 min. PZ2 (optional) or rest	Threshold 1 mi. PZ3 2.5 mi. PZ6 1 mi. PZ3	X-train 20 to 30 min. PZ2 (optional) or rest	Progression 9 mi. PZ3 1 mi. PZ4
11	Off	Base 6 mi. PZ3 plus 6 × 10 sec. HS PZ10	Lactate 1 mi. PZ2 4 × 1K PZ8 (AR = 400 m PZ2) 1 mi. PZ2	X-train 20 to 30 min. PZ2 (optional) or rest	Threshold 1 mi. PZ3 3 mi. PZ6 1 mi. PZ3	X-train 20 to 30 min. PZ2 (optional) or rest	Progression 9 mi. PZ3 2 mi. PZ4
12	Off	Base 6 mi. PZ3 plus 6 × 10 sec. HS PZ10	Lactate 1 mi. PZ2 5 × 1K PZ8 (AR = 400 m PZ2) 1 mi. PZ2	X-train 20 to 30 min. PZ2 (optional) or rest	Threshold 1 mi. PZ3 4 mi. PZ6 1 mi. PZ3	X-train 20 to 30 min. PZ2 (optional) or rest	Progression 10 mi. PZ3 2 mi. PZ4
13	Off	Base 6 mi. PZ3 plus 6 × 10 sec. HS PZ10	Mixed 1 mi. PZ2 200 m/400 m/ 800 m/400 m/ 200 m PZ8 or PZ10 (AR = 400 m PZ2) 1 mi. PZ2	X-train 20 to 30 min. PZ2 (optional) or rest	Threshold 1 mi. PZ3 5 mi. goal half marathon pace 1 mi. PZ3	X-train 20 to 30 min. PZ2 (optional) or rest	Progression 9 mi. PZ3 3 mi. PZ4
14	Off	Base 6 mi. PZ3 plus 6 × 10 sec. HS PZ10	Mixed 1 mi. PZ2 300 m/600 m/ 1K/600 m/ 300 m PZ8 or PZ10 (AR = 400 m PZ2) 1 mi. PZ2	X-train 20 to 30 min. PZ2 (optional) or rest	Threshold 1 mi. PZ3 6 mi. goal half marathon pace 1 mi. PZ3	X-train 20 to 30 min. PZ2 (optional) or rest	Progression 8 mi. PZ3 4 mi. PZ4
15	Off	Base 6 mi. PZ3 plus 6 × 10 sec. HS PZ10	Mixed 1 mi. PZ2 400 m/800 m/ 1K/800 m/ 400 m PZ8 or PZ10 (AR = 400 m PZ2) 1 mi. PZ2	X-train 20 to 30 min. PZ2 (optional) or rest	Threshold 1 mi. PZ3 10K goal half marathon pace 1 mi. PZ3	X-train 20 to 30 min. PZ2 (optional) or rest	Progression 7 mi. PZ3 5 mi. PZ4
16	Off	Base 5 mi. PZ3 plus 4 × 10 sec. HS PZ10	Lactate 1 mi. PZ2 3 × 800 m PZ8 (AR = 400 m PZ2) 1 mi. PZ2	X-train 20 to 30 min. PZ2 (optional) or rest	Threshold 1 mi. PZ3 1 mi. goal half marathon pace 1 mi. PZ3	Off	Race Half marathon

Table 8.9 Half Marathon Level 2 Training Plan

Week	Mon.	Tues.	Wed.	Thurs.	Fri.	Sat.	Sun.
1	Off	Base 3.5 mi. PZ3 plus 1 × 10 sec. HS PZ10	Hills 1.5 mi. PZ2 4 × 400 m PZ8 (AR = 400 m PZ2) 1 mi. PZ2	X-train 20 to 30 min. PZ2 (optional) or rest	Fartlek 4 mi. PZ3 with 6 × 30 sec. PZ10	Base 4 mi. PZ3	Base 6 mi. PZ3
2	Off	Base 4 mi. PZ3 plus 2 × 10 sec. HS PZ10	Hills 1.5 mi. PZ2 7 × 2400 m PZ8 (AR = 400 m PZ2) 1 mi. PZ2	X-train 20 to 30 min. PZ2 (optional) or rest	Fartlek 4.5 mi. PZ3 with 10 × 30 sec. PZ10	Base 4 mi. PZ3	Base 7 mi. PZ3
3	Off	Base 5 mi. PZ3 plus 3 × 10 sec. HS PZ10	Hills 1.5 mi. PZ2 9 × 400 m PZ8 (AR = 400 m PZ2) 1 mi. PZ2	X-train 20 to 30 min. PZ2 (optional) or rest	Fartlek 5 mi. PZ3 with 8 × 45 sec. PZ10	Base 4.5 mi. PZ3	Progression 7 mi. PZ3 1 mi. PZ4
4	Off	Base 5 mi. PZ3 plus 4 × 10 sec. HS PZ10	Hills 1.5 mi. PZ2 6 × 600 m PZ8 (AR = 600 m PZ2) 1 mi. PZ2	X-train 20 to 30 min. PZ2 (optional) or rest	Fartlek 5 mi. PZ3 with 6 × 1 min. PZ10	Base 4 mi. PZ3	Progression 6 mi. PZ3 1 mi. PZ4
5	Off	Base 6 mi. PZ3 plus 5 × 10 sec. HS PZ10	Hills 1.5 mi. PZ2 8 × 600 m PZ8 (AR = 600 m PZ2) 1 mi. PZ2	X-train 20 to 30 min. PZ2 (optional) or rest	Fartlek 6 mi. PZ3 with 8 × 1 min. PZ10	Base 5 mi. PZ3	Progression 8 mi. PZ3 1 mi. PZ6
6	Off	Base 6.5 mi. PZ3 plus 6 × 10 sec. HS PZ10	Hills 1.5 mi. PZ2 10 × 400 m PZ10 (AR = 400 m PZ2) 1 mi. PZ2	X-train 20 to 30 min. PZ2 (optional) or rest	Threshold 1 mi. PZ3 3 × 1 mi. PZ6 (AR = 400 m PZ2) 1 mi. PZ3	Base 5 mi. PZ3	Progression 8 mi. PZ3 1 mi. PZ6
7	Off	Base 7 mi. PZ3 plus 7 × 10 sec. HS PZ10	Speed 1 mi. PZ2 9 × 400 m PZ10 (AR = 400 m PZ2) 1 mi. PZ2	X-train 20 to 30 min. PZ2 (optional) or rest	Threshold 1 mi. PZ3 4 × 1 mi. PZ6 (AR = 400 m PZ2) 1 mi. PZ3	Base 5 mi. PZ3	Fartlek 10 mi. PZ3 with 6 × 45 sec. PZ8
8	Off	Base 6 mi. PZ3 plus 6 × 10 sec. HS PZ10	Speed 1 mi. PZ2 6 × 400 m PZ10 (AR = 400 m PZ2) 1 mi. PZ2	X-train 20 to 30 min. PZ2 (optional) or rest	Threshold 1 mi. PZ3 3 × 1 mi. PZ6 (AR = 400 m PZ2) 1 mi. PZ3	Base 5 mi. PZ3	Fartlek 10 mi. PZ3 with 6 × 45 sec. PZ8
9	Off	Base 7 mi. PZ3 plus 7 × 10 sec. HS PZ10	Speed 1 mi. PZ2 12 × 400 m PZ10 (AR = 400 m PZ2) 1 mi. PZ2	X-train 20 to 30 min. PZ2 (optional) or rest	Threshold 1 mi. PZ3 5 × 1 mi. PZ6 (AR = 400 m PZ2) 1 mi. PZ3	Recovery 6 mi. PZ2	Fartlek 11 mi. PZ3 with 6 × 1 min. PZ8

Week	Mon.	Tues.	Wed.	Thurs.	Fri.	Sat.	Sun.
10	Off	Base 7 mi. PZ3 plus 8 × 10 sec. HS PZ10	Lactate 1 mi. PZ2 5 × 800 m PZ8 (AR = 400 m PZ2) 1 mi. PZ2	X-train 20 to 30 min. PZ2 (optional) or rest	Threshold 1.5 mi. PZ3 3 mi. PZ6 (AR = 400 m PZ2) 1.5 mi. PZ3	Recovery 6 mi. PZ2	Progression 11 mi. PZ3 1 mi. PZ4
11	Off	Base 7 mi. PZ3 plus 8 × 10 sec. HS PZ10	Lactate 1 mi. PZ2 5 × 1K PZ8 (AR = 400 m PZ2) 1 mi. PZ2	X-train 20 to 30 min. PZ2 (optional) or rest	Threshold 1.5 mi. PZ3 4 mi. PZ6 (AR = 400 m PZ2) 1.5 mi. PZ3	Recovery 6 mi. PZ2	Progression 11 mi. PZ3 2 mi. PZ4
12	Off	Base 6 mi. PZ3 plus 8 × 10 sec. HS PZ10	Lactate 1 mi. PZ2 5 × 800 m PZ8 (AR = 400 m PZ2) 1 mi. PZ2	X-train 20 to 30 min. PZ2 (optional) or rest	Threshold 1.5 mi. PZ3 3 mi. PZ6 (AR = 400 m PZ2) 1.5 mi. PZ3	Recovery 6 mi. PZ2	Progression 11 mi. PZ3 1 mi. PZ4
13	Off	Base 8 mi. PZ3 plus 8 × 10 sec. HS PZ10	Mixed 1 mi. PZ2 300 m/600 m/ 1K/600 m/ 300 m PZ8 ot PZ10 (AR = 400 m PZ2) 1 mi. PZ2	X-train 20 to 30 min. PZ2 (optional) or rest	Threshold 1 mi. PZ3 6 mi. goal half marathon pace 1 mi. PZ3	Recovery 6 mi. PZ2	Progression 12 mi. PZ3 2 mi. PZ4
14	Off	Base 8 mi. PZ3 plus 8 × 10 sec. HS PZ10	Mixed 1 mi. PZ2 300 m/300 m 600 m/1K/ 600 m/300 m/ 300 m PZ8 or PZ10 (AR = 400 m PZ2) 1 mi. PZ2	X-train 20 to 30 min. PZ2 (optional) or rest	Threshold 1 mi. PZ3 6.5 mi. goal half marathon pace 1 mi. PZ3	Recovery 6 mi. PZ2	Progression 13 mi. PZ3 2 mi. PZ4
15	Off	Base 8 mi. PZ3 plus 8 × 10 sec. HS PZ10	Mixed 1 mi. PZ2 200 m/400 m/ 800 m/1K/ 800 m/400 m PZ8 or PZ10 (AR = 400 m PZ2) 1 mi. PZ2	X-train 20 to 30 min. PZ2 (optional) or rest	Threshold 1 mi. PZ3 7 mi. goal half marathon pace 1 mi. PZ3	Recovery 6 mi. PZ2	MP 1 mi. PZ3 8 mi. PZ4 1 mi. PZ3
16	Off	Base 7 mi. PZ3 plus 5 × 10 sec. HS PZ10	Lactate 1 mi. PZ2 4 × 800 m PZ8 (AR = 400 m PZ2) 1 mi. PZ2	X-train 20 to 30 min. PZ2 (optional) or rest	Threshold 1 mi. PZ3 1.5 mi. goal half marathon pace 1 mi. PZ3	Base 3 mi. plus 4 × 100 m strides PZ10	Race Half mara-thon

Table 8.10 Half Marathon Level 3 Training Plan

Week	Mon.	Tues.	Wed.	Thurs.	Fri.	Sat.	Sun.
1	Base 4 mi. PZ3 plus 1 × 10 sec. HS PZ10	Hills 1.5 mi. PZ2 6 × 400 m PZ8 (AR = 400 m PZ2) 1.5 mi. PZ2	Base 4 mi. PZ3	Progression 5 mi. PZ3 1 mi. PZ4	Fartlek 6 mi. PZ3 with 8 × 30 sec. PZ10	Base 4 mi. PZ3	Base 8 mi. PZ3
2	Base 4.5 mi. PZ3 plus 2 × 10 sec. HS PZ10	Hills 1.5 mi. PZ2 10 × 400 m PZ8 (AR = 400 m PZ2) 1.5 mi. PZ2	Base 4.5 mi. PZ3	Progression 5 mi. PZ3 1.5 mi. PZ4	Fartlek 6 mi. PZ3 with 12 × 30 sec. PZ10	Base 4.5 mi. PZ3	Base 9 mi. PZ3
3	Base 5 mi. PZ3 plus 3 × 10 sec. HS PZ10	Hills 1.5 mi. PZ2 12 × 400 m PZ10 (AR = 400 m PZ2) 1.5 mi. PZ2	Base 4.5 mi. PZ3	Progression 5 mi. PZ3 1 mi. PZ6	Fartlek 6 mi. PZ3 with 12 × 45 sec. PZ10	Base 5 mi. PZ3	Progression 9 mi. PZ3 1 mi. PZ4
4	Base 5 mi. PZ3 plus 4 × 10 sec. HS PZ10	Hills 1.5 mi. PZ2 8 × 600 m PZ8 (AR = 600 m PZ2) 1.5 mi. PZ2	Base 4 mi. PZ3	Progression 4 mi. PZ3 1 mi. PZ6	Fartlek 6 mi. PZ3 with 8 × 1 min. PZ10	Base 4.5 mi. PZ3	Progression 7 mi. PZ3 1 mi. PZ4
5	Base 6.5 mi. PZ3 plus 5 × 10 sec. HS PZ10	Hills 1.5 mi. PZ2 10 × 600 m PZ8 (AR = 600 m PZ2) 1.5 mi. PZ2	Recovery 6 mi. PZ2	Progression 6 mi. PZ3 1 mi. PZ6	Fartlek 7 mi. PZ3 with 12 × 1 min. PZ10	Base 6 mi. PZ3	Progression 9 mi. PZ3 2 mi. PZ4
6	Base 6.5 mi. PZ3 plus 6 × 10 sec. HS PZ10	Hills 1.5 mi. PZ2 12 × 400 m PZ10 (AR = 400 m PZ2) 1.5 mi. PZ2	Recovery 6 mi. PZ2	Progression 5 mi. PZ3 2 mi. PZ4	Threshold 1.5 mi. PZ3 4 × 1 mi. PZ6 (AR = 400 m PZ2) 1.5 mi. PZ3	Base 6 mi. PZ3	Progression 10 mi. PZ3 2 mi. PZ4
7	Base 7 mi. PZ3 plus 7 × 10 sec. HS PZ10	Speed 1 mi. PZ2 12 × 400 m PZ10 (AR = 400 m PZ2) 1 mi. PZ2	Recovery 6 mi. PZ2	Progression 6 mi. PZ3 2 mi. PZ4	Threshold 1.5 mi. PZ3 5 × 1 mi. PZ6 (AR = 400 m PZ2) 1.5 mi. PZ3	Base 6 mi. PZ3	Fartlek 12 mi. PZ3 with 6 × 45 sec. PZ8
8	Base 6 mi. PZ3 plus 6 × 10 sec. HS PZ10	Speed 1 mi. PZ2 8 × 400 m PZ10 (AR = 400 m PZ2) 1 mi. PZ2	Recovery 6 mi. PZ2	Progression 6 mi. PZ3 2 mi. PZ4	Threshold 1.5 mi. PZ3 4 × 1 mi. PZ6 (AR = 400 m PZ2) 1.5 mi. PZ3	Base 6 mi. PZ3	Fartlek 12 mi. PZ3 with 6 × 45 sec. PZ8

Week	Mon.	Tues.	Wed.	Thurs.	Fri.	Sat.	Sun.
9	Base 8 mi. PZ3 plus 7 × 10 sec. HS PZ10	Speed 1.5 mi. PZ2 8 × 600 m PZ10 (AR = 400 m PZ2) 1.5 mi. PZ2	Recovery 6 mi. PZ2	Progression 6 mi. PZ3 2 mi. PZ4	Threshold 1 mi. PZ3 6 × 1 mi. PZ6 (AR = 400 m PZ2) 1 mi. PZ3	Recovery 6 mi. PZ2	Fartlek 13 mi. PZ3 with 8 × 1 min. PZ8
10	Base 8 mi. PZ3 plus 8 × 10 sec. HS PZ10	Lactate 1.5 mi. PZ2 6 × 800 m PZ8 (AR = 400 m PZ2) 1.5 mi. PZ2	Recovery 7 mi. PZ2	Progression 6 mi. PZ3 2 mi. PZ4	Threshold 1.5 mi. PZ3 4 mi. PZ6 (AR = 400 m PZ2) 1.5 mi. PZ3	Recovery 7 mi. PZ2	Progression 13 mi. PZ3 1 mi. PZ4
11	Base 8 mi. PZ3 plus 9 × 10 sec. HS PZ10	Lactate 1.5 mi. PZ2 5 × 1K PZ8 (AR = 400 m PZ2) 1.5 mi. PZ2	Recovery 7 mi. PZ2	Progression 6 mi. PZ3 2 mi. PZ4	Threshold 1.5 mi. PZ3 5 mi. PZ6 (AR = 400 m PZ2) 1.5 mi. PZ3	Recovery 7 mi. PZ2	Progression 13 mi. PZ3 2 mi. PZ4
12	Base 7 mi. PZ3 plus 8 × 10 sec. HS PZ10	Lactate 1.5 mi. PZ2 6 × 800 m PZ8 (AR = 400 m PZ2) 1.5 mi. PZ2	Recovery 7 mi. PZ2	Progression 6 mi. PZ3 2 mi. PZ4	Threshold 1.5 mi. PZ3 4 mi. PZ6 (AR = 400 m PZ2) 1.5 mi. PZ3	Recovery 7 mi. PZ2	Progression 13 mi. PZ3 1 mi. PZ4
13	Base 10 mi. PZ3 plus 9 × 10 sec. HS PZ10	Mixed 1 mi. PZ2 300 m/300 m/ 600 m/600 m/ 1K/600 m/ 600 m/300 m/ 300 m PZ8 or PZ10 (AR = 400 m PZ2) 1 mi. PZ2	Recovery 8 mi. PZ2	Progression 6 mi. PZ3 2 mi. PZ4	Threshold 2 mi. PZ3 6 mi. goal half marathon pace 2 mi. PZ3	Recovery 8 mi. PZ2	Progression 14 mi. PZ3 2 mi. PZ4
14	Base 10 mi. PZ3 plus 10 × 10 sec. HS PZ10	Mixed 1 mi. PZ2 200 m/400 m/ 600 m/800 m/ 1K/800 m/ 600 m/400 m/ 200 m PZ8 or PZ10 (AR = 400 m PZ2) 1 mi. PZ2	Recovery 8 mi. PZ2	Progression 6 mi. PZ3 2 mi. PZ4	Threshold 2 mi. PZ3 7 mi. goal half marathon pace (AR = 0.5 mi. PZ2) 2 mi. PZ3	Recovery 8 mi. PZ2	Progression 16 mi. PZ3 2 mi. PZ4

(continued)

Table 8.10 Half Marathon Level 3 Training Plan *(continued)*

Week	Mon.	Tues.	Wed.	Thurs.	Fri.	Sat.	Sun.
15	Base 10 mi. PZ3 plus 10 × 10 sec. HS PZ10	Mixed 1 mi. PZ2 300 m/300 m/ 600 m/600 m/ 1K/1K/ 600 m/600 m/ 300 m/300 m PZ8 or PZ10 (AR = 400 m PZ2) 1 mi. PZ2	Recovery 6 mi. PZ2	Progression 5 mi. PZ3 2 mi. PZ4	Threshold 2 mi. PZ3 2 × 4 mi. goal half marathon pace (AR = 0.5 mi. PZ2) 2 mi. PZ3	Recovery 6 mi. PZ2	MP 1 mi. PZ3 10 mi. PZ4 1 mi. PZ3
16	Base 8 mi. PZ3 plus 6× 10 sec. HS PZ10	Lactate 1.5 mi. PZ2 5 × 800 m PZ8 (AR = 400 m PZ2) 1.5 mi. PZ2	Base 5 mi. PZ3	Threshold 1 mi. PZ3 2 mi. goal half mara-thon pace 1 mi. PZ3	Base 4 mi. PZ3	Base 3 mi. PZ3 plus 4 × 100 m strides PZ10	Race Half mara-thon

Table 8.11 Marathon Level 1 Training Plan

Week	Mon.	Tues.	Wed.	Thurs.	Fri.	Sat.	Sun.
1	Off	Base 3 mi. PZ3	Hills 1 mi. PZ2 2 × 200 m PZ10 (AR = 200 m PZ2) 1 mi. PZ2	X-train 20 to 30 min. PZ2 (optional) or rest	Fartlek 3 mi. PZ3 with 4 × 30 sec. PZ8	X-train 20 to 30 min. PZ2 (optional) or rest	Progression 3 mi. PZ3 1 mi. PZ4
2	Off	Base 3.5 mi. PZ3 plus 1 × 10 sec. HS PZ10	Hills 1 mi. PZ2 4 × 400 m PZ8 (AR = 400 m PZ2) 1 mi. PZ2	X-train 20 to 30 min. PZ2 (optional) or rest	Fartlek 3.5 mi. PZ3 with 6 × 30 sec. PZ8	X-train 20 to 30 min. PZ2 (optional) or rest	Progression 4.5 mi. PZ3 0.5 mi. PZ6
3	Off	Base 4 mi. PZ3 plus 2 × 10 sec. HS PZ10	Hills 1 mi. PZ2 4 × 400 m PZ10 (AR = 400 m PZ2) 1 mi. PZ2	X-train 20 to 30 min. PZ2 (optional) or rest	Fartlek 4 mi. PZ3 with 5 × 45 sec. PZ8	X-train 20 to 30 min. PZ2 (optional) or rest	Progression 5 mi. PZ3 1 mi. PZ6
4	Off	Base 4.5 mi. PZ3 plus 3 × 10 sec. HS PZ10	Hills 1 mi. PZ2 4 × 400 m PZ10 (AR = 400 m PZ2) 1 mi. PZ2	X-train 20 to 30 min. PZ2 (optional) or rest	Fartlek 4.5 mi. PZ3 with 4 × 1 min. PZ8	X-train 20 to 30 min. PZ2 (optional) or rest	Progression 6.5 mi. PZ3 0.5 mi. PZ6
5	Off	Base 5 mi. PZ3 plus 4 × 10 sec. HS PZ10	Speed 1 mi. PZ2 6 × 300 m PZ10 (AR = 300 m PZ2) 1 mi. PZ2	X-train 20 to 30 min. PZ2 (optional) or rest	Fartlek 4.5 mi. PZ3 with 5 × 1 min. PZ8	X-train 20 to 30 min. PZ2 (optional) or rest	Progression 7 mi. PZ3 1 mi. PZ6
6	Off	Base 5.5 mi. PZ3 plus 5 × 10 sec. HS PZ10	Speed 1 mi. PZ2 6 × 400 m PZ10 (AR = 400 m PZ2) 1 mi. PZ2	X-train 20 to 30 min. PZ2 (optional) or rest	Lactate 1 mi. PZ2 7 × (1 min. PZ8, 1 min. PZ2) 1 mi. PZ2	X-train 20 to 30 min. PZ2 (optional) or rest	Progression 9 mi. PZ3 1 mi. PZ6
7	Off	Base 5.5 mi. PZ3 plus 6 × 10 sec. HS PZ10	Speed 1 mi. PZ2 4 × 600 m PZ10 (AR = 400 m PZ2) 1 mi. PZ2	X-train 20 to 30 min. PZ2 (optional) or rest	Lactate 1 mi. PZ2 8 × (1 mi.n. PZ8, 1 mi.n. PZ2) 1 mi. PZ2	X-train 20 to 30 min. PZ2 (optional) or rest	Progression 10 mi. PZ3 1 mi. PZ6

(continued)

159

Table 8.11 Marathon Level 1 Training Plan *(continued)*

Week	Mon.	Tues.	Wed.	Thurs.	Fri.	Sat.	Sun.
8	Off	Base 5 mi. PZ3 plus 4 × 10 sec. HS PZ10	Speed 1 mi. PZ2 4 × 400 m PZ10 (AR = 400 m PZ2) 1 mi. PZ2	X-train 20 to 30 min. PZ2 (optional) or rest	Fartlek 4.5 mi. PZ3 with 5 × 1 min. PZ8	X-train 20 to 30 min. PZ2 (optional) or rest	Race 10K
9	Off	Base 5.5 mi. PZ3 plus 6 × 10 sec. HS PZ10	Lactate 1 mi. PZ2 8 × 600 m PZ8 (AR = 400 m PZ2) 1 mi. PZ2	X-train 20 to 30 min. PZ2 (optional) or rest	Threshold 1 mi. PZ3 3 × 1 mi. PZ6 (AR = 400 m PZ2) 1 mi. PZ3	X-train 20 to 30 min. PZ2 (optional) or rest	Base 12 mi. PZ3
10	Off	Base 6 mi. PZ3 plus 6 × 10 sec. HS PZ10	Lactate 1 mi. PZ2 4 × 800 m PZ8 (AR = 400 m PZ2) 1 mi. PZ2	X-train 20 to 30 min. PZ2 (optional) or rest	Threshold 1 mi. PZ3 2.5 mi. PZ6 1 mi. PZ3	X-train 20 to 30 min. PZ2 (optional) or rest	Base 13 mi. PZ3
11	Off	Base 6 mi. PZ3 plus 6 × 10 sec. HS PZ10	Lactate 1 mi. PZ2 4 × 1K PZ8 (AR = 400 m PZ2) 1 mi. PZ2	X-train 20 to 30 min. PZ2 (optional) or rest	Threshold 1 mi. PZ3 3 mi. PZ6 1 mi. PZ3	X-train 20 to 30 min. PZ2 (optional) or rest	Base 14 mi. PZ3
12	Off	Base 6 mi. PZ3 plus 6 × 10 sec. HS PZ10	Lactate 1 mi. PZ2 3 × 1K PZ8 (AR = 400 m PZ2) 1 mi. PZ2	X-train 20 to 30 min. PZ2 (optional) or rest	Threshold 1 mi. PZ3 4 mi. PZ6 1 mi. PZ3	Off	Race Half marathon
13	Off	Base 6 mi. PZ3 plus 6 × 10 sec. HS PZ10	Mixed 1 mi. PZ2 200 m/400 m/ 800 m/400 m/ 200 m PZ8 to PZ10 (AR = 400 m PZ2) 1 mi. PZ2	X-train 20 to 30 min. PZ2 (optional) or rest	Threshold 1 mi. PZ3 5 mi. PZ6 1 mi. PZ3	X-train 20 to 30 min. PZ2 (optional) or rest	Base 16 mi. PZ3
14	Off	Base 6 mi. PZ3 plus 6 × 10 sec. HS PZ10	Fartlek 7 mi. PZ3 with 6 × 1 min. PZ8	X-train 20 to 30 min. PZ2 (optional) or rest	Threshold 1 mi. PZ3 2 mi. PZ4 2 mi. PZ6 1 mi. PZ3	X-train 20 to 30 min. PZ2 (optional) or rest	Base 17 mi. PZ3

Week	Mon.	Tues.	Wed.	Thurs.	Fri.	Sat.	Sun.
15	Off	Base 5 mi. PZ3 plus 4 × 10 sec. HS PZ10	Mixed 1 mi. PZ2 400 m/800 m/ 1K/800 m/ 400 m PZ8 or PZ10 (AR = 400 m PZ2) 1 mi. PZ2	X-train 20 to 30 min. PZ2 (optional) or rest	MP 1 mi. PZ3 10K PZ4 1 mi. PZ3	X-train 20 to 30 min. PZ2 (optional) or rest	Base 13 mi. PZ3
16	Off	Base 6 mi. PZ3 plus 6 × 10 sec. HS PZ10	Fartlek 8 mi. PZ3 with 6 × 1 min. PZ8	X-train 20 to 30 min. PZ2 (optional) or rest	Progression 3 mi. PZ3 2 mi. PZ4 1 mi. PZ6	Off	Base 20 mi. PZ3
17	Off	Base 6 mi. PZ3 plus 6 × 10 sec. HS PZ10	Mixed 1 mi. PZ2 1K/600 m/ 300 m PZ8 or PZ10 (AR = 400 m PZ2) 1 mi. PZ2	X-train 20 to 30 min. PZ2 (optional) or rest	Progression 3 mi. PZ3 3 mi. PZ4 1 mi. PZ6	Off	Base 15 mi. PZ3
18	Off	MP 1 mi. PZ3 2 mi. PZ4 1 mi. PZ3	Base 3 mi. PZ3	Threshold 1 mi. PZ3 1.5 mi. PZ6 1 mi. PZ3	Base 3 mi. PZ3	Off	Race Marathon

Table 8.12 Marathon Level 2 Training Plan

Week	Mon.	Tues.	Wed.	Thurs.	Fri.	Sat.	Sun.
1	Off	Base 3.5 mi. PZ3 plus 1 × 10 sec. HS PZ10	Hills 1.5 mi. PZ2 4 × 200 m PZ10 (AR = 200 m PZ2) 1 mi. PZ2	X-train 20 to 30 min. PZ2 (optional) or rest	Fartlek 4 mi. PZ3 with 6 × 30 sec. PZ8	Base 4 mi. PZ3 plus 3 × 100 m strides PZ10	Progression 5 mi. PZ3 1 mi. PZ4
2	Off	Base 4 mi. PZ3 plus 2 × 10 sec. HS PZ10	Hills 1.5 mi. PZ2 7 × 400 m PZ8 (AR = 400 m PZ2) 1 mi. PZ2	X-train 20 to 30 min. PZ2 (optional) or rest	Fartlek 4.5 mi. PZ3 with 10 × 30 sec. PZ8	Base 4 mi. PZ3	Progression 6.5 mi. PZ3 0.5 mi. PZ6
3	Off	Base 5 mi. PZ3 plus 3 × 10 sec. HS PZ10	Hills 1.5 mi. PZ2 7 × 400 m PZ10 (AR = 400 m PZ2) 1 mi. PZ2	X-train 20 to 30 min. PZ2 (optional) or rest	Fartlek 5 mi. PZ3 with 6 × 45 sec. PZ8	Base 4.5 mi. PZ3 plus 4 × 100 m strides PZ10	Progression 9 mi. PZ3 1 mi. PZ6
4	Off	Base 5 mi. PZ3 plus 4 × 10 sec. HS PZ10	Hills 1.5 mi. PZ2 6 × 400 m PZ10 (AR = 400 m PZ2) 1 mi. PZ2	X-train 20 to 30 min. PZ2 (optional) or rest	Fartlek 5 mi. PZ3 with 6 × 1 min. PZ8	Base 4 mi. PZ3	Progression 9.5 mi. PZ3 0.5 mi. PZ6
5	Off	Base 6 mi. PZ3 plus 5 × 10 sec. HS PZ10	Speed 1 mi. PZ2 8 × 300 m PZ10 (AR = 400 m PZ2) 1 mi. PZ2	X-train 20 to 30 min. PZ2 (optional) or rest	Fartlek 6 mi. PZ3 with 8 × 1 min. PZ8	Base 5 mi. PZ3	Progression 11 mi. PZ3 1 mi. PZ6
6	Off	Base 6.5 mi. PZ3 plus 6 × 10 sec. HS PZ10	Speed 1.5 mi. PZ2 10 × 400 m PZ10 (AR = 400 m PZ2) 1 mi. PZ2	X-train 20 to 30 min. PZ2 (optional) or rest	Lactate 1.5 mi. PZ2 10 × (1 min. PZ8, 1 min. PZ2) 1.5 mi. PZ2	Base 5 mi. PZ3	Progression 11.5 mi. PZ3 1.5 mi. PZ6
7	Off	Base 6.5 mi. PZ3 plus 7 × 10 sec. HS PZ10	Speed 1.5 mi. PZ2 5 × 600 m PZ10 (AR = 400 m PZ2) 1 mi. PZ2	X-train 20 to 30 min. PZ2 (optional) or rest	Lactate 1.5 mi. PZ2 12 × (1 min. PZ8, 1 min. PZ2) 1.5 mi. PZ2	Base 5 mi. PZ3	Progression 12.5 mi. PZ3 1.5 mi. PZ6

Week	Mon.	Tues.	Wed.	Thurs.	Fri.	Sat.	Sun.
8	Off	Base 6 mi. PZ3 plus 6 × 10 sec. HS PZ10	Speed 1 mi. PZ2 6 × 400 m PZ10 (AR = 400 m PZ2) 1 mi. PZ2	X-train 20 to 30 min. PZ2 (optional) or rest	Fartlek 6 mi. PZ3 with 8 × 1 min. PZ8	Recovery 3 mi. PZ2	Race 10K
9	Off	Base 7 mi. PZ3 plus 7 × 10 sec. HS PZ10	Lactate 1 mi. PZ2 8 × 600 m PZ10 (AR = 400 m PZ2) 1 mi. PZ2	X-train 20 to 30 min. PZ2 (optional) or rest	Threshold 1 mi. PZ3 5 × 1 mi. PZ6 (AR = 400 m PZ2) 1 mi. PZ3	Recovery 6 mi. PZ2	Base 16 mi. PZ3
10	Off	Base 7 mi. PZ3 plus 8 × 10 sec. HS PZ10	Lactate 1 mi. PZ2 5 × 800 m PZ8 (AR = 400 m PZ2) 1 mi. PZ2	X-train 20 to 30 min. PZ2 (optional) or rest	Threshold 1.5 mi. PZ3 3 mi. PZ6 (AR = 400 m PZ2) 1.5 mi. PZ3	Recovery 6 mi. PZ2	Base 17 mi. PZ3
11	Off	Base 7 mi. PZ3 plus 8 × 10 sec. HS PZ10	Lactate 1 mi. PZ2 5 × 1K PZ8 (AR = 400 m PZ2) 1 mi. PZ2	X-train 20 to 30 min. PZ2 (optional) or rest	Threshold 1.5 mi. PZ3 4 mi. PZ6 (AR = 400 m PZ2) 1.5 mi. PZ3	Recovery 6 mi. PZ2	Base 18 mi. PZ3
12	Off	Base 6 mi. PZ3 plus 8 × 10 sec. HS PZ10	Lactate 1 mi. PZ2 4 × 1K PZ8 (AR = 400 m PZ2) 1 mi. PZ2	X-train 20 to 30 min. PZ2 (optional) or rest	Threshold 1.5 mi. PZ3 3 mi. PZ6 (AR = 400 m PZ2) 1.5 mi. PZ3	Recovery 3 mi. PZ2	Race Half marathon
13	Off	Base 8 mi. PZ3 plus 8 × 10 sec. HS PZ10	Mixed 1 mi. PZ2 300 m/600 m/ 1K/600 m/ 300 m PZ8 or PZ10 (AR = 400 m PZ2) 1 mi. PZ2	X-train 20 to 30 min. PZ2 (optional) or rest	Threshold 1 mi. PZ3 6 mi. PZ6 1 mi. PZ3	Recovery 6 mi. PZ2	Base 20 mi. PZ3
14	Off	Base 8 mi. PZ3 plus 8 × 10 sec. HS PZ10	Fartlek 10 mi. PZ3 with 8 × 1 min. PZ8	X-train 20 to 30 min. PZ2 (optional) or rest	Threshold 1 mi. PZ3 3 mi. PZ4 2 mi. PZ6 1 mi. PZ3	Recovery 6 mi. PZ2	Progression 13 mi. PZ3 3 mi. PZ4

(continued)

Table 8.12 Marathon Level 2 Training Plan *(continued)*

Week	Mon.	Tues.	Wed.	Thurs.	Fri.	Sat.	Sun.
15	Off	Base 6 mi. PZ3 plus 6 × 10 sec. HS PZ10	Mixed 1 mi. PZ2 200 m/400 m/ 800 m/1K/ 800 m/400 m PZ8 or PZ10 (AR = 400 m PZ2) 1 mi. PZ2	X-train 20 to 30 min. PZ2 (optional) or rest	Threshold 1 mi. PZ3 4 mi. PZ6 1 mi. PZ3	Recovery 6 mi. PZ2	Progression 10 mi. PZ3 4 mi. PZ4
16	Off	Base 8 mi. PZ3 plus 8 × 10 sec. HS PZ10	Fartlek 12 mi. PZ3 with 8 × 1 min. PZ8	X-train 20 to 30 min. PZ2 (optional) or rest	Progression 4 mi. PZ3 3 mi. PZ4 1 mi. PZ6	Base 6 mi. PZ3	MP 10 mi. PZ3 10 mi. goal marathon pace
17	Off	Base 8 mi. PZ3 plus 8 × 10 sec. HS PZ10	Mixed 1 mi. PZ2 300 m/600 m/ 1K/600 m/ 300 m PZ8 or PZ10 (AR = 400 m PZ2) 1 mi. PZ2	X-train 20 to 30 min. PZ2 (optional) or rest	Progression 4.5 mi. PZ3 4 mi. PZ4 1.5 mi. PZ6	Base 6 mi. PZ3	Progression 10 mi. PZ3 4 mi. PZ4
18	Off	MP 1 mi. PZ3 4 mi. PZ4 1 mi. PZ3	Base 4 mi. PZ3	Threshold 1 mi. PZ3 2.5 mi. PZ6 1 mi. PZ3	Base 4 mi. PZ3	Base 3 mi. PZ3 plus 4 × 100 m strides PZ10	Race Marathon

Table 8.13 Marathon Level 3 Training Plan

Week	Mon.	Tues.	Wed.	Thurs.	Fri.	Sat.	Sun.
1	Base 4 mi. PZ3 plus 1 × 10 sec. HS PZ10	Hills 1.5 mi. PZ2 6 × 400 m PZ8 (AR = 400 m PZ2) 1.5 mi. PZ2	Base 4 mi. PZ3	Progression 5 mi. PZ3 1 mi. PZ4	Fartlek 6 mi. PZ3 with 8 × 30 sec. PZ8	Base 4 mi. PZ3 plus 4 × 100 m strides PZ10	Progression 3 mi. PZ3 1 mi. PZ4
2	Base 4.5 mi. PZ3 plus 2 × 10 sec. HS PZ10	Hills 1.5 mi. PZ2 10 × 200 m PZ10 (AR = 200 m PZ2) 1.5 mi. PZ2	Base 4.5 mi. PZ3	Progression 5 mi. PZ3 1.5 mi. PZ4	Fartlek 6 mi. PZ3 with 12 × 30 sec. PZ8	Base 4.5 mi. PZ3	Progression 10 mi. PZ3 1 mi. PZ6
3	Base 5 mi. PZ3 plus 3 × 10 sec. HS PZ10	Hills 1.5 mi. PZ2 10 × 400 m PZ10 (AR = 400 m PZ2) 1.5 mi. PZ2	Base 4.5 mi. PZ3	Progression 5 mi. PZ3 1 mi. PZ4	Fartlek 7 mi. PZ3 with 7 × 45 sec. PZ8	Base 5 mi. PZ3 plus 6 × 100 m strides PZ10	Progression 11 mi. PZ3 1 mi. PZ6
4	Base 5 mi. PZ3 plus 4 × 10 sec. HS PZ10	Hills 1.5 mi. PZ2 8 × 400 m PZ10 (AR = 400 m PZ2) 1.5 mi. PZ2	Base 4 mi. PZ3	Progression 4 mi. PZ3 1 mi. PZ6	Fartlek 6 mi. PZ3 with 8 × 1 min. PZ8	Base 4.5 mi. PZ3	Base 11 mi. PZ3
5	Base 6.5 mi. PZ3 plus 5 × 10 sec. HS PZ10	Hills 1.5 mi. PZ2 10 × 300 m PZ10 (AR = 400 m PZ2) 1.5 mi. PZ2	Recovery 6 mi. PZ2	Progression 6 mi. PZ3 1 mi. PZ6	Fartlek 7 mi. PZ3 with 12 × 1 min. PZ8	Base 6 mi. PZ3	Progression 13 mi. PZ3 1 mi. PZ4
6	Base 6.5 mi. PZ3 plus 6 × 10 sec. HS PZ10	Speed 1.5 mi. PZ2 12 × 400 m PZ10 (AR = 400 m PZ2) 1.5 mi. PZ2	Recovery 6 mi. PZ2	Progression 5.5 mi. PZ3 1.5 mi. PZ6	Lactate 2 mi. PZ2 12 × (1 min. PZ8, 1 min. PZ2) 2 mi. PZ2	Base 6 mi. PZ3	Progression 14 mi. PZ3 2 mi. PZ4
7	Base 6.5 mi. PZ3 plus 7 × 10 sec. HS PZ10	Speed 1.5 mi. PZ2 6 × 600 m PZ10 (AR = 400 m PZ2) 1.5 mi. PZ2	Recovery 6 mi. PZ2	Progression 5.5 mi. PZ3 1.5 mi. PZ6	Lactate 2 mi. PZ2 14 × (1 min. PZ8, 1 min. PZ2) 2 mi. PZ2	Base 6 mi. PZ3	Progression 16 mi. PZ3 2 mi. PZ4

(continued)

Table 8.13 Marathon Level 3 Training Plan *(continued)*

Week	Mon.	Tues.	Wed.	Thurs.	Fri.	Sat.	Sun.
8	Base 6 mi. PZ3 plus 6 × 10 sec. HS PZ10	Speed 1 mi. PZ2 8 × 400 m PZ10 (AR = 400 m PZ2) 1 mi. PZ2	Recovery 6 mi. PZ2	Progression 6 mi. PZ3 2 mi. PZ4	Fartlek 7 mi. PZ3 with 12 × 1 min. PZ8	Recovery 4 mi. PZ2	Race 10K
9	Base 8 mi. PZ3 plus 7 × 10 sec. HS PZ10	Lactate 1.5 mi. PZ2 9 × 600 m PZ10 (AR = 400 m PZ2) 1.5 mi. PZ2	Recovery 6 mi. PZ2	Progression 6 mi. PZ3 2 mi. PZ4	Threshold 1 mi. PZ3 6 × 1 mi. PZ6 (AR = 400 m PZ2) 1 mi. PZ3	Recovery 6 mi. PZ2	Base 20 mi. PZ3
10	Base 8 mi. PZ3 plus 8 × 10 sec. HS PZ10	Lactate 1.5 mi. PZ2 6 × 800 m PZ8 (AR = 400 m PZ2) 1.5 mi. PZ2	Recovery 7 mi. PZ2	Progression 6 mi. PZ3 2 mi. PZ4	Threshold 1.5 mi. PZ3 4 mi. PZ6 (AR = 400 m PZ2) 1.5 mi. PZ3	Recovery 7 mi. PZ2	Progression 14 mi. PZ3 4 mi. PZ4
11	Base 8 mi. PZ3 plus 9 × 10 sec. HS PZ10	Lactate 1.5 mi. PZ2 5 × 1K PZ8 (AR = 400 m PZ2) 1.5 mi. PZ2	Recovery 7 mi. PZ2	Progression 6 mi. PZ3 2 mi. PZ4	Threshold 1.5 mi. PZ3 5 mi. PZ6 (AR = 400 m PZ2) 1.5 mi. PZ3	Recovery 7 mi. PZ2	Base 22 mi. PZ3
12	Base 7 mi. PZ3 plus 8 × 10 sec. HS PZ10	Lactate 1.5 mi. PZ2 5 × 1K PZ8 (AR = 400 m PZ2) 1.5 mi. PZ2	Recovery 7 mi. PZ2	Progression 6 mi. PZ3 2 mi. PZ4	Threshold 1.5 mi. PZ3 4 mi. PZ6 (AR = 400 m PZ2) 1.5 mi. PZ3	Recovery 4 mi. PZ2	Race Half marathon
13	Base 10 mi. PZ3 plus 9 × 10 sec. HS PZ10	Mixed 1 mi. PZ2 300 m/300 m/ 600 m/600 m/ 1K/600 m/ 600 m/300 m/ 300 m PZ8 or PZ10 (AR = 400 m PZ2) 1 mi. PZ2	Recovery 8 mi. PZ2	Progression 6 mi. PZ3 2 mi. PZ4	Threshold 2 mi. PZ3 6 mi. PZ6 2 mi. PZ3	Recovery 8 mi. PZ2	Base 24 mi. PZ3

Week	Mon.	Tues.	Wed.	Thurs.	Fri.	Sat.	Sun.
14	Base 10 mi. PZ3 plus 10 × 10 sec. HS PZ10	Fartlek 12 mi. PZ3 with 10 × 1 min. PZ8	Recovery 8 mi. PZ2	Progression 6 mi. PZ3 2 mi. PZ4	Threshold 2 mi. PZ3 3 mi. PZ4 3 mi. PZ6 (AR = 0.5 mi. PZ2) 2 mi. PZ3	Recovery 8 mi. PZ2	MP 2 mi. PZ3 8 mi. goal marathon pace 2 mi. PZ3
15	Base 7 mi. PZ3 plus 8 × 10 sec. HS PZ10	Mixed 1 mi. PZ2 200 m/400 m/ 600 m/800 m/ 1K/800 m/ 600 m/400 m/ 200 m PZ8 or PZ10 (AR = 400 m PZ2) 1 mi. PZ2	Recovery 6 mi. PZ2	Progression 5 mi. PZ3 2 mi. PZ4	Threshold 2 mi. PZ3 2 × 3 mi. PZ6 (AR = 0.5 mi. PZ2) 2 mi. PZ3	Recovery 6 mi. PZ2	Progression 12 mi. PZ3 4 mi. PZ4
16	Base 10 mi. PZ3 plus 10 × 10 sec. HS PZ10	Fartlek 15 mi. PZ3 with 8 × 1 min. PZ8	Base 6 mi. PZ3	Base 9 mi. PZ3	Progression 6 mi. PZ3 3 mi. PZ4 1 mi. PZ6	Base 6 mi. PZ3	MP 1 mi. PZ3 14 mi. goal marathon pace 1 mi. PZ3
17	Base 10 mi. PZ3 plus 10 × 10 sec. HS PZ10	Mixed 1 mi. PZ2 400 m/800 m/ 1 mi./ 800 m/400 m at PZ6 or PZ10 (AR = 400 m PZ2) 1 mi. PZ2	Base 8 mi. PZ3	Base 7 mi. PZ3	Progression 6 mi. PZ3 4 mi. PZ4 2 mi. PZ6	Base 7 mi. PZ3	Progression 12 mi. PZ3 4 mi. PZ4
18	Base 7 mi. PZ3 plus 6 × 10 sec. HS PZ10	MP 1 mi. PZ3 6 mi. PZ4 1 mi. PZ3	Base 5 mi. PZ3	Threshold 1 mi. PZ3 3 mi. PZ6 1 mi. PZ3	Base 4 mi. PZ3	Base 3 mi. PZ3 plus 4 × 100 m strides PZ10	Race Marathon

CUSTOMIZING THE PLANS TO FIT INDIVIDUAL NEEDS

As suggested earlier, no ready-made training plan is ever a perfect fit for any runner. Some amount of customization is always necessary. Five basic types of adjustments can be made to the plan you choose from among those presented in this chapter:

Rearranging Days

No rule says you have to do your long runs on Sundays where we've put them. If you prefer to rest on Sundays, or you work on Sundays, or you prefer not to do your long runs on Sundays for any other reason, you can move them to another day. The same principle applies to the remaining days in the week. Feel free to shuffle workouts around within the week as necessary to make the plan work with your schedule. Just avoid doing key workouts, such as high-intensity runs and long runs, on back-to-back days.

Adding or Subtracting Weeks

You need not confine yourself to the fixed length of these ready-made plans. If your current fitness level is a little below the level required at the start of a given plan, take a few weeks to gradually ramp up your training to the level of week 1 and then start the plan officially. On the other hand, if the race you want to peak for is too soon for you to complete a full plan in preparation for that race, and your fitness level is higher than the level required at its beginning, you may choose to start a few weeks into it. Be careful not to get in over your head, though. All of these plans include a fair amount of high-intensity running, which you might not be used to doing. So even if the total mileage in, say, week 5 of the level 3 half-marathon training plan is not greater than what you've been doing, it may overwhelm you if most of the running you've been doing is fairly easy.

Adding Runs

If the key workouts in a given training plan seem like a good fit for you, but you are accustomed to running more frequently, go ahead and insert additional runs into the plan as appropriate. All of these additional runs should be base and recovery runs. The plans already have all the higher-intensity running you should do. If you insert more than one additional run into each week, be sure to distribute them evenly so that your running is not too concentrated within a few days.

Adjusting Individual Workouts

You can adjust the challenge level of individual key workouts to make them better suited to your fitness level. If a given workout seems a little too easy, make it more challenging; if it seems a bit too hard, dial it back somewhat. Naturally, the more experienced you are, the more reliably you can judge the appropriateness of the key workouts in a ready-made plan. You can use the workout tables in chapter 4 to help you make these adjustments.

Making Reactive Adjustments

When executing any training plan, it is always necessary to make adjustments to future workouts based on how your body responds to completed workouts. When you feel more fatigued than expected or an injury seems imminent, replace planned runs with days off or easier runs. When you identify an aspect of your fitness that needs more attention than the plan is giving it, modify the plan to shore up that weakness. Use the guidelines in chapter 7 to steer this process.

CHAPTER

Developing In-Race Strategies for Faster Times

Speed and distance devices are as useful in racing as they are in training. The process of using your speed and distance device to benefit your racing actually begins in training. Proper use of your device will help you establish an appropriate goal pace for an upcoming race. Also, you can use your speed and distance device in training to improve your pacing ability and to perform race-pace workouts that put the finishing touches on your fitness development. These workouts provide the additional benefit of getting your body accustomed to the challenge of prolonged running at your goal race pace. During the race itself, of course, you can use your speed and distance device to monitor and control your pace. However, it's important not to rely too much on technology to govern your pacing during races. In the end, you will race best if you run by feel—and simply run as hard as you can! When racing it's best to use technology to guide your efforts, rather than to dictate them.

DETERMINING YOUR RACE PACE

Establishing an appropriate goal pace is relatively easy for shorter races such as 5K and 10K. The simplest way to go about it is to run a tune-up race of the same distance before you run your peak race. Your finishing time for the tune-up race will give you a solid basis to choose a goal time for your peak race. Once you have that goal time, it's easy to calculate the average pace you need to sustain to achieve that goal. Just how much faster you can expect to run in your peak race than in your tune-up race of the same distance depends primarily on how much time separates the two races and on how much fitter you can expect to be for your peak race based on the training you have planned. Your prediction will be most accurate if you make a ballpark guess immediately after running your tune-up race and then fine-tune it as you move closer to the peak race based on how your fitness progresses. Comparing your performance in recent key workouts against your performance in key workouts done before the tune-up race will give you a good measure of your improvement.

If you can't find an appropriate tune-up race to run, you can run a time trial on your own instead. Be sure to run your time trial in a fairly fresh state so that your performance is not limited by preexisting fatigue. Also be sure to run on a favorable course for fast running. Using a track as your venue will give you the most favorable conditions for fast running and a slightly more accurate measurement than you would get from your speed and distance device, which will probably be 1 to 2 percent inaccurate in one direction or the other. Another option is to run a time trial on a course that is similar to that of your peak race, which, in the case of hillier peak race courses, will give you a more accurate prediction of your likely pace. But we favor flat and fast routes because it is often difficult to find routes that closely match the elevation profiles of hillier race courses and because flat-route time trials provide a truer measure of your actual fitness level.

Equal-distance tune-up races and time trials are not a viable option when your peak race is a half marathon or a marathon. However, you can still use a 5K or 10K tune-up race or time trial along with a race time equivalence table or calculator to generate a reasonably reliable predicted finish time for a half marathon or marathon. There's a good race time equivalence table in *Daniels' Running Formula,* and coach Greg McMillan has a good calculator at www.mcmillanrunning.com. For example, suppose you are training for a half marathon and along the way you run a 10K tune-up race in 37:55. When you punch this number into McMillan's running calculator, you get a predicted half-marathon finish time of 1:24:22, or 6:27 per mile. If your half-marathon peak race is still several weeks away, you can expect to run somewhat faster—perhaps in the low 1:23:00s or high 1:22:00s.

Be forewarned, however, that these tables and calculators assume optimal training for each race distance. Optimal training for a marathon includes a lot more mileage than optimal training for a 10K. However, most runners train far closer to optimally for shorter races than they do for the marathon. They are unwilling or unable to increase their mileage enough to make their marathon training truly equivalent to their training for shorter races. Thus, we have found that the race performance equivalence calculators tend to be very accurate from the 5K to the half marathon but overestimate performance for the marathon. Keep this in mind when using them.

LEARNING THE ART OF PACING

If you're like most runners, you learned the art of pacing the hard way. You started way too fast in your first kids' fun run or 1-mile running test in high school and hit the wall long before you reached the finish line, staggering and wheezing. But you learned your lesson and held yourself back a bit at the start of your next run, and today you're able to avoid an early bonk in most of your hard workouts and races.

Until recently, the phenomenon of pacing received very little attention from exercise scientists. That's probably because it's clearly seated in the subconscious brain: Every runner knows that pacing is guided by a mysterious sense of feel, making it difficult to access. But new technologies and ideas have given some of today's brightest young exercise scientists a window into how pacing really works. One of the leading researchers on pacing in endurance sports is Ross Tucker, PhD, associate professor of exercise physiology at the University of Cape Town, South Africa. Tucker prefers to refer to the physiological pacing mechanism as *anticipatory regulation* because he feels it's based on an anticipated endpoint of exercise—the finish line, in the case of running races. According to Tucker and Noakes (2009), the whole premise for pacing is that the brain is regulating exercise performance in order to protect the body from reaching a limit or a failure point or a potentially harmful level before the end of exercise, which is a controversial viewpoint in the field of exercise physiology.

In other words, pacing is the brain's way of enabling you to run as hard as you can without actually running yourself to death. But how does your brain know and enforce this limit? According to Tucker and Noakes, the brain is constantly receiving inputs and signals from every system in the body and then interpreting those signals in the context of the exercise bout. It then alters the exercise intensity by changing the degree of muscle activation to either slow you down or allow you to speed up.

Although controversial, there is some evidence to support the notion of anticipatory regulation, some of which comes from Tucker's studies of exercise in hot environments. In one such study, cyclists predictably took longer to complete a time trial in the heat than in a cool environment. But their core body temperature rose to the same level in both trials. While the cyclists started both trials at the same pace, they slowed down unconsciously within five minutes of starting the hot time trial, when their core body temperature was still well below the safety limit. The fact that this happened so early suggests that the pacing decision was made well before the physiological factors forced the athletes to slow down. In this scenario, anticipatory regulation enabled the athletes to complete the time trial much faster than they would have completed it if they had continued at their normal power-output level despite the heat, in which case they would have become overheated halfway through the time trial and slowed down precipitously. Tucker suggests that the brain senses the skin temperature and the rate of body temperature increase and uses this information to calculate how hard it can drive the muscles given the anticipated duration of the time trial. In cool environments, he adds, other factors such as the pH level of the muscles and the glucose concentration in the blood are likely used in making similar calculations.

According to Tucker, anticipatory regulation becomes more reliable with experience. The more you experience fatigue in training and racing, the more your brain becomes tuned into your true limits, even as those limits change because of increasing fitness. As a result, you become better able to start races at just the right speed to ensure you neither slow down before the finish line nor cross it feeling as though you could have run harder. This view is supported by the research of Carl Foster, PhD, presented later in this chapter.

While pacing is done by feel, technology can accelerate the process of learning the art of pacing because, again, anticipatory regulation is based on knowledge of an expected end point of exercise (the finish line), and a speed and distance device provides constant real-time information about progress toward the end of exercise. The value of such feedback is shown in a 2009 study by researchers at the University of Exeter, England (Mauger, Jones, and Williams 2009). Eighteen competitive cyclists were divided into two groups, each of whom performed a series of four 4-kilometer cycling time trials separated by 17-minute recovery periods. Both groups were instructed to complete each time trial in the shortest time possible, but members of one group were told the distance of the time trials before starting and were given distance feedback information throughout each trial, whereas members of the second group completed all four time trials blindly, although aware that the distance (whatever it was) of the four time trials was the same.

As you probably could have predicted, in the first time trial members of the blind group were far more conservative than members of the aware group and completed the time trial much more slowly. But with each subsequent repetition of the time trial, the blind cyclists went a little faster until, in the fourth and last time trial, the average finish times of the two groups were identical. So members of the blind group were able to catch up to those with distance information, but this information gave the latter group a big head start. In a similar way, wearing a speed and distance device in training can accelerate your gaining a feel for the fastest pace you can run over any given distance.

Dr. Charles Pedlar on Training Elite Runners With Speed and Distance Technology

Dr. Charles Pedlar is an exercise physiologist employed by the English Institute of Sport to provide physiological support to elite British endurance athletes. This support consists of administering physiological testing, consulting with coaches, and helping both coaches and athletes plan training and troubleshoot problems on the basis of the data he collects.

Among the elite distance runners Pedlar has worked with are 2008 Olympic 1500-meter finalist Andy Baddeley, 2008 world junior 1500-meter champion Stephanie Twell, 2009 London Marathon runner-up Mara Yamauchi, and 2009 European indoor 3000-meter champion Mo Farah. All of these runners and the many others Pedlar works with use speed and distance devices and embrace their use. "They like the ease of use and to have a training log very easily constructed," he says. "They like to know how far they've run, how fast they're running, and what their heart rate is. Some athletes use it for every single run while others use it only for runs during which they want to target a certain intensity."

Pedlar uses the data he collects from runners primarily to determine the effectiveness of their training. "We're trying to be as objective as possible with the information that we provide to our athletes and the training methods that they're using," he explains. "So if you have quality data on training volume and training intensity, then it helps you understand what's working and what's not working. Then when we apply other testing methods and protocols that measure adaptation, we can make more informed guesses as to exactly what is causing adaptation."

When asked whether speed and distance data is often used as the basis for significant training adjustments, Pedlar answers, "All the time. Usually I will talk to the coach about what his or her hunch is about training, and then we will address it. So, for example, if we have an athlete who we believe is training too hard in much of his or her lower-intensity work and is unable to complete more intense work effectively, we may set heart rate limits. Very often we have to set limits on what intensity various types of runs should be. On a weekly basis, we check those intensities and increase or decrease them as appropriate."

While Pedlar finds that elite runners often need to be held back and prevented from trying to push too hard in their training, he says that speed and distance devices are equally useful in pushing athletes harder when appropriate. "We have a development athlete at the moment and we have a question mark over him about whether he's training hard enough," he says. "We think maybe he can do more. So we're trying to get him to do as much work as possible in certain workouts by setting intensity targets to reach and hold."

Pedlar continues, "Another thing that happens is that, as athletes tend to improve rapidly over the first few weeks of training, they then find a comfort zone and sit there. We use intensity targets to push them on."

Genetically elite runners are very different from the rest of us. But they're still human, and so the same general training methods that work best for us work best for them, too. As Charles Pedlar has shown, these methods include the use of speed and distance devices for performance management.

USING CALIBRATION WORKOUTS

According to Carl Foster, PhD, professor of exercise and sport science at the University of Wisconsin at La Crosse and an expert on the science of pacing, the workouts that do the best job of calibrating your pacing mechanism are those that most closely simulate the challenges of a coming race. His research has shown that most people have to race three or four times at a certain distance to really nail down the pacing. So anything you can do in training to get a head start on this learning process is helpful. And while you may have already done more than three or four races at the distance of your next race, if your fitness level has changed markedly since your previous one, you'll need to take a step back and learn to pace yourself appropriately for your current fitness level.

To calibrate or recalibrate your pacing mechanism, roughly 10 days before a race complete a workout that challenges you to run an extended distance at your goal race pace. Use your speed and distance device to ensure that you stay consistently on target. This will help you develop a feel for that pace and get your brain accustomed to the feedback signals it will receive from your body during sustained running at that pace. Here are suggested calibration workouts for four distances:

5K

> 1-mile easy warm-up
>
> 5 × 1K at 5K race pace with 400-meter jogging recoveries
>
> 1-mile easy cool-down

10K

> 1-mile easy warm-up
>
> 5 × 2K at 10K race pace with 400-meter jogging recoveries
>
> 1-mile easy cool-down

Half Marathon

> 1-mile easy warm-up
>
> 4 × 2 miles at half-marathon race pace with 0.5-mile jogging recovery
>
> 1-mile easy cool-down

Marathon

> 1-mile easy warm-up
>
> 13.1 miles at marathon pace
>
> 1-mile easy cool-down

PLANNING RACE STRATEGY

Once you have determined your appropriate target pace for an upcoming race and have trained appropriately to meet that target, it's time to plan your specific pacing strategy. The need for this step arises from the fact that races of different distances require slightly different pacing strategies.

As part of his ongoing research on the science of pacing, Ross Tucker and colleagues (2006) have exhaustively studied world-record performances at various race distances. Making the safe assumption that it's hard to break a world record with poor pacing, they looked for patterns at each distance that could serve as a general pacing strategy for the rest of us. As you might expect, running at a fairly steady pace is best at every distance, but a specific pattern of slight variations in speed appears to be optimal at most distances.

These guidelines assume a flat race course. Any race course with hills will require an altered pacing strategy. Even pacing becomes a very poor pacing strategy when keeping an even pace requires sharp fluctuations in your rate of energy expenditure. And when you're running uphill, you have to expend much more energy to hold the same pace you were holding on the level terrain that preceded the hill, whereas when you're running downhill you can go faster with less energy than you can on level terrain.

Try to keep your energy expenditure relatively even throughout a race, which means you have to slow down when running uphill and speed up when running downhill. This is something you will tend to do naturally, but instead of just taking the hills as they come, you should study the race course beforehand so you can factor the placement of hills into your pacing strategy. For example, almost the entire first half of the Boston Marathon is downhill, while the second half is not. Therefore, you should plan to run the first half at a pace that's slightly faster than your target pace for the whole event. By contrast, the San Francisco Marathon is much hillier in the first half than in the second, so a planned negative split is definitely the way to go in this event. The London Marathon is a good example of a marathon that is almost perfectly flat and for which you may therefore plan to run at a perfectly even pace from start to finish.

If you want to get fancy, you can use the normalized graded pace feature in Training Peaks to determine exactly how much you need to slow down to maintain a consistent effort on big hills in an upcoming race. On a training run, approach a hill that is similar to the biggest hill in your upcoming race at your target race pace; as you run the hill, use heart rate and perceived exertion to maintain a steady effort that's equivalent to your race-pace effort on the flats. Later, when you analyze your workout graph, compare your actual pace on the hill to your normalized graded pace on the hill. If your normalized graded

2008 London Marathon. Martin Lei of Kenya, the eventual winner, is at the far right.

pace on the hill is equal to your target race pace, then you judged your effort correctly. In this case, in the race itself you should aim to maintain the actual pace you ran on the hill in practice. If your normalized graded pace on the hill does not match your target race pace, then adjust your actual pace on the hill proportionately in the race. For example, suppose you ran the hill at 7:44 per mile. Your normalized graded pace for the same stretch is 6:09. Your goal pace for the race is 6:15. In this case, you'll want to run the hill at an actual pace that's six to eight seconds per mile slower than in practice, or 7:50 to 7:52 per mile. You'll have to make up the time as much as possible coming down the other side.

5K and 10K: Fast-Slow-Fast

Interestingly, in world-record performances at the 5K and 10K distances, the first and last miles are almost always faster than the middle miles. Research by Carl Foster at the University of Wisconsin at La Crosse suggests that endurance athletes adjust their pacing throughout races based on ongoing comparisons between how they expected to feel at any given point and how they actually feel. When they feel better than expected, they speed up or hold pace; when they feel worse than expected, they slow down. But at the beginning of a race, there's no basis for comparison, and because of intense fight or flight nervous stimulation runners tend to feel superhuman and consequently start fast. After a few minutes they have enough sensory feedback to realize they cannot continue at that pace, so they settle in a bit. Then, at the end of the race, the brain's anticipatory regulation mechanism relaxes a bit, having calculated that a higher level of muscle activation (that is, a finishing kick) cannot cause catastrophic harm in the short distance left to be covered.

To emulate this fast-slow-fast pacing pattern, aim to run your first mile five seconds faster than your goal pace for the full race, then find a steady groove for the next few miles, and finally put everything you have left into the last mile.

Half Marathon: Steady as She Goes

World-record performances in the half marathon usually result from very even pacing from start to finish. It seems that runners come out ahead at this distance when they run hard enough so that they're just hanging on in the last mile, making a final surge impossible. In your next half marathon, try to run the first mile at precisely your goal pace and then continue like a metronome.

Marathon: Positively Negative

The most common pacing pattern for marathon world records is a slightly negative split, in which the second half is run roughly 30 seconds faster than the first. The marathon is so long that there's no margin for error in terms of running too fast in the early miles. To avoid a precipitous slowdown at the end, runners may need to run conservatively enough in the beginning that they can actually speed up very slightly at the end.

To run your optimal marathon, run the first half at two to four seconds per mile slower than your goal pace, then run the second half by feel—which, if all goes well, will be a little faster.

CONTROLLING YOUR PACE DURING RACES

While it's obvious that a speed and distance device can be used for monitoring and controlling your pace during races, you need to use your device somewhat differently in races of different distances, and you must avoid succumbing to the temptation to rely on it too heavily.

First, before you race, try to get a good sense of your device's specific degree of accuracy. Most devices are inaccurate by a consistent degree in one direction—either too long or too short. Test your device on measured courses whenever possible to determine its pattern. Races themselves afford some of the best opportunities, but be aware that it's actually normal to run approximately 0.5 percent too far on certified road race courses because these courses are measured by the shortest possible distance a runner could cover in completing it (that is, by running every turn and tangent perfectly), and nobody ever does that.

Pacing During a 5K

If your device model has an option to display the average pace for the current lap or run, set the display in this mode before the race starts. If you're running a 5K, ignore your watch for the first several hundred yards, when it's crowded and your main priority is to find a rhythm. Once you have found your rhythm, take a quick glance at your average pace. It almost certainly will not match your target pace for the first mile, but that doesn't mean you have to actively speed up or slow down. Just absorb the number you see, think about it in relation to how you feel, and let your gut tell you how to adjust.

Sometimes this early quick glance can save the day. When adrenaline gets the better of you and you start way too fast, it gives you the chance to rein in your legs and save your race before it's too late. If you waited until the first mile split to discover your mistake, it would be too late. On the other hand, if you start way too slowly, the quick glance at your average pace may remind you that, in fact, you are not working as hard as you could be, and you have an opportunity to speed up before you've dug too deep a hole to climb out of. But most often that early, quick glance will merely confirm that you're more or less on pace.

Pacing During a 10K

When running 10K races, do the same early glance at your average pace as soon as you've settled into a rhythm and adjust, if necessary. After that point, ignore your device (but pay attention to your mile splits) until the second half of the race, during which you should check the device whenever you find yourself worrying that fatigue is causing you to slip off your goal pace. The benefit of doing this is that it almost always motivates you to run harder, no matter whether the display tells you that you're right on pace, have fallen a second or two per mile behind pace, or are ahead of pace. The only circumstance in which it's likely to be demoralizing is when you're having a bad race and have fallen far behind your target pace. In these circumstances, you're going to end up demoralized anyway.

Pacing During a Half Marathon

Half marathons are long enough that your mile split times become almost meaningless after you've run several miles and brain fatigue has crippled your mathematical faculties. So don't even bother paying attention to your splits after 10K. Instead, glance at your average pace at each mile mark to check whether you're still on track toward your goal. As in 10K races, this type of monitoring is likely to keep a fire under you—there's just something about chasing numbers that makes us work harder!

Pacing During a Marathon

In the marathon, all measures taken to control your pacing with objective data go out the window after the halfway mark. You have to run by feel. But properly controlling your pace with objective data in the first half is critical to setting yourself up for success in the second half. The marathon distance is just too long for your anticipatory regulation mechanism to make reliable decisions about how fast you ought to be running in the early miles. Instead, rely on setting an appropriate time goal and target pace and check your speed and distance device as often as necessary to ensure that you stay on this pace through the first half.

While a speed and distance device certainly can help you pace yourself more effectively in races, it is no substitute for your body's built-in pacing mechanism. While this mechanism is poorly developed in beginning runners, it is highly refined and more reliable than objective pacing controls in experienced runners. If you are ready for a breakthrough race performance, your anticipatory regulation mechanism will tell you so by causing you to feel better than anticipated as you proceed through the miles. It would be a mistake in this situation to trust your pacing plan and your speed and distance device more than your body and resist the urge to run faster. Likewise, on those days when you just don't have it in a race, you need to heed your body's message of unexpected discomfort and run slower than planned instead of stubbornly persisting at your target pace only to suffer a disastrous bonk late in the race.

WHAT ABOUT HEART RATE?

It is not useful to monitor your heart rate during races. In fact, the only thing you're likely to accomplish in doing so is to hold yourself back artificially. Because of the stimulation of the sympathetic nervous system that is associated with the excitement and anxiety of racing, your heart rate is likely to be 5 to 10 beats per minute faster in races than it is at an equivalent pace in training. This does not mean you're working harder any more than your elevated heart rate on a roller coaster means you're working harder than you are when sitting in front of the television. Thus, if you try to keep your heart rate from rising above the race-pace heart rate you established in training, you will miss your goal time by a large margin.

Also, because you are at a high fitness level and well rested when you race, you will be able to work harder than you ever do in training. The harder you work, the higher your heart rate climbs. In this sense, it is a good thing to have a higher heart rate in a 10K race than in a 10K time trial workout. It simply means you're able to run faster. The advantage of being able to maintain a higher heart rate over a race distance is often unrecognized by runners who are accustomed to heart rate-based training, in which target heart rates are used as ceilings to prevent a person from running too hard. This is a primary argument against using heart rate as a governor, or limiter, to pace during races. You will likely obtain a poorer performance than if you used pace, or perception, and went as hard as you could.

Keep this point in mind whenever you're tempted to use your heart rate as a pacing control in races: The winner of every race you run has one of the highest average heart rates, if not the highest average heart rate, in the entire field of competitors, precisely because he or she is the runner who is able to work the hardest.

ANALYZING YOUR RACE PERFORMANCES

After you complete each race, download your data from your device to your computer. Look at your pace graph and highlight 1-mile or 1-kilometer segments of the race from start to finish to assess the evenness of your pacing. If the race course was flat or almost flat throughout, any segments will do. If the race course included hills, choose flat segments to compare.

Don't expect your pace to be perfectly steady in each segment throughout the race, but it should be relatively even. In a perfect race, the pace of your first and last kilometers in a 5K or 10K race will be roughly three seconds faster than those in the middle. In a half marathon there will be minimal pace sag in the middle of the race and only a very slight acceleration at the finish. In a marathon, a pace that's one second per mile faster in the second half than in the first is the ideal, but it's not realistic for most runners. If you can hold a steady pace through 20 miles, and if your pace in the final 10K is no more than 15 seconds per mile slower, call it a victory.

If you use TrainingPeaks WKO+ software, use the feature Fix Elevation Profile using GPS to improve the accuracy of the elevation change data and hence also the normalized graded pace (NGP). Recall that NGP, or flat pace, is a calculated level-ground equivalent of the actual pace you ran on any terrain, whether uphill or downhill. When you analyze races in terms of flat pace, you can ignore hills and compare paces at any points throughout the race.

10

Using Technology for Triathlon Success

L et's face it: Triathletes tend to be more technologically savvy than runners, and they are also generally willing to spend more money on their sport. For these reasons, a much higher percentage of triathletes than pure runners run with speed and distance devices. Many triathletes also train with power meters on their bikes, and these devices offer the same performance management capabilities as speed and distance devices. Perhaps you've already dabbled in multisport, or maybe you're a pure runner who's considering branching into triathlon for a new challenge. In either case, you'll want to know how the performance management system we've shown you in this book can be modified to meet your multisport training needs. This topic deserves a book of its own, but in this chapter we give you some specific tips that will get you started.

Swimming currently lacks the technological equivalent of running's speed and distance devices and cycling's power meters. Therefore we focus our discussion on training with a power meter and tracking combined cycling and running workout data with performance management software. However, in the final section we show you how, with a little creativity, you can include swim workout data in the mix.

FINDING THE PERFECT MEASUREMENT

In physics, *work* has a very precise meaning: force times distance. Power is force times distance over time, or force times velocity. In cycling, power is a function of the force you apply to the pedals and your pedal speed. Power—usually expressed in watts—is therefore a pure measurement of your work rate when cycling.

Speed, by contrast, is only an approximate expression of work rate, because it doesn't account for the force that is required to sustain a given speed. For example, wind and hills often increase the amount of force a cyclist has to generate to hold speed—or, more often, reduce a cyclist's speed at a constant work rate. Suppose you are riding your bike at 20 mph and 300 watts on level terrain. You reach a hill and begin climbing it at the same effort level at which you were previously riding on the flat. In this scenario, your speed will drop to, say, 12 mph while your watts remain steady at 300. That's because your power meter will register an increase in force applied to the pedals that makes up for your loss of speed. Thus a 300-watt effort is the same in all conditions, whether it is uphill, flat, or downhill, in a headwind, in a tailwind, or in crosswinds. But a 20 mph effort in one situation might be equivalent to a 12 mph in another situation, and one 20 mph effort may be very different from another in different conditions.

The variable of normalized graded pace (NGP) accounts for the effects of hills on running pace, making it more like a power measurement than absolute pace. However, no device exists that makes the conversion from absolute pace to NGP in real time, and NGP cannot account for the effects of wind resistance on running pace, whereas a bike power meter does account for the effects of wind resistance on cycling power. Aside from this difference, though, you can use a bike power meter to monitor, analyze, and plan your training in generally the same ways you use your speed and distance device to manage your running performance.

CHOOSING A POWER METER

The five major manufacturers of power meters are SRM, PowerTap, Polar, Ergomo, and iBike. There are significant differences among the four brands. The devices made by each manufacturer have a distinct set of advantages and disadvantages relative to the others. It's important to know about these differences, advantages, and disadvantages before you buy.

SRM

SRM, a German company, was the first manufacturer to bring a power meter to market. The SRM power meter is integrated into a crank and crank arm assembly that you simply install on your bike as you would any other such unit. Sensors inside the crank arm measure the force applied by the right foot to the right pedal. These data are run through a complex calculation that generates a real-time power estimate (in watts) that is transmitted to the handlebar display, which also shows heart rate, cadence, speed, distance, and elapsed time in various modes.

The SRM power meter is considered one of the most reliable and durable power meters on the market. It is susceptible to becoming inaccurate, however, as temperature changes expand and contract the metal of the crank arm and as aging and wear change its internal structure. Fortunately, there are recalibrating procedures you can use to counteract these factors. The biggest disadvantage of the SRM is its price. SRM models start at approximately $2,300.

PowerTap

Whereas SRM chose to put its strain gauges inside the crank arm, PowerTap chose to put its own inside the back wheel hub. Different calculations are required to generate wattage estimates from the torsion measurements taken by its sensors, but otherwise it works much like the SRM. PowerTap's power measurements tend to be 5 to 10 watts lower than SRM's, however, because of the different positioning of the two devices.

PowerTap's location in the rear wheel hub is problematic for riders who use more than one set of wheels. If you ride with the PowerTap in your everyday training wheels but want to switch to carbon aero wheels for racing without giving up power monitoring, you'll have to dismantle both wheels and transfer the hub.

Retail pricing for PowerTap units starts at approximately $900 plus the cost of a wheel to mount it on.

Polar

Polar's bike power meters gather data from yet another location on the bike— actually, two locations. A sensor mounted on the chainstay measures tension on the chain, while a second sensor located on the rear derailleur measures chain speed. A handlebar-mounted computer calculates power in watts as the product of the tension on the chain and its speed. This system is more difficult to install correctly than the SRM and PowerTap offerings, and incorrect installation results in inaccurate power readings. Some mechanics at performance bike shops are qualified to perform these installations, but they will charge you for the service, because few bike shops actually sell the units. Nevertheless, Polar power meters are attractive to many riders because of their affordability. You can get one for as little as $350 plus the cost of a Polar monitor capable of interfacing with it.

Polar is best known for its heart-rate monitors and, as you know, Polar makes speed and distance devices for runners, too. One great advantage of Polar power meters for triathletes is that the display unit doubles as a heart-rate monitor that you can detach and wear when swimming and running. In fact, Polar's high-end multisport computer is a GPS-based speed and distance device with integrated heart-rate monitor that can also be linked up with power sensors, allowing you to truly do it all with a single device.

Ergomo

Ergomo, another German company, makes power meters that use an optical sensor located inside the bike's bottom bracket spindle to measure torsional strain resulting from pressure on the left pedal and translates this measurement into a wattage estimate. The fact that the Ergomo measures power only from the left leg makes it perhaps a little less accurate than other power meters, because there almost certainly will be discrepancies between legs that may not be consistent among individuals or even within the same individual. Another serious limitation with the Ergomo is the fact that it cannot be externally calibrated against a known standard in a similar fashion to the Powertap and SRM models.

One characteristic of the Ergomo's functioning that owners appreciate is that its data are smoother, or less noisy, than those of most units. In other words, the display shows more consistent wattage numbers, whereas others show numbers that tend to fluctuate far above and below an average. This characteristic also makes for clearer workout graphs after the data have been downloaded.

The current retail price for the Ergomo power meter is approximately $1,650.

iBike

Velocomp's iBike is the newest player in the bike power meter market. It actually doesn't measure power directly at all but instead estimates power output by measuring wind, road, and gravitational resistance as the total amount of resistance overcome per unit time is equal to power output. This is actually a very complex and elegant way to derive power and because of the unique way it works, the ibike can do a lot of things that other power meters can't. For example, you can instantaneously test the effects of a change in your bike setup or riding position on wind resistance—a sort of at-home wind tunnel testing.

The iBike is also the easiest power meter to install and the least expensive after Polar at approximately $400 for the base model. Although the iBike's approach to deriving power is elegant, it also imposes serious limitations on the device that are difficult to overcome. Its chief drawback is that the device must be calibrated with the rider in a position that will be maintained consistently for the duration of data collection. Any change in position will result in erroneous power numbers. Further, drafting will have a dramatic effect on the derived power number that is reported and will be erroneous. Also situations that subject the bike to high levels of vibration—such as riding over rough roads—result in less accurate power estimates.

GETTING STARTED

After you've purchased your power meter, but before you can use it effectively for performance management, you must first get comfortable with it. The process of getting comfortable with a power meter mirrors that of getting comfortable with a speed and distance device, which is laid out in chapter 2. Here are the basic steps:

1. **Read the user's manual.** Nobody likes to read user's manuals. The last thing you want to do after you pull a shiny new gadget out of its box is ignore

it for the next hour while you read a bunch of technical mumbo-jumbo. But that's exactly what we urge you to do. It will save you a lot more than an hour's frustration later. Not everyone is able to learn best by reading. That's okay. You don't have to absorb it all. Just absorb as much as you can.

2. **Install your power meter.** Follow the instructions for installing your power meter on your bike. If you run into trouble, call the shop where you bought it and ask whether a mechanic there can install it for you.

3. **Try it out.** Don't use your power meter for the first time on some complex interval workout. Instead, try it first on a low-key base or recovery ride and just fiddle with the display options as you go.

4. **Download your ride data onto your computer.** To do this, of course, you will have to have first installed the performance management software that came with your device. Don't wait to accumulate a bunch of workouts on your power meter before completing your first download. Analyzing your power data is just as important as using the power meter on the bike. You don't want to delay the process of getting comfortable with your software.

5. **Explore your performance management software.** After you've downloaded your first workout, start fiddling around with the various features of the application to get a basic feel for how it works. Use any instructions included with the software to facilitate this process. A platform such as Training Peaks WKO+ will allow you to integrate swim, bike, and run data, either instead of your device software or alongside it. Most triathletes prefer to use just one all-encompassing program, but if your device software has some unique features you like, there's no harm in downloading your power data into both programs.

ESTABLISHING POWER ZONES

If you use your power meter for only one purpose, it should be to monitor and control your riding intensity to ensure you get the desired benefit from each workout. To do this, you must first establish target power zones, much as you established target pace zones with your running speed and distance device. There are various systems out there. We recommend that you use the system created by Hunter Allen and Andrew Coggan, which is the most popular and is fully explained in their book *Training and Racing With a Power Meter* (2006).

Allen and Coggan recommend that cyclists and triathletes use a 20-minute max test to establish their power zones. After a thorough warm-up, ride for 20 minutes as hard as you can. Be sure to pace yourself so that you're not fading in the final minutes of the test. After cooling down, find your power average for the 20-minute maximum effort. The power zones are based on the functional threshold (FT) power, which is analogous to the one-hour pace used in the running system described in this book, and is defined as the maximum power sustainable for one hour. Therefore, the power derived from the 20-minute test will need to be adjusted by multiplying by 0.95 (one-hour power is generally 95 percent of 20-minute power) to arrive at the FT power.

Next, use this number, a calculator, and table 10.1 to calculate your target power range for each of seven training intensity levels. For example, if the 20-minute effort resulted in a power of 275 and an adjusted value for 60 minutes of 260 watts, multiply 260 watts by 91 percent (0.91) and 105 percent (1.05) to establish your lactate threshold power range, which in the case of this example is (260 × 0.91= 235 to 260 × 1.05 = 273 watts. The right-hand column provides an example based on a hypothetical athlete who averaged 275 watts in the 20-minute max test. Note that the numbers are adjusted very slightly in some cases to leave no gaps between zones. Note also that power is not needed as a guide to training at level 7 (neuromuscular power) intensity because it corresponds to absolute maximum pedaling efforts that a person can maintain for only a few seconds.

Once you've worked out your target power ranges, use them during all of your cycling workouts, each of which should focus on one or two specific intensity levels. Don't be a slave to the numbers, however. If the target range is too hard on a given day, go a little easier; if it's too easy, go a little harder. When the target power zones become consistently too easy, do another 20-minute max test to establish new zones.

Table 10.1   Power-Based Training Levels

Level	Name	Target power range (as % of average watts in 20:00 max test)	Example based on 275 watts average power in 20:00 max test
1	Active recovery	≤55%	≤143
2	Endurance	56–75%	144–195
3	Tempo	76–90%	196–234
4	Lactate threshold	91–105%	235–273
5	V\od\O2max	106–120%	274–312
6	Anaerobic capacity	≥121%	≥313
7	Neuromuscular power	N/A	

Courtesy of TrainingPeaks (www.trainingpeaks.com).

ANALYZING YOUR POWER FILES

You can—and should—analyze the cycling workout data you download from your power meter generally in the same ways you analyze your run workout data. The differences are all at the level of details. The three most important types of analysis to perform regularly are tracking your fitness level, monitoring your training load, and determining your strengths and weaknesses.

Gale Bernhardt on Intensity Guidelines for Triathlon Training

Gale Bernhardt has long been one of America's premier coaches of runners, cyclists, mountain bikers, and triathletes. Based in Colorado, she coached the U.S. Olympic triathlon team for the Sydney Games. Bernhardt has also authored several books, including *Training Plans for Multisport Athletes* (2006) and *The Female Cyclist* (1999). She serves as a consultant and spokesperson for Timex, working to develop and market tools for the company's training devices.

Bernhardt uses a single training intensity system for athletes in all endurance sports. "The advantage of this system for triathletes is that it's a lot simpler than having a different set of guidelines for each discipline," she says. Because the pace zone index applies only to running, and Coggan and Allen's power guidelines apply only to cycling, you might want to switch to Bernhardt's system for triathlon training. Coach Joe Friel uses the same system Bernhardt uses and incorporated it into Training Peaks WKO+, so you can set this application to prescribe and analyze your swim, bike, and run workouts in terms of its seven zones.

To use the Bernhardt and Friel system, you must determine your lactate threshold pace in swimming, your lactate threshold heart rate in running, and your lactate threshold power in cycling. In all three disciplines, your lactate threshold is equivalent to your one-hour maximum performance. But you don't have to do a one-hour maximum effort to determine it. Instead you can do a 20-minute time trial and divide your average speed, heart rate, or power output by 1.04. Then use table 10.2 to find your training zones.

Table 10.2 Training Zones for Swimming, Cycling, and Running

Zone	Swim pace relative to lactate threshold pace	Percent of lactate threshold power (cycling)	Percent of lactate threshold heart rate (running)
1	NA	≤55%	≤84
2	T-pace + 10 sec. per 100	56–75%	85–91
3	T-pace + 5 sec. per 100	76–90%	92–95
4	T-pace	91–97%	96–99
5a	T-pace	98–105%	100–102
5b	T-pace – 5 sec. per 100	106–120%	103–106
5c	As fast as possible	≥121%	≥107

To learn workouts and find training plans based on this intensity system, check out Bernhardt's book *Training Plans for Multisport Athletes,* or visit www.galebernhardt.com.

The disadvantage of Bernhard's uniform intensity control system is that running workouts are based on heart rate, and we know about the flaws and limitations of heart rate–based training. There is a way around this disadvantage, however. After you

(continued)

Gale Bernhardt *(continued)*

establish your heart rate–based running zones, perform workouts in each zone and use your speed and distance device to record pace and heart rate data in each. Next, analyze the file on your performance management software and find the pace ranges that correlate with the seven heart rate zones. Now you can perform pace-based runs within the structure of Bernhardt's intensity system.

Track Your Fitness Level

Your target power zones are among the best indicators of your current fitness level. After all, they are based on a maximal time-trial effort. During periods of race-focused training when your fitness level is increasing steadily, you can repeat the 20-minute max test as often as once every four weeks. But there are other ways to track your fitness level, and indeed it's possible for your cycling fitness to improve even when your 20-minute max test does not. For example, if you are training properly for a long-distance triathlon such as the Ironman, your 20-minute max test performance might plateau many weeks before the race as you focus on improving your speed over longer distances. In this case, you'll want to focus on comparing your performance in each long ride to your past performances in similar rides to look for evidence of improving fitness.

You can do the same with your key workouts of every type (threshold rides, intervals, hill repetitions) throughout the training process. As you do with running, establish a benchmark with your first workout of each type and then try to slightly improve on your performance in each subsequent workout of the same type. Suppose you are training for an Olympic-distance triathlon. Your bike training includes a series of lactate interval workouts on the bike. These workouts consist of intervals of three to five minutes performed at roughly 10-mile maximum intensity (that is, the fastest pace you could sustain for 10 miles in race conditions) with three-minute active recoveries between them. Your first such workout will be relatively manageable, with fewer and shorter intervals, to get your body accustomed to this particular type of training stress. It will also have to be paced by feel (that is, you'll have to consciously ride the intervals at a pace that feels like the fastest pace you could sustain for 10 miles) because you don't yet have data from previous workouts to go by and because three-minute intervals are too short to govern by heart rate anyway (your heart rate will climb throughout each interval).

Let's also suppose that you have a power meter and that your average power output in these intervals is 292 watts. This number becomes the standard that you will try to match or beat in subsequent lactate interval workouts, even as you gradually add intervals and increase the interval duration. If your average power output is 295 watts in your second lactate interval workout, you will then try to match or beat that number in the third, and so forth.

Changes in your heart rate–power relationships provide evidence of changing cycling fitness just as changes in your heart rate–pace relationships provide evidence of changes in running fitness. Your heart rate at any given power output level should gradually decrease over the course of a training cycle, and your power output level at any given heart rate should increase. These changes tend to be very slight in experienced cyclists, though. The duration for which you can sustain a higher heart rate and the maximum heart rate you can sustain over a given distance will increase more significantly as you build toward peak fitness.

In chapter 5, under the heading Raw Endurance (page 97), we showed you how to calculate your heart rate decoupling index for long runs and use this metric to quantify changes in your running endurance. Use the same formula to calculate your heart rate decoupling index for long rides and quantify changes in your cycling endurance.

Monitor Your Training Load

Your power monitor is a very useful tool that helps you monitor how hard you are training and your state of recovery. The concepts of training stress score (TSS), acute training load (ATL), chronic training load (CTL), and training stress balance (TSB) translate raw power data into simple numbers and graph lines that make this type of monitoring very easy to do. TrainingPeaks WKO+ calculates these variables automatically from the power meter data you download to the program. You can also do the calculations yourself. Training stress score is calculated the same way for cycling as for running (as described on page 38) except that power is used instead of pace. There is no need to correct power for elevation change, however, because hills do not affect power as they do pace.

TrainingPeaks WKO+ allows you to graph the training loads of your biking and running independently and in sum. We recommend that you do both. Tracking your bike training independently will give you a better sense of how your specific cycling fitness is developing than tracking the sum of your bike and run training. But tracking the two together will give you a better sense of the total effect of your training on your body and your recovery status. After all, since running and cycling are both leg-dominant activities, fatigue from running affects your cycling and vice versa. So when making decisions about such things as when to reduce your training load for recovery, look at your combined TSB, not your TSB for running or cycling alone.

Identify Weaknesses

Like running fitness, cycling fitness is not a single, uniform phenomenon. There are various components of cycling fitness, which match the components of running fitness: raw endurance (or the ability to bike far at a moderate to moderately fast speed), lactate threshold (the ability to sustain a fast pace for one hour), intensive endurance (the ability to resist fatigue at paces exceeding your threshold speed), and speed (the ability to ride very fast over short distances). The relative proportions of each component that you need depends on what type of racing you do. The specific type of fitness desired by triathletes is time-trialing fitness, or the ability to ride for a prolonged period at a steady and high intensity. If you are a sprint triathlete, your time-trialing fitness needs to include more speed than endurance. If you're a long-distance triathlete, your time-trialing fitness needs to include more endurance than speed. But regardless of your specialty, you need a high level of threshold fitness.

A weakness is a component of your cycling fitness that is lower than it should be relative to your race goals or that inhibits the development of your overall cycling fitness. A way to identify a weakness in your cycling fitness is to analyze your power profile. Developed by Hunter Allen and Andrew Coggan, a power profile is a comparison of your power output in maximum efforts lasting 5 seconds, 1 minute, 5 minutes, and 60 minutes. You may establish your power profile either by performing periodic test workouts featuring maximal efforts of these durations or by analyzing your power files from regular workouts and locating your highest 5-second wattage, 1-minute wattage, and so forth. Power profiling is easier to do with TrainingPeaks WKO+, which can be set to show your best 5-second, 1-minute, 5-minute, and 60-minute power outputs from recent training. By using this feature, you can create a power profile without doing any formal test workouts, provided your normal training includes maximum efforts spanning all of these durations.

To complete the process, divide your best recent average power output over each of these durations by your weight in kilograms and then find your watts-per-kilogram score for each duration in figure 10.1. You should find that all of them are at close to the same level, although it's unlikely that they will all be at exactly the same level. Different types of cyclists tend to have different power profiles. Strong time-trial specialists have an upward-sloping power profile, with their 5-second watts per kilogram at the lowest level and their 60-minute watts per kilogram at the highest. Triathlon cycling is time-trial cycling, so your power profile should fit this pattern.

A 60-minute power score that is lower than any of your other scores may indicate that you need to do more threshold-intensity training. However, if you are a natural sprinter, your 5-second or 1-minute power scores may always be your best no matter how you train, so don't let your training become too lopsided in the direction of threshold training. A score in any column that is three or more levels below another indicates a weakness that is very likely limiting your overall cycling fitness. If you spot such an outlier, increase your training at that intensity to address that weakness.

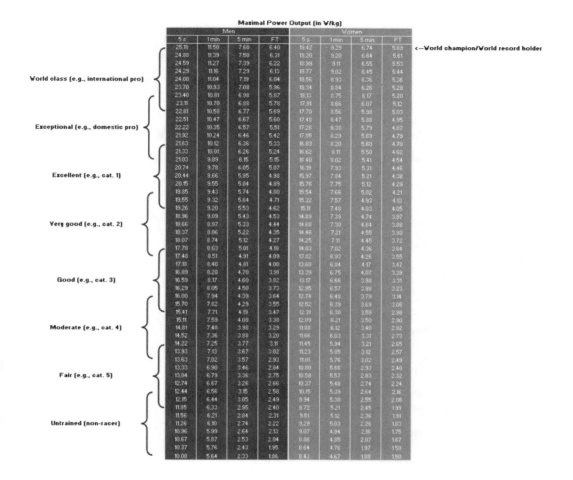

Figure 10.1   Watts-per-kilogram score for male and female cyclists based on maximum efforts at 5 seconds, 1 minute, 5 minutes, and 20 minutes.
Courtesy of TrainingPeaks (www.trainingpeaks.com).

BALANCING YOUR BIKE AND RUN TRAINING

Bike training and run training affect each another in positive and negative ways. On the positive side, the fitness you gain from training in either discipline carries over to some degree to the other. So, for example, if an injury prevents you from running for two weeks but does not prevent you from continuing to bike (and swim), then your running performance will not decline as much as it would if the injury prevented you from riding also. On the negative side, the fatigue you accrue from workouts in any discipline also carries over to the other disciplines, affecting your performance therein. Indeed, the fatigue carries over more than the fitness does. For example, your running performance would be hampered by a 100-mile ride done the previous day more than your running performance would be improved by a training program that included lots of cycling and no running whatsoever.

In light of these realities, it is best to track your ATL, CTL, and TSB for cycling and running both individually and together throughout the training process. Use individual tracking for cycling and running primarily to monitor the development of your fitness in each discipline. In particular, the CTL for your running alone will tell you more about your running fitness than your combined CTL for cycling and running, whose value could come mostly from the former if your training is not well balanced. All of the guidelines for using the CTL, ATL, and TSB for running analysis in chapter 6 apply to cycling analysis and combined cycling and running analysis. However, expect to find that your maximum rate of increase in training load, maximum CTL, and other such values for cycling are not the same as they are for running.

Use combined tracking of cycling and running primarily to manage your training stress balance (figure 10.2). This perspective is especially important when it comes to planning and executing a taper. It does you no good to have your running TSB in the optimal range of +5 to 10 the day before a triathlon if your combined bike–run TSB is still negative because of failure to sufficiently reduce your bike training.

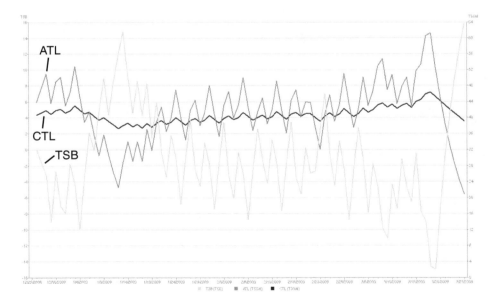

Figure 10.2 Sample graph of combined bike and run ATL, CTL, and TSB.
Courtesy of TrainingPeaks (www.trainingpeaks.com).

WHAT ABOUT THE SWIM?

Currently there is no equivalent to the bike power meter and the run speed and distance device in swimming. It's not that the technology is lacking. The technology for creating such a device already exists. It could be done with a wristwatch accelerometer, for example. Every time you did a flip turn, the accelerometer would register a change in direction. That's the way the device would tell us the time we were swimming for every 25- or 50-meter lap in a pool. We'll probably see devices like that on the market within the next few years. Indeed, accelerometers designed for use in scientific research could be used for swimming, but they do not meet the usability needs of athletes.

The reason such devices don't exist already is simply a lack of demand. The pool environment is so well controlled, and tracking speed and distance is already so easy, that swimmers are not exactly clamoring for a tool that enables them to check their pace anytime, rather than merely every 25 or 50 yards, especially considering that most swimmers would not check their pace halfway through a length even if they could. Indeed, it's fair to ask whether there is any need for a swimming speed and distance device at all.

We believe that there is one major advantage of such technology over conventional means of tracking speed and distance in the pool, which is the ability to effortlessly capture a complete set of workout data and download it into performance management software. In other words, while we concede that a swimming accelerometer would not be as useful for monitoring and controlling workout intensity as a bike power meter or a running speed and distance device, it would be every bit as useful for analysis and planning. When swimming accelerometers do become available, they will probably be most popular among triathletes who are already downloading bike and run data and want completeness in their performance management.

Some heart-rate monitors work in the pool, but we don't see much use for them without speed and distance data. And so, while we wait for swimming accelerometers to come along, it is necessary to log swim workout data manually. That hasn't stopped some coaches and swimmers from developing formulas to generate swimming-specific training stress scores (TSS) for use with Training Peaks. These formulas allow triathletes to monitor their training loads and fatigue levels in swimming as they do with their cycling and running.

At first blush, it seems tempting to apply the TSS system to swimming the same way it is applied to running. After all, like running, swimming is a discipline in which pace is commonly used as a training metric, both as a gauge of intensity and as a means of quantifying training load. However, in running there is an essentially linear relationship between oxygen demand ($\dot{V}O_2$) and speed on a level surface, meaning that oxygen demand increases at more or less the same rate that speed does. But because of the viscosity of water (compared to air), the relationship between oxygen demand and speed is not linear in swimming as it is in running, but exponential, meaning that oxygen demand increases faster than speed does. Since TSS calculations are based on these relationships, it is necessary to modify the calculations used in running to make them accurate for swimming.

The simplest, if not the most accurate, way to account for this difference in calculating TSS scores is to weight the intensity factor of swim workouts differently than it is weighted for run workouts. Since the $\dot{V}O_2$–power–speed relationship is exponential in swimming, then the intensity factor (IF) should be weighted more heavily in the TSS determination—specifically, we suggest, cubed as opposed to squared. You'll see this in the formula for swim TSS calculation presented later.

Determining Functional Threshold Speed in Swimming

Training stress calculations in running and cycling are scaled according to the individual athlete's current functional threshold pace (FTP), which corresponds roughly to the lactate threshold running pace or cycling power. The lactate threshold can be determined only through laboratory testing, while the functional threshold is determined through field tests that are known to yield roughly equivalent results. In running, a recent race or time-trial result and the pace zone index chart will reveal your current functional threshold pace. In cycling, as we've just seen, a 20-minute timed effort can be used to yield your current functional threshold power.

Similarly, the functional threshold pace for swimming is a stand-in for the laboratory-determined lactate threshold pace for swimming. Two approaches are most appropriate for the determination of swimming FTP. The first is the straightforward timed effort, in which you swim as far as possible in a given time (such as 30 or 60 minutes). So, if you swim for 30 minutes and cover 1,000 meters, then you can use the value of 33.3 m/min. as your FTP. (Divide 1,000 by 30 to arrive at that figure.) Since the actual FTP is closer to the one-hour effort, it might be more advisable to perform a 60-minute test or to take the value obtained for 30 minutes, multiply by 2, and subtract 2.5 percent, because most trained swimmers swim roughly 2.5 percent slower in a 60-minute maximal effort than in a 30-minute maximal effort. So again, if you cover 1,000 meters in 30 minutes, your 60-minute FTP would be 1,950 m/hr or 32.5 m/min. This may seem like a minor difference, but due to the resistive aspect of swimming, small differences can have a substantial impact.

If you are less inclined to perform such long, exhaustive efforts in the pool, you may alternatively perform a critical velocity (CV) test. This particular method has been validated by a research group in Japan (Wakayoshi 1992). This method consists of two all-out test efforts at different distances (such as 200 m and 400 m) separated by a complete rest. Because complete rest is required for the results of a CV test to be valid, it is best to perform the first all-out effort at the beginning of one workout (after warming up, of course) and the next at the beginning of another, say two days later. Record the time required to complete each effort and simply plot the results on a graph (see figure 10.3) as distance versus time. The slope of that line is your critical speed. Alternatively, a simple equation yields the same result:

Critical speed = Distance of longer test swim – distance of shorter test swim

Time of longer test swim – time of shorter test swim

For example, suppose you swim your 200-meter test swim in 2:02 (2.04 minutes) and your 400-meter test swim in 4:21 (4.35 minutes). To translate times, divide the seconds by 60. For example, to change 4:21 (minutes:seconds), divide 21 by 60 to get 0.35 and tack on the decimal to the number of minutes (4.35). To translate minutes and seconds, divide the seconds by 60 (21 ÷ 60 = 0.35) and then divide the total (4.35) by 60. In this example, that would yield 0.0725 hours. Your critical velocity, then, is (400 meters – 200 meters) ÷ (4.35 minutes – 2.02 minutes) = 85.8 meters per minute.

The results of your critical speed determination should yield a result that is very close to a 60-minute test or a laboratory-determined lactate threshold pace. Either of these results can then be used as the FTP for determination of TSS and performance modeling.

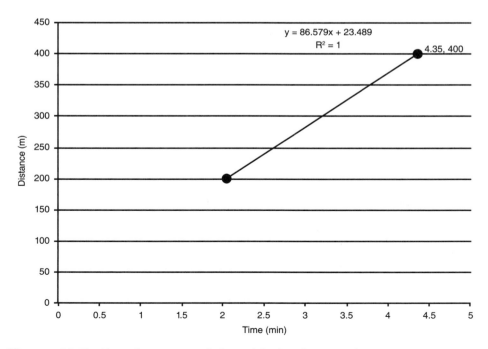

Figure 10.3 Sample test graph for critical swim speed.

Calculating TSS for the Swim

Now that you know your swim FTP, you can easily calculate the TSS for any swim workout. The steps for the determination of a TSS for a swimming workout are as follows:

1. Measure total distance covered for the workout.
2. Determine time to cover total distance (not including rest periods).
3. Express distance versus time in m/min. to obtain normalized swim speed (NSS), which is analogous to the normalized power and normalized graded pace in cycling and running, respectively.
4. Divide NSS by FTP to obtain IF.
5. Calculate swim TSS = $IF^3 \times$ hours $\times$ 100.

Once you have determined the swim TSS, you can manually input values in Training Peaks WKO+ and then use the program's analysis features for swimming as you do with running and cycling. Let's look at an example of a specific workout. First, let's suppose that your swim FTP is 75 meters per minute. Next, let's suppose you complete the following workout (remember, rest periods are not counted):

Warm-up: 200 meters at 3:20, 30-second rest (3:20 total)

Drills: 4 × 50 meters at 1:00, 10-second rest (4:00 total)

Main set: 10 × 100 meters at 1:15, 20-second rest (12:30 total)

Cool-down: 200 meters at 3:20 (3:20 total)

Total workout distance: 1,600 meters

Total workout time: 23:10 (or 0.386 hour)

The average pace for the complete workout is 1,600 meters divided by 23:10 (23.16 minutes or 0.386 hours) or 69 m/min. The intensity factor for the complete workout is the average pace (69 m/min.) divided by the athlete's functional threshold pace (75 m/min.) or 0.92. To cube IF, multiply it by itself three times (so, in this example, 0.92 × 0.92 × 0.92). So the TSS for the workout is 0.778 × 0.386 hours × 100 = 30.1.

Understanding the Limitations

You need to bear in mind some important limitations of our do-it-yourself method of swim TSS calculation. First of all, although this simplistic approach can be effective, it should be noted that by simply tracking distance and time swum, the effects of rest periods on the sustainable efforts are neglected, whereas in cycling and running they are not, because power meters and speed and distance devices capture coasting and nonmovement as part of the workout. Similarly, our rough-and-ready method of calculating swim TSS lacks the exponential weighting of higher intensities that is done automatically with pace and power in the digital calculation of normalized cycling power and normalized graded pace, which are important means of capturing the exponentially greater stress imposed by higher intensities. That being said, the cubed weighting of the IF counterbalances this limitation to a certain extent.

These calculations ignore the differences between various swim strokes and the rather substantial differences in efficiency that result from good or poor technique. Finally, the impact of flip turns and push-offs is essentially neglected using this approach.

If you choose to calculate TSS for your swims, we recommend that you monitor your swimming independently of your cycling and running in the performance management chart, for two reasons. First, there is little crossover fitness or fatigue effect between swimming, on the one hand, and cycling and running, on the other. Second, the global perspective of the performance management chart requires that the same calculation be used for chronic training load for all sports included. However, whereas the optimal constant for cycling and running is seven days, the optimal constant for swimming is only three days, because recovery from swimming occurs much more quickly.

Nevertheless, some triathletes like to see at least occasionally how their combined swim, bike, and run training looks. Figure 10.4 presents the global perspective of a triathlete's performance management chart.

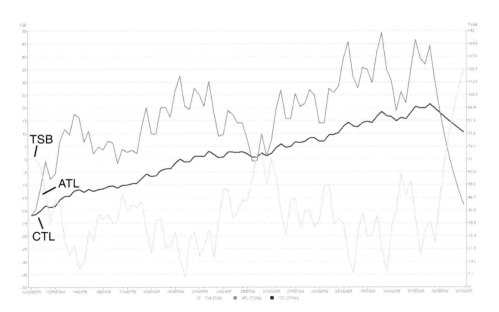

Figure 10.4 Changes over time in individual swim, bike, and run fitness levels (TSB values) for a triathlete.
Courtesy of TrainingPeaks (www.trainingpeaks.com).

Training effectively for a triathlon is not a simple matter, because it requires balancing three separate disciplines. Making progress in each discipline requires careful monitoring, analysis, and planning. Speed and distance devices, power meters, performance management software, and concepts such as training stress balance can help you manage this complexity. But working with these technologies and concepts can itself be overwhelming for beginners, and it's not for everyone. Some of the best triathletes in the world train simply by feel with the aid of nothing more than a paper training log. Others make full use of the latest technologies and concepts. Either path, or some middle path, may work best for you. We believe in the high-tech route, but we encourage every triathlete to be patient in the process of becoming comfortable taking it and understand that the learning process never ends.

Appendix: Pace Zone Index Scores in Kilometers

Pace Zone Index Scores (Metric Measurements)

RECENT RACE (MIN:SEC)				TARGET TRAINING PACE ZONES (MIN:SEC PER KILOMETER)					
3K	5K	10K	PZI	2: Low aerobic	3: Moderate aerobic	4: High aerobic	6: Threshold	8: V̇O₂max	10: Speed
18:10- 17:41	32:55- 32:01	68:04- 66:21	50	9:11-8:21	8:20-7:39	7:39-7:16	6:53-6:41	6:20-6:14	6:01-1:40
17:40- 17:13	32:00- 31:06	66:20- 64:37	49	8:59-8:09	8:08-7:28	7:28-7:04	6:42-6:30	6:09-6:03	5:51-1:40
17:12- 16:46	31:05- 30:15	64:36- 62:55	48	8:47-7:57	7:56-7:17	7:16-6:54	6:33-6:21	5:59-5:53	5:41-1:40
16:45- 16:21	30:14- 29:33	62:54- 61:17	47	8:36-7:46	7:45-7:06	7:06-6:43	6:23-6:11	5:49-5:43	5:31-1:40
16:20- 15:57	29:32- 28:42	61:16- 59:40	46	8:24-7:34	7:34-6:56	6:55-6:33	6:13-6:01	5:39-5:33	5:21-1:40
15:56- 15:34	28:41- 28:00	59:39- 58:10	45	8:14-7:24	7:24-6:46	6:46-6:24	6:04-5:53	5:32-5:26	5:14-1:40
15:33- 15:12	27:59- 27:19	58:09- 56:44	44	8:01-7:11	7:11-6:36	6:36-6:15	5:56-5:44	5:24-5:18	5:06-1:40
15:11- 14:51	27:18- 26:41	56:43- 55:23	43	7:56-7:06	7:05-6:28	6:28-6:07	5:48-5:37	5:17-5:11	4:58-1:40
14:50- 14:31	26:40- 26:04	55:22- 54:07	42	7:46-6:56	6:55-6:19	6:19-5:58	5:40-5:29	5:09-5:04	4:49-1:40
14:30- 14:12	26:03- 25:29	54:06- 52:48	41	7:37-6:47	6:47-6:11	6:11-5:51	5:33-5:23	5:02-4:56	4:43-1:40
14:11- 13:54	25:28- 24:55	52:47- 51:43	40	7:29-6:39	6:39-6:03	6:02-5:42	5:26-5:16	4:54-4:49	4:36-1:40
13:53- 13:37	24:54- 24:24	51:42- 50:36	39	7:22-6:32	6:31-5:56	5:56-5:36	5:20-5:09	4:49-4:44	4:31-1:40
13:36- 13:20	24:23- 23:53	50:35- 49:32	38	7:11-6:24	6:24-5:49	5:48-5:29	5:13-5:03	4:44-4:39	4:26-1:40

(continued)

Pace Zone Index Scores *(continued)*

RECENT RACE (MIN:SEC)				TARGET TRAINING PACE ZONES (MIN:SEC PER KILOMETER)					
3K	5K	10K	PZI	2: Low aerobic	3: Moderate aerobic	4: High aerobic	6: Threshold	8: $\dot{V}O_2$max	10: Speed
13:19-13:03	23:52-23:24	49:31-48:31	37	7:04-6:17	6:17-5:42	5:42-5:23	5:06-4:56	4:39-4:34	4:21-1:40
13:02-12:48	23:23-22:55	48:30-47:33	36	6:57-6:10	6:09-5:36	5:35-5:16	5:00-4:50	4:34-4:29	4:16-1:40
12:47-12:40	22:54-22:28	47:32-46:37	35	6:51-6:04	6:04-5:29	5:29-5:10	4:54-4:45	4:29-4:24	4:11-1:40
12:39-12:19	22:27-22:02	46:36-45:43	34	6:44-5:57	5:56-5:23	5:23-5:04	4:48-4:39	4:24-4:19	4:06-1:40
12:18-12:05	22:01-21:38	45:42-44:50	33	6:38-5:51	5:51-5:18	5:17-4:58	4:43-4:34	4:16-4:11	4:01-1:40
12:04-11:52	21:37-21:13	44:49-44:01	32	6:32-5:45	5:44-5:11	5:11-4:53	4:38-4:29	4:14-4:09	3:56-1:40
11:51-11:39	21:12-20:51	44:00-43:13	31	6:26-5:39	5:38-5:06	5:06-4:48	4:33-4:24	4:09-4:04	3:51-1:40
11:38-11:27	20:50-20:29	43:12-42:27	30	6:20-5:33	5:33-5:01	5:01-4:43	4:28-4:19	4:04-3:59	3:46-1:40
11:26-11:15	20:28-20:07	42:26-41:43	29	6:15-5:28	5:29-4:56	4:55-4:38	4:24-4:16	4:00-3:56	3:43-1:40
11:14-11:04	20:06-19:46	41:42-41:00	28	6:07-5:23	5:23-4:51	4:51-4:33	4:21-4:13	3:56-3:52	3:39-1:40
11:03-10:53	19:45-19:26	40:59-40:19	27	6:02-5:19	5:18-4:46	4:46-4:28	4:17-4:08	3:52-3:48	3:36-1:40
10:52-10:42	19:25-19:08	40:18-39:40	26	5:57-5:13	5:13-4:42	4:41-4:24	4:13-4:05	3:51-3:46	3:33-1:40
10:41-10:32	19:07-18:49	39:39-39:01	25	5:53-5:09	5:08-4:38	4:37-4:20	4:09-4:01	3:47-3:43	3:30-1:40
10:31-10:22	18:48-18:31	39:00-38:24	24	5:48-5:04	5:04-4:33	4:32-4:16	4:05-3:58	3:43-3:39	3:27-1:40
10:21-10:13	18:30-18:13	38:23-37:49	23	5:44-5:00	4:59-4:29	4:29-4:12	4:01-3:54	3:39-3:35	3:24-1:40
10:12-10:03	18:12-17:57	37:48-37:14	22	5:39-4:56	4:55-4:25	4:24-4:08	3:58-3:51	3:35-3:31	3:20-1:40
10:02-9:54	17:56-17:41	37:13-36:41	21	5:35-4:51	4:51-4:21	4:21-4:04	3:54-3:48	3:33-3:29	3:18-1:40
9:53-9:46	17:40-17:25	36:40-36:08	20	5:31-4:48	4:47-4:18	4:17-4:01	3:51-3:44	3:30-3:26	3:13-1:40
9:45-9:37	17:24-17:10	36:07-35:37	19	5:28-4:44	4:43-4:13	4:12-3:57	3:48-3:41	3:28-3:24	3:11-1:40

3K	5K	10K	PZI	2: Low aerobic	3: Moderate aerobic	4: High aerobic	6: Threshold	8: $\dot{V}O_2$max	10: Speed
9:36-9:29	17:09-16:55	35:36-35:07	18	5:21-4:40	4:39-4:09	4:09-3:54	3:44-3:38	3:25-3:21	3:08-1:40
9:28-9:21	16:54-16:41	35:06-34:38	17	5:16-4:36	4:35-4:07	4:06-3:51	3:42-3:36	3:23-3:19	3:06-1:40
9:20-9:13	16:40-16:27	34:37-34:09	16	5:13-4:32	4:32-4:04	4:03-3:48	3:39-3:33	3:20-3:17	3:03-1:40
9:12-9:06	16:26-16:14	34:08-33:42	15	5:09-4:29	4:28-4:01	4:00-3:44	3:36-3:31	3:18-3:14	3:01-1:40
9:05-8:59	16:13-16:01	33:41-33:15	14	5:06-4:26	4:25-3:58	3:57-3:41	3:33-3:28	3:15-3:12	2:58-1:40
8:58-8:52	16:00-15:48	33:14-32:48	13	5:03-4:22	4:21-3:54	3:54-3:38	3:30-3:25	3:13-3:09	2:56-1:40
8:51-8:45	15:47-15:36	32:47-32:23	12	4:59-4:19	4:18-3:51	3:51-3:36	3:28-3:23	3:10-3:07	2:53-1:40
8:44-8:38	15:35-15:23	32:22-31:59	11	4:56-4:15	4:14-3:48	3:48-3:33	3:25-3:21	3:07-3:04	2:51-1:40
8:37-8:31	15:22-15:12	31:58-31:35	10	4:53-4:13	4:12-3:46	3:45-3:30	3:23-3:18	3:04-3:02	2:48-1:40
8:30-8:25	15:11-15:01	31:34-31:11	9	4:50-4:09	4:09-3:43	3:43-3:28	3:20-3:16	3:02-2:59	2:46-1:40
8:24-8:19	15:00-14:50	31:10-30:49	8	4:44-4:07	4:06-3:41	3:40-3:25	3:18-3:14	2:59-2:57	2:43-1:40
8:18-8:13	14:49-14:39	30:48-30:27	7	4:41-4:03	4:03-3:38	3:37-3:23	3:15-3:11	2:57-2:54	2:41-1:40
8:12-8:07	14:38-14:28	30:26-30:06	6	4:38-4:01	4:00-4:13	4:12-3:20	3:13-3:09	2:55-2:53	2:38-1:40
8:06-8:01	14:27-14:18	30:05-29:46	5	4:36-3:58	3:58-3:33	3:32-3:18	3:11-3:08	2:54-2:53	2:36-1:40
8:00-7:56	14:17-14:08	29:45-29:24	4	4:32-3:55	3:54-3:30	3:29-3:15	3:09-3:06	2:52-2:49	2:35-1:40
7:55-7:51	14:07-13:58	29:23-29:05	3	4:30-3:53	3:52-3:28	3:28-3:13	3:07-3:04	2:49-2:47	2:32-1:40
7:50-7:46	13:57-13:49	29:04-28:45	2	4:28-3:50	3:49-3:26	3:25-3:11	3:04-3:01	2:47-2:45	2:31-1:40
7:45-7:40	13:48-13:40	28:44-28:27	1	4:24-3:47	3:46-3:23	3:23-3:08	3:02-2:59	2:44-2:43	2:29-1:40
7:39-7:35	13:39-13:31	28:26-28:09	0	4:23-3:45	3:44-3:21	3:21-3:06	3:00-2:58	2:44-2:48	2:28-1:40

Courtesy of TrainingPeaks (www.trainingpeaks.com).

References

Allen, H., and Coggan, A. 2006. *Training and racing with a power meter.* Boulder, CO: VeloPress.

Bernhardt, G. 1999. *The female cyclist.* Boulder, CO: VeloPress.

Bernhardt, G. 2006. *Training plans for multisport athletes.* 2nd edition. Boulder, CO: VeloPress.

Billat, V., Sirvent, P., Lepretre, P.M., and Koralsztein, J.P. 2004. Training effect on performance, substrate balance and blood lactate concentration at maximal lactate steady state in master endurance-runners. *European Journal of Physiology* Mar;447(6):875-83.

Esteve-Lanao, J., Foster, C., Sieler, S., and Lucia, A. 2007. Impact of training intensity distribution on performance in endurance athletes. *Journal of Strength and Conditioning Research* Aug;21(3):943-9.

Karnazes, D. 2006. *Ultramarathon man: Confessions of an all-night runner.* Tarcher.

Mauger, A.R., Jones, A.M., and Williams, C.A. 2009. Influence of feedback and prior experience on pacing during a 4-km cycle time trial. *Medicine and Science in Sports and Exercise* Feb;41(2):451-8.

McGregor, S.J., R.K. Weese, and I.K. Ratz, Peformance Modeling in an Olympic 1500 m finalist: A practical approach. *Journal of Strength and Conditioning Research, 2008.* In Press.

Tucker, R., Lambert, M.I., Noakes, T.D. 2006. An analysis of pacing strategies during men's world-record performances in track athletics. *International Journal of Sports Physiology and Performance* Sep;1(3):233-45.

Tucker, R, and Noakes, T.D. 2009. The anticipatory regulation of performance: The physiological basis for pacing strategies and the development of a perception-based model for exercise performance. *British Journal of Sports Medicine Epub* Feb 17.

Wakayoshi, K., Yoshida, T., Udo, M., Kasai, T., Moritani, T., Mutoh, Y., and Miyashita, M. 1992. A simple method for determining critical speed as swimming fatigue threshold in competitive swimming. *International Journal of Sports Medicine* July;13(5):367-71.

Index

Note: The italicized *t* and *f* following page numbers refer to tables and figures, respectively.

About the Authors

Stephen J. McGregor, PhD, is a pioneer in the development of training concepts and software designed to maximize the benefits of running with a speed and distance device. Most notably, Dr. McGregor created the normalized graded pace (NGP) algorithm and the run training stress score (rTSS). The NGP algorithm accounts for changes in grade that affect running speed and reports an adjusted pace that is more reflective of the actual effort exerted by the athlete and helps runners determine the true physiological stress level of each run. Dr. McGregor is the director of the Applied Physiology Laboratory at Eastern Michigan University and has published and presented numerous research papers examining muscle injury, nutritional supplements, performance modeling, and running physiology.

Dr. McGregor is a former intercollegiate soccer player, triathlete, and elite competitive cyclist. He has coached endurance athletes for almost 15 years and has a doctorate in exercise physiology. He is on the science and education faculty for USA Cycling and serves as a consultant to numerous international-caliber cyclists and runners, including Olympians.

Matt Fitzgerald is the author of numerous books on running, triathlon, nutrition, and weight loss. A prolific health and fitness journalist, Fitzgerald writes regularly for such national publications as *Bicycling, Experience Life, Her Sports, Maxim, Men's Fitness, Men's Health, Outside,* and *Runner's World.* He is currently a senior editor with *Triathlete,* is a featured running expert on Active.com, and contributes to the Active Runner e-mail newsletter. Fitzgerald has written extensively on performance-enhancing drugs and how to excel without them for publications including *Muscle Media* and *Running Times.*

Fitzgerald serves as a communications consultant to a number of sports nutrition companies. He is the editor of PoweringMuscles.com, an online nutrition information resource for athletes and exercisers. In 2006 he became a certified sports nutritionist licensed by the International Society of Sports Nutrition. Outside of writing, Fitzgerald is a featured coach with TrainingPeaks, the leader in providing online training services to endurance athletes and coaches. In this capacity, he creates interactive training plans for runners and triathletes.